TITLE & CL

Island Music:

The History of AIR Montserrat

ISBN: 9798354832231

TABLE OF CONTENTS

Title & Copyright..1

FORWARD 4

PROLOGUE 6

MONTSERRAT HISTORY 11

LIFE IN MONTSERRAT 14

A BRIEF HISTORY OF AIR STUDIOS 22

THE CONCEPT 24

THE RIDGE 27

STUDIO CONSTRUCTION 31

STUDIO DETAILS 44

THE NEVE 54

THE GUINEA PIGS 60

OPENING DAY 67

DENNY TAKES THE HELM..72

THE JACKSONS 83

YVONNE 91

THE ISLAND STAFF 98

JOHN SILCOTT..108

TAPPY MORGAN 112

BOSUN 118

A UNIQUE OPPORTUNITY 124

THE CYCLE OF A SESSION 147

TIDBITS 152

PRODUCERS...157

TUG OF WAR 165

SYNCHRONIZING GHOSTS..170

ELTON...174

BROTHERS IN ARMS...179

ARTISTS...190

A PARADIGM SHIFT..195

NATURAL DISASTER..209

THE END OF AN ERA..214

AFTER THE HURRICANE 219

THANK YOU! 232

PHOTO SECTION..239

FORWARD

Some people might think that we were crazy to attempt to establish a fully professional studio on a remote tropical island! History has shown though that this incredible project was created because of a mad idea dreamt up by George Martin. This idea was formed during a number of remote recordings which George successfully carried out in the most wonderful exotic locations with the expert assistance of both Geoff Emerick and Bill Price.

George wanted his own remote studio and having discovered the ideal situation in Montserrat, following Christopher Columbus, George decided that this would be the place to recreate his dream.

This happened to be the most amazing project that Malcolm Atkin and I could ever be asked to undertake, and we were very fortunate to be given the opportunity to put together what was to become one of the foremost studios in the world. Being situated in so perfect a place, given the remoteness, one imagined the hurdles and problems that we would need to overcome: The unknown situation of finding oneself over four thousand miles from AIR in London, the realisation that this was a massive gulf, especially when considering that all the information and intricate components that had to be collated, ensuring with much organisation and pre-planning that everything was included, combined with the associated contemplation of all the difficulties and problems which could and did ensue.

Being situated in The West Indies surrounded by the Caribbean Ocean, all the equipment had to be of the highest standard. The major basis on which it was to be judged would be a combination of convenience of situation, ease of maintenance and of course exceptional reliability. In addition, sound quality had to be second to none in order to satisfy George Martin together with, in particular, the two "golden ears," Geoff Emerick and Bill Price. An incredible masterstroke of electronic design from none other than Rupert Neve himself ensured excellence in sound quality produced by the revolutionary circuit design that he developed for us. I truly believe that the three special consoles that he supplied for our studios in Montserrat and London were probably the very best ever built.

George's dream had been fulfilled with absolute success, sadly nature with all its totally unexpected foibles ultimately ensured that this thing was not destined to last. In the famous words of Jimmy Buffet, recorded in that studio, "I don't know where I'm gonna go when the volcano blows"!

Many great memories still live with the many stars, producers and engineers who visited. I'm deeply honoured to have been part of their creation.

The author of this book, Brian Sallerson, has for several years gone to exceptional lengths to ensure that the reader can enjoy the ultimate insight into the creation and day-to-day management of George Martin's unique dream studio. From the outset, Brian was determined that his work should celebrate with the most accurate and detailed description this very special period in the history of recording. Tirelessly he has researched and collated far-reaching and detailed facts and stories from the many interviews with artists, producers and engineers, as well as ensuring the inclusion of tales from as many people as possible who were involved from day one. Much time was spent in meetings and telephone calls and emails to enable the telling of the tale in this most absorbing manner. This book then is the absolute bible of how to create and run a crazy, enthralling, and extraordinary project from inception to sad conclusion. Please enjoy!

Dave Harries - AIR Studios Studio Director and AIR Montserrat Managing Director during the time of the studio's construction

July 2022

PROLOGUE

Whether we realize it or not, the music that we listen to becomes the soundtrack of our lives. For most people, it has meaning far beyond its lyrics or melodies. A popular song can be enjoyed by millions of people around the world but for each individual person, it becomes a unique emotional time capsule. When a popular song from your youth starts playing over a store's PA system, it catches your attention not only because you enjoy its melody or lyrics, but because of the emotions forever tied to it. You can close your eyes and be transported back in time, remembering the moment when that song became an integral part of your life. Memories and emotions tied to that era can come flooding back and, for good or bad, that song will always bring you to that place in time. Whenever I hear Elton John's "I Guess That's Why They Call It The Blues," I am instantly filled with the bittersweet memory of a wonderful family vacation to Disney World when I was twelve years old. This seminal 80s hit was in heavy rotation on the radio at the time and to this day, Elton's song conjures up strong emotions for me. It brings me back to 1983 again and I can almost see the flashing colorful screens and hear the wonderous cacophony of the video arcades that my brother and I practically lived in during that trip. Such fun! The song also transports me into the seats of roller coasters in the theme parks we went to that year; hands in the air, wind in my hair, and screaming in fear and exhilaration. Little did I know but this was to be the last holiday our family spent together before my parents' separation a few months later so Elton's track also brings a bit of sadness as well. Strong emotions of love and loss come flooding back to me by simply hearing that song from over 35 years ago.

It was these emotional ties to music that led me from my home on the east coast of the U.S.A. to currently being behind the wheel of an old creaking rental car on the small island of Montserrat in the East Caribbean. I had never expected to be here. In fact, I did not even know that Montserrat existed until three months ago and yet here I am navigating the tight twisting steep roads of the island, dodging wild goats, chickens, and potholes the size of moon craters, while also trying not to be distracted by the breathtaking vistas that seem to suddenly appear around every turn. I am in Montserrat to interview AIR Studios staff members and island locals who were here during the studio's heyday and to experience the culture of Montserrat, which was key to Sir George Martin's decision to build the studio here over forty years ago. Although the studio has been shuttered for decades, the inspiration for my book about the history of AIR Montserrat had started just a few short months ago.

When exploring ideas for a new writing endeavor, I had an idea for a project: to track down the origins of the songs, albums, and artists that have strong emotional ties to my childhood. Being a musician, I always like to know the backstory of the music I listen to. What was the artists' reason for writing a song? What technology and instruments were used in producing the music? Where and when was the music recorded and how did the times and culture influence the process? By knowing how a recording came to be, it gives context to the music far beyond its lyrics or melody. Once I started digging into the subject matter, I began noticing the name of a recording studio that I had never heard of before: AIR Studios Montserrat. Many albums that were a big part of my teenage years were recorded there: Dire Straits' "Brothers in Arms" album, The Police's "Synchronicity," Rush's "Power Windows," and of course, Elton John's "Too Low for Zero" which spawned the hit that transports me back to that vacation in 1983. Having knowledge of many of the major recording studios of that time period, I asked myself, "With all of these huge records being recorded there, why had I not heard of Air Studios Montserrat?" Researching the background of the studio quickly led to frustration. There seemed to be an extensive list of recordings that were produced there during the 1980s, yet there was so little information available about its history. My hypothesis about this dearth of historical documentation was that the studio had been in operation from 1979 until 1989 which precedes the Internet and digital media age by almost a decade. If someone had not taken the time to digitally archive media from the studio and place it on the Internet, it is not going to be found. That was certainly the case here. Coupling that with the fact that the studio was located on a remote island in the Caribbean with the express purpose of being "off the radar" made finding anything close to a comprehensive history nearly impossible. What little information I did find had really piqued my interest:

· The studio was owned by Sir George Martin who had built it on Montserrat because of the beautiful, isolated location and its uniquely warm and welcoming people.
· Many of the biggest hits of the 1980s were recorded there. Prime examples being "Ebony and Ivory," "Every Breath You Take," and "Money For Nothing."
· The island was ravaged by Hurricane Hugo in 1989 causing incredible hardship for the people of Montserrat and a sudden end to AIR Studios' illustrious run of recordings.
· The studio was never reopened, and the once beautiful property is currently in a decrepit state as the jungle reclaims the land and structures once occupied by many renowned musicians and producers.
· Research indicated that many of the key individuals, staff members, and artists involved with the studio were in their twilight years or had passed.
· After forty years, many photos and physical documents of the studio are fading or are lost.

What became clear to me was that if no one took the time and effort to compile and record the history of AIR Studios Montserrat immediately, it would soon be lost to time. For something so significant to both music history and world culture to disappear without ever being documented properly seemed like a travesty to me. I realized that I needed to know more about this influential studio and that I wanted to share what I found with everyone who was similarly touched by the music that was recorded there. It was clear that this had to be my next project. Within a month, I had booked a trip to Montserrat and headed 2000 miles south towards the equator on a quest to collect as much information as I could about the studio directly from the source.

And so I have been on the island for more than a week and am flying home tomorrow so it is a bittersweet moment to be tracking down the last lead on my trip to Montserrat, knowing that I will be leaving such a beautiful place and its wonderful people so soon. I have been treated with a kindness that I have never experienced before. Without exception, everyone on the island that I have had contact with has been inviting, warm, and excited to assist with my book project. Air Studios was and still is an important part of Montserrat's history and is remembered fondly by those who were here during the decade it was operating on the island. The fact that someone had taken an interest in Montserrat and the studio's history has led to many a smile and invitations to talk about AIR this past week.

I park my rental car along the side of Friths Road, just outside of the village of Salem. Parking is a relative term on most of the streets here. Almost all the roads are the width of two small cars with about a foot of clearance between lanes which feels claustrophobic to me. This is quite different from the wide multilane roads that I am used to in the United States. With a current population of only five thousand people, many of whom do not own a vehicle, there is no need for large thoroughfares here. Parking in Montserrat simply means leaving your car in one of the lanes of traffic. This would warrant a ticket for double parking at home which is why it feels so strange to leave my car parked clearly blocking traffic, but for the relaxed culture of Montserrat, this is quite normal.

Standing here, I am within walking distance of the exclusion zone where travel is restricted due to the dangers of the active volcano on the island. Many years ago, Montserrat was known to have had the best roads in the Caribbean, but natural disasters and a depressed economy have caused them to fall into disrepair, especially as you approach the edge of the exclusion zone where the population gets sparse. The crumbling asphalt of Friths Road descends into the Belham Valley that was once home to the island's beautiful (and only) golf course. Sadly, it has been buried under many layers of ash, rock, and debris over the past twenty years as the volcano woke up and began erupting after 350 years of slumber. Luckily for me, the volcano is quiet today and the bright clear skies allow me to see the peak of Soufriere Hills with its plumes of steam and ash wicking off its dome. I am also less than a half mile from the decaying ruins of AIR Studios Montserrat, the subject of my book, but its physical remains are not why I have travelled to the island. I am here to meet the people whose lives were affected by the studio and to immerse myself in the culture of Montserrat.

The reason for being here on Friths Road is that I am searching for the home of Minetta Francis, the head of housekeeping at the studio whose tenure spanned almost the entire decade of its operations. No one I had previously interviewed knew where she was currently residing or if she was still alive. Extensive searches on the Internet revealed no definitive clues of her whereabouts. She had been in her 50s when she was working at AIR Studios and it has been almost 30 years since the studio shuddered its doors. A quick calculation reveals that she would likely be in her 80s at this point. This is one of the challenges of researching a story so far in the past but still within the span of a lifetime. The studio's staff and clients have been scattered across the globe since its closing in 1989 and the relentless passing of time is now starting to lay claim to some of those who were involved with the studio so many years ago.

Serendipity is on my side though. Just five minutes prior to stepping out of the car onto Friths Road, I had been interviewing Lloyd Francis, better known as "X" to locals on the island. He had been a driver for AIR Studios, carting recording artists around the island to clubs, beaches, or wherever they wanted to go while recording at the studio. As I was leaving, he said "You know. Minetta is on the island." I was shocked! "Minetta Francis? She's here?" I said, to which he replied, "Yes, she and I went to see Judy Martin yesterday at Olveston House. You should go see her." I was flabbergasted! It turns out that both X and Minetta had emigrated to England over twenty years ago after the volcanic eruptions started devastating the island but by some freak streak of luck, both happened to be visiting friends and family on Montserrat while I am here. Serendipity indeed! X gave me directions to Minetta's neighborhood which led me to where I am currently standing in Friths at the edge of the exclusion zone.

X's directions get me close but without a house number, I am not sure which of the several homes surrounding me would be Minetta's. Houses on Montserrat are not numbered which I find odd but considering that everyone here seems to know the whereabouts of everyone else on the island, there does not appear to be a need to number houses. I look around at the few single-story island houses in the neighborhood. All are in need repair: roofs are old, some windows are covered with plywood, paint is peeling. These houses are quite different than the grand villas that I have seen this week when I interviewed some of the well-to-do islanders and snowbirds who spend their winters here. This neighborhood has seen better days and yet I feel completely at ease. Montserrat does that to you.

I stand in the street for a moment, deciding which door I'm going to rap on first when I notice a female voice singing. I do not recognize the tune but its sweet melody seems to be the perfect complement to the rolling green hills surrounding me. It reminds me of an old Irish folk song which would be very appropriate here in Montserrat considering that the island is often referred to as the "Emerald Isle" due to its physical resemblance to one of its main cultural influences, Ireland. With no obvious clue as to where to go, I start heading toward the house of the neighborhood vocalist with the thought that she might be able to point me in the right direction. The friendliness of

Montserratians is legendary, and I knew that whoever was unknowingly serenading me would lend a helping hand in finding Minetta.

As I approach the house, it takes some effort to get through the old wooden gate. Like many houses on the island, it is old and in need of repair, but the yard is clean and organized. The residents in this village may be poor but the owner of this house obviously takes pride in her home. As I approach the front of the house, I notice that the front door is open with a thin sheet of translucent fabric covering the entrance. I can see the faint shadow of the singing woman behind the curtain. As I approach the doorway, I tentatively call out "Hello?" Her singing stops and the curtain is pulled back revealing an old woman sitting in a simple straight back chair. She is dressed casually but with that hint of elegance that many people of her generation cherish: a beautiful blouse, a long colorful skirt that contrasts and compliments her dark skin, and sensible shoes. Her coarse dark hair is combed back neatly. She is not expecting a visitor but looks as if she is ready to be a hostess at a moment's notice. She greets me with a broad smile and kind eyes. I say to her, "Excuse me but I am looking for Minetta Francis. Do you happen to know which house she lives in?" To which she replies in a strong Caribbean accent, "I am Minetta Francis. Please come in."

I am ecstatic! I have found the elusive Minetta Francis! She is here in front of me alive and with a radiant smile. She is 81 years old and residing in the house that she bought over 35 years ago while working for AIR Studios. She may not currently live on the island, but she maintains her home here to have a familiar place to return to when she visits Montserrat. I find out later that too many good memories keep her from selling the house. The room is spotlessly clean and sparsely furnished with a small desk, a couch covered in protective plastic, and two chairs set facing each other as if ready for a pair of friends to have a conversation. She offers me a seat and I sit across from her as if I were a neighbor coming for a visit. Something about her greeting makes me feel that I am welcome in her home, that I could actually be her neighbor. Such is Montserrat.

I introduce myself and explain the reason for my visit: I am here to interview people who were involved with AIR Studios for my book. Again, a smile flashes across her face and when she speaks, her succinct reply validates everything I feel about this project and why I am compelled to take up the mantle of documenting the history of AIR Studios Montserrat. She says to me, "I was wondering when someone was going to ask me about AIR Studios." I was stunned. In the forty years since she first became a stalwart member of its staff, I was about to be the first person ever to interview her about her many years working for AIR Studios. In this moment, I knew that documenting the studio's history was a project worth pursuing, preserving its history for posterity before it is lost to time.

Brian Sallerson
January 2019

MONTSERRAT HISTORY

When addressing the subject of AIR Studios Montserrat, I would be remiss if I did not include a brief history of the island of Montserrat since the island's past led to the environment and culture that convinced George Martin that Montserrat would be the ideal location for his new studio. George could have built the studio anywhere in the world and yet he specifically chose Montserrat for this remote studio project. The island's history is critical to the story of how the studio came to be.

Columbus

Montserrat was "discovered" in 1493 by Christopher Columbus on his second Spanish-sponsored voyage across the Atlantic. He did not actually make landfall on the island but merely viewed the island in the distance from his ship as he made his way through the Leeward Islands. He named the island 'Santa Maria de Montserrat' due to its resemblance to the mountainous area surrounding the Abbey of Montserrat near Barcelona, Spain. He was told by his local guides that the island was uninhabited at the time, so Columbus continued his voyage westward and the Spaniards never colonized the island.

Not much is known about the history of Montserrat prior to Columbus' trip though the Leeward Islands. Evidence of habitation has been discovered by archeologists, indicating that the island was used as a home or possibly as a point of harbor by small local island tribes such as the Arawaks and Caribs, but there is not significant evidence of substantial human use of the island in previous centuries.

Irish Ties Begin As Does Slavery

The deep ties that the island has with Ireland began in the 17th century when Irish Catholics found sanctuary in Montserrat after being forced from the island of St. Kitts by their Protestant countrymen. News of the Catholic haven in the Leeward islands made its way to the United States and in 1633, persecuted Catholics from the state of Virginia immigrated to the island. More than a decade later, Irish prisoners were sent to the island as indentured servants.

Later in the 17th century, a plantation economy emerged with the island's main export crop being sugar. As with many agricultural Caribbean colonies, slaves from Africa were brought to Montserrat to work the fields. Due to the oppression suffered by the slaves and indentured servants, they decided to revolt on St. Patrick's Day 1768, knowing that their masters would be distracted, celebrating the traditional Irish holiday. Unfortunately, the slave revolt was not successful and many slaves were killed for the act of rebellion. Today, St. Patrick's Day is a national holiday in Montserrat, not celebrating the famous Catholic saint, but instead paying tribute to the slaves who lost their lives while trying to gain their freedom in 1768.

Economy Evolves

During the 17th and 18th centuries, the island changed hands several times between the French and British until Montserrat became a permanent colony of England with the signing of the Treaty of Versailles in 1783. (It remains a British territory to this day.) The plantation economy began to wane throughout the 18th century due to natural disasters such as hurricanes, droughts, earthquakes, and with the emancipation of slaves when slavery was abolished by Britain in 1834. The plantations, which were often burdened with debt from the crop losses, were then tended by former slave sharecroppers who grew their own crops on plantation lands. As the sugar industry collapsed in the mid-1800s, there was a shift to limes as the local mainstay crop. Several decades later, a hurricane devastated the lime orchards in 1899. Afterwards, there was a subsequent shift to cotton which continued to be the main export of the island until the middle of the 20th century. Montserratian cotton was known for its high quality within the textile industry.

Into The 20th Century and The Rise of Tourism

In the 1940s and 1950s, the decline of agriculture industries, such as cotton and fruit production, caused a large emigration away from Montserrat as many people left to find employment overseas. Over 5,000 Montserratians moved to England between the mid-1940s and mid-1960s which represented a loss of almost 20% of the population of the island. It was during this time that many of the large plantation estates in Montserrat were broken up into smaller land plots in order to build vacation homes for expatriates, most of them coming from England, Canada, and America. Many of these villas were used as winter homes and this began what local island historian and poet Sir Howard Fergus calls "residential tourism." This term refers to the fact that the tourism industry in Montserrat was based on expatriates staying in homes they had built on the island for longer periods of time rather than short stays in conventional hotels as you would find with a traditional tourism-based economy. Many of these expatriates are called "snowbirds" as they tend to stay on the island during the winter months, escaping the harshness of the weather in their home countries in the north. Since they lived on the island long term, their needs were closer to locals rather than traditional tourists so there was not the demand for trinket shops, large dance clubs, or car and boat rentals. With the boom in residential tourism came an influx of real estate and construction investment from these tourists who made Montserrat their home for part of the year. This economic boom also provided work for locals in many areas such as construction, maintenance, hospitality, etc. As such, there was a very high employment rate and little poverty on the island during this period. Montserrat was in an economic upswing in the 1970s and it was into this environment that AIR Studios Montserrat was developed.

LIFE IN MONTSERRAT

To comprehend what the experience of working at the studio was like, you must understand the island culture of Montserrat that was an essential part of the studio experience. Montserrat is unique amongst most of the islands in the Caribbean and its culture was an integral part of why the experience of recording or working at AIR Montserrat left such a strong imprint on those who were there.

The Way The Caribbean Used To Be

The major misconception of the legend of AIR Montserrat is that the island was a playground for the rich artists with many outlets for rock star debauchery that you might imagine happening during the freewheeling 1970s and 1980s. Seeing pictures of bands lounging around the pool, drinks in hand, surrounded by the beauty of the Caribbean can give that impression, but the reality is that Montserrat was quite different than many of the neighboring islands in the Caribbean. Other Caribbean islands relied on tourism for their economies and thus had built up resorts and entertainment industries to cater to those travelers who came to party and to tour the islands. Montserrat was an outlier among its island neighbors in that traditional tourism was not a major economic force. Since the influence of tourism on the local economy was minimal, Montserrat's culture remained stable throughout the 20th century, changing little as other islands moved from agriculture to tourism. Montserrat was, and still is today, referred to by many as "The way the Caribbean used to be."

Plymouth, the island's capital and central hub for business and socialization, was more like a small country town than a bustling city. The population of Plymouth in the early 1980s was about 1,500 residents with the remaining 10,000 Montserratians scattered across the island in little villages made up of small houses, humble shacks with corrugated galvanized roofing, or tracts of upscale villas for expatriates. The streets of Plymouth were narrow and many were made of cobblestone. The town's architecture consisted mostly of 19th century colonial buildings clustered tightly around the roads, some painted with bright pastel colors but unlike other islands, this was more for the enjoyment of the locals rather than for attracting tourists.

Downtown Plymouth Circa Mid-1980s
Photo: Anna Dam

Island visitors could spend some time wandering through town and visiting some of the local shops, but these businesses were mainly selling goods and services for local consumption, not catering to tourists. There were only a handful of small hotels on the island and 5-star restaurants were non-existent. Bars tended to be single room shacks scattered around the island in local villages or open aired clubs, such as "The Plantation" or "The Yacht Club" (that curiously did not have a place for docking yachts) that catered to locals and snowbird expats. Those fancying an afternoon at the links could play a round at the Belham Valley golf course. For a night of dancing, there was one small disco in town, appropriately called "Le Cave" that was in the basement of a building in Plymouth.

La Cave's Rules-Always Smartly Dressed
Photo: Anna Dam

If someone wanted watersports, they could visit Danny Sweeney at his beach shack to rent a windsurfing board or a small dinghy. There was hiking to the Soufriere volcano crater or to the island's large waterfall or perhaps hanging out at one of the island's black sand beaches. Fishing trips could be arranged with locals. Beyond these limited entertainment avenues, there were not many other activities that might have appealed to tourists on the island.

The pier in Plymouth was not large enough to accommodate the docking of large cruise ships so if tourists wanted to visit the island, they had to take smaller boats that would ferry them from the cruise ships to the island. Midge Ure of the band Ultravox described the situation as "There was nothing for cruise ship tourists to do. They'd come off the ship and buy a coconut or a pair of maracas...but [the island] wasn't set up for [tourism]...The fact was it didn't have a fantastic marina or a Kentucky Fried Chicken or McDonalds or any of that stuff." Maureen Hodd, resident of the island for fifty years said that "Many people come to Montserrat once but don't come back because they say it is too quiet, but that is the beauty of it."

The influence of the Irish connection with Montserrat was (and still is) prevalent throughout the culture of the island. Like I stated previously, the biggest holiday in Montserrat is Saint Patrick's Day which is a weeklong festival celebrating the slave uprising and Irish traditions. Clover shamrocks could be found painted on buildings all over the island, even adorning the peak of the roof of Government House. Towns and villages were named after prominent Irish towns such as Cork and Kinsale. The Irish influence was even reflected in the surnames of the those whose families had been on the island for generations, names like Riley, Farrell, and Sweeney.

Montserratians celebrated together during several annual festivals which included "Festival" in late December and Saint Patrick's Day in March. The festivals were known for their colorful parades and partying in the streets. These moving caravans of merriment did not only occur during specific festivals but could spontaneously start up at any time and were known on the island as "Jump-Ups." AIR Engineer Ken Blair explained: "The way it worked in Montserrat was...from time to time sporadically a Jump Up would start and it was basically a party that was a rolling party through the streets. So they put a sound system on the back of a truck and then it would slowly move [through town]. Everyone would just line up behind it with a beer, dancing and gradually moving...From where I'm from, if someone tried to run a party in the middle of town, the police would shut it down. In Montserrat, police would close the road so that the party could happen. Everyone would spend hours dancing along the street and we took part in some of those parties and there was always just a feeling that you were absolutely welcome in those parties which were essentially local affairs."

Law Enforcement

Montserratians had great pride in their community and could be quite strict with their laws, despite the laid-back attitude of the island. Despite the small size of the airport and the low volume of visitors to the island, immigration and customs was taken quite seriously. AIR Engineer Matt Butler said that "[Studio manager] Yvonne warned us, all of us that visited, to be very careful of the airport. No swaggering in saying 'You there.' We had to be very respectful at the airport. More than anywhere else on the island because they had the power to let us through or not. So I remember...going every time to that airport thinking, 'Don't blow it Butler. Don't do anything wrong...It was definitely not the moment to joke about having a bomb in your luggage. They were very proud of the job they were doing and if you're lucky, you'd get a stamp in your passport which is the cloverleaf which I'm very proud to have." Although the island had no stop lights and a light load of road traffic, even traffic laws were enforced rigorously. Again, a story from Matt Butler. Matt, and AIR staffers Paul Rushbrooke, and Malcolm Atkin were driving into Plymouth to buy some vanilla essence for Malcolm's wife. They reached the intersection where the store was a stone's throw around the corner from where they had come to a stop. Matt said that "We came across probably the only crossroads in Plymouth...and there was a Montserratian policeman there. He stopped us and Malcolm, a very deadpan kind of guy, looked at him and said 'I'm going left.' [the officer said] 'You cannot turn left.' [Malcolm says] 'It's only there. I just want to go there.' 'No. You can't turn left.' And of course, Paul Rushbrooke and I were having fits of laughter because Malcolm was just looking at this guy saying, 'What are you talking about?' But the policeman was saying 'REALLY! YOU CAN NOT TURN LEFT!'...This was such a surprise on this idyllic island to be told what we could and couldn't do. But, of course as I say, [they were] very proud people and they had their laws and rules like anywhere else."

Drugs were highly illegal and were not tolerated by the police. Those who dealt drugs or used them openly were swiftly arrested. A long-time resident of the island told me that the police pulled the proprietor of the local record shop over and found a few marijuana seeds in his car. He was promptly deported. Since the island was physically small and its population was limited, criminals had no place to hide and incidents were easily solved which kept criminality at a minimum. There were only two points of entry, the airport and Plymouth's port, so the local authorities knew the comings and goings of visitors and locals and thus, everyone who was on the island at all times. With limited ways to leave the island, security for prisoners was quite lax. Stuart Breed, AIR Engineer told me, "You used to see the prisoners on the beach, manacled together, picking up deadwood...They'd all have machetes and there'd be two guards with bamboo sticks. So you got 5, 8, 10 people with machetes and two guys [guards] with bamboo sticks. They didn't think about trying to escape. Where you going to go? It was incredible." Local Montserratian broadcaster Rose Willock said that, "In Montserrat...you don't want to be seen as somebody that's a troublemaker. And it's because of the smallness and the intimacy, that peacefulness that is part of who we are."

A "Small" Community

A story that really captures the attitude of the "smallness" of Montserrat was told to me by artist Anna Dam. She spent many summers in Montserrat in the 1980s and 1990s, living in local villages and capturing the vibrant landscape and architecture on canvas. Regarding the politics of the island, she told me: "This is a funny thing about [Montserratians.] They know their British governor [personally] because they ran into him on the street yesterday...They know their chief minister because they grew up with him and they know everything about him. If they want to ask something about their government or what's happening or what's going on, they just talk to him about it. So I would walk [into a bar] and sit down and they would say, [in a Montserratian accent] 'So Anna, what do you think your president is going to do about the bombing everybody and everything?' And I'm like, 'How am I [supposed to know]?' They just assumed I talk to the president. I swear to God. And I'm sitting there and they're all wanting to know what Bush is going to do. 'What's he going to do? I don't know what he's going to do. I'm here!'...They literally think we all are as involved with our government as they are with theirs." Another example of the "smallness" of Montserrat is the fact that many people knew each others' cars by their license plate numbers. Since there were a very limited number of cars on the island and only four digits on a license plate, it was quite easy to remember the tag numbers of many of their neighbors.

Classism In Society

Although most black and white locals would often socialize with each other in everyday life, one negative aspect of Montserratian culture during the time of AIR Montserrat was a layer of classism that ran beneath the outwardly cordial interactions of the upper-class white residents and the Afro-Caribbean native islanders. While one might try to label it as racism due its apparent appearance of "white versus black," it was described to me as a "snobbery" of the well-to-do expats and white Montserratians who tended to only socialize within their own socio-economic stratum. This can be attributed to the colonial history of the island as well as the social norms in the home countries where these local expats hailed from. Dave Harries, AIR Managing Director, was quite candid about the situation and had this to say: "Some of the 'whiteys' did not like me because I mixed [with the locals.] I used to go down to the Seaway bar and play darts with the locals and drink with them...It wasn't like other places [that had overt racism] but maybe you had to behave in a certain way. It wasn't racist. It was snobbery...They would think you were 'going below yourself.' It was criticism from that." I was told that when one of the white owners would have a party, "anyone who is somebody on the island" would be invited. This meant people such as the Governor, Chief Minister, and other well-to-do white expats and islanders would be in attendance with the local black islanders serving the party. With that said, this was not the case with most of the AIR staff that came to the island to work at the studio. Yes, they would be invited to the "elite" parties because of the perceived exclusivity and panache of the studio but they spent considerable time socializing with local Montserratians and integrating into the island's culture. They effectively straddled the line between the socio-economic stratums of Montserrat.

Almost Paradise

Irrespective of this classism, Montserratians are a warm, friendly, and welcoming people. One of the nicknames that I have heard for Montserrat is "Strangers' Paradise." AIR Montserrat employee and native Montserratian Stephanie Francis said that "If you are a stranger, you get treated pretty well. If they see you on the street, somebody is going to say hello and find out who you are. If you look lost, somebody is going to help you." Trust and caring for one another is paramount in Montserratian culture. Most people did not lock their cars or homes. Dave Harries said that while Malcolm Atkin and he were on the island building the studio, they lost the key to their rented house. It was filled with very expensive high-end audio equipment like amplifiers and microphones and yet no one tried stealing anything. He said that "the only thing that would come up missing on occasion [was] something

19

out of the fridge." In fact, it was considered an insult to lock up your vehicles as Geoff Irons, AIR technical manager, found out on his first day on the island. He told me: "My first encounter was coming from London. I turned up in the studio van one day...I think was going to the customs house and I shut it and locked it. A habit. And I guy came up to me and said, 'Why did you lock it?' I said, 'Well you have to, don't you?' He said, 'No you don't. You're insulting us if you lock this van. It means you are locking it because you think we're going to steal from it and we're not.' So I said, 'Ok. I'll unlock it then.' And that was my first contact with the local Montserratians...It was only because I've come from London. If you don't lock it, you lose it. And forever after that I...never took the keys out of the car. Just leave the car and...nobody ever touched anything, ever."

Montserratians looked after one another. Stephanie Francis told me that "We looked after the older people as well, in the community. So if I know that there's an old person that lived there, I'd pass, say hello, see if they want some shopping. So there's somebody always helping. We always help each other out. So if you are [in need], and I've got stuff in my garden, I'd come bring you some bananas. You didn't have to ask me. I would think, 'Let me go carry him some bananas to get friendly, to say hello.' So I'd bring you some of my fruits, my vegetables and we do that often. We share with each other what we have."

Religion played a large role in many of the Montserratians' lives. Churches were plentiful considering the small population and they were a major source of communal socialization and celebration. The beauty of the congregations' choirs singing was noted by many in interviews. Producer Chris Neil told me a great story about Gerry Rafferty's experience with the splendor of one church service he happened upon. "Gerry Rafferty told me a lovely story. It was one Sunday morning when he was there and it was glorious. He just went for a walk. He walked past this church. It was like a tin church, put together. He heard the singing coming out...He said the singing was beautiful. So Gerry crept into the back of the church. He was in shorts. [They] were in 3 piece suits and ties and he said they were all there all dressed up to the nines. Everyone singing and he said it was stunning. The choir was just beautiful. Evangelical hymns they were singing. One of the guys at the back saw Gerry and Gerry [was] in a t-shirt, flip-flops, and shorts. 'Come in, brother. Come in.' And Gerry went 'No. No. Can I just listen?' He said 'Come in! Doesn't matter. Come in.' So Gerry went into this church and stood at the back and [was] just in awe. He said 'I wish I'd had a microphone. Set it up and let them sing.' He said, 'It was beautiful...Lovely people.'"

In the 1970s, Montserrat was in an economic upswing. Unemployment was almost nonexistent due to the flourishing construction business caused by the residential tourism boom. The island's schools provided a high-quality education. The island's roads were known to be the best in the Caribbean. The American Medical University campus on the island brought many overseas medical students to Montserrat for their education. AIR Montserrat also contributed greatly to the local economy bringing money to the island in many different ways. The studio directly employed locals for various jobs at the facility such as bartenders, gardeners, chefs, and housekeeping. Local craftsmen and engineers were hired to maintain the electrical and HVAC systems at the studio. Local food and goods were purchased for the artists and staff from the island's merchants. Artists rented villas and cars when staying on the island and visited local businesses for entertainment and dining. The studio had a cascading positive economic benefit for the island and the prestige of famous artists coming to Montserrat to record there elevated its image throughout the world.

With that said, let's take a step back and talk about the history of AIR Studios leading up to George Martin's decision to build a studio on the island.

A BRIEF HISTORY OF AIR STUDIOS

The history of AIR Studios begins with George Martin's dissatisfaction of working for EMI records. George had been head of EMI's Parlophone record label, which was known for their comedy record releases in the late 1950s and early 1960s. George's life trajectory changed in 1962 when he signed a contract with a very talented yet unknown band hailing out of Liverpool, The Beatles. George became the band's producer and together, they dominated the worldwide music landscape throughout the 1960s. With dozens of number one records released over the first few years with The Beatles, you may think that George, as the person responsible for signing the Beatles and producing their music, would have a stake in the financial success of the band. Sadly, this was not the case. He was being paid a meager yearly salary of about 3,000 English pounds (about $4,000 U.S.) at the time, which is about £22,000 English pounds ($33,000 U.S.) in 2020. George, who was integral to the artistic and financial success of the band, knew his value to EMI and tried renegotiating his contract to obtain a more equitable part of the profits that EMI was raking in with each subsequent Beatles hit. This idea of a producer receiving royalties represented a sea change in the recording industry as producers such as George were compensated as company employees rather than part of the creative team that made records. When EMI balked at his idea of sharing the profits with producers, George decided to strike out on his own, forever changing producers' place in the recording industry. He hatched a plan to create his own company representing the interest of record producers, giving them the power, prestige, and profit sharing that they deserved. When he left EMI, he took three other prominent producers of the time with him to start his new venture: Peter Sullivan from Decca Records (Tom Jones, Engelbert Humperdinck), Ron Richards from EMI (The Hollies, Gerry and the Pacemakers), and John Burgess from EMI (Freddie and the Dreamers, Manfred Mann). The four of them formed Associated Independent Recording (or AIR) in 1965. This new company would be controlled by the producers and it would also finance their recording projects, with the producers being compensated through a share of the profits of album sales. This new "freelance producer" compensation model changed the industry forever.

The start of the new company was not quite as glamorous as it may seem. Carol Weston, John Burgess' secretary describes the start of AIR: "I was the baby at the company. We left EMI: George, John, Ron, Shirley who worked for George and Ron, and myself. We left EMI with their stationary sort of tucked in our knickers to start again. And we started in a little garage over a bank in Baker Street. We had no furniture to start with. We were sitting on boxes and it was just such a wonderful adventure. My boss, John, I'd only been working for him for about 18 months then. I started in July of '64...and by September '65, we'd started up AIR. And he said to me, 'I'm leaving' and I thought 'Oh!' I was so disappointed because I thought, 'I like this job.' He said, 'Do you want to come with me?' I didn't even know what he was going to do. And I didn't know he was going to George because it was all kept very, very secret. And I had no idea and I just said 'Yes!' From then on, [it was] a wonderful big adventure that lasted right until '93 when John and I both left AIR."

AIR Grows

Throughout the late 1960s, AIR had much success with their freelance production business and by 1970, they took the "independent" part of their namesake to the next level. Their stellar reputation for production and financial success allowed them to design and open their own recording studio in London. Previously, they had been using recording studios owned by record labels, such as Abbey Road Studios which were owned by EMI. Having their own studios to record artists managed by AIR would allow them to have control over costs, technology, and the creative process. They opened their Oxford Circus Studios in London in October 1970. The studio complex was located on the upper floor of a department store in a central London shopping district. It had three separate recording studios that could accommodate everything from solo artists to full orchestras. Many new technologies were pioneered there including 24-track recording. The studio would host a large variety of artists over the decade including Pink Floyd, Queen, The Pretenders, Paul McCartney, and The Sex Pistols.

In the early part of the 1970s, Ron and Peter moved on from AIR leaving John and George as the principals of the company.

With Oxford Circus well established as a premier recording studio by the mid-1970s, George had started to think beyond London. He had an idea for a recording studio far from the bustling cities such as Paris, Los Angeles, and New York. The seas were calling...

THE CONCEPT

n the early-1970s, George Martin was contemplating building a studio away from the bustle of large cities where many of the prominent studios of the day were located. A key factor in his decision to expand beyond AIR Studios in London was the fact that his own Oxford Circus studio was so popular that it was causing scheduling issues for his own recording projects. He said that "AIR London had been going for a while and had been so busy and successful that I could not get into it...more and more of my work was being done abroad."1 George began to explore possible options for building a facility away from England.

The High Seas

One of the early options for a destination studio that was explored by George and his staff at AIR was the concept of building a mobile studio on a ship. Former AIR studio manager Dave Harries explained that George had considered using a "big boat" for a recording studio "...so you could go anywhere in the world and record. That was the theory of it." George called this idea 'world mobile,' and his original concept of a mobile marine recording studio was to be based in the Mediterranean with destinations in Greece and Italy. During the period of 1972 to 1974, significant research was performed regarding the technical issues, logistics, and economics of such an endeavor. A 160 ft. ship was selected by George, but eventually he had to abandon the idea of recording at sea due to the problems caused by the movement of the ship and the sounds of the ship's motors that reverberated through the hull. He then pivoted from the concept of at-sea sessions to recording while docked which solved many of these technical issues. Another logistical problem that George foresaw was American artists' reluctance to travel the long distance to the Mediterranean for recording, so he again pivoted the idea of 'world mobile' from Europe to the Caribbean. His idea was to have pre-negotiated deals with island governments and hospitality industries so that he could bring the mobile studio to whatever Caribbean Island an artist would prefer. Although many of the logistics and technical issues had viable solutions, what finally killed the project was economics. In 1974, England was in an economic crisis and AIR's new financial partner, Chrysalis Records, decided it was not comfortable with the amount of investment that would have been required to complete George's unique and financially risky project. The 'world mobile' concept was shelved.

A "Destination" Studio

In the mid-1970s, "destination studios" became en vogue in the recording industry. Producer Chris Neil explained that at that time, "It became the fashion or the thing to do to be recording in some exotic location." He continued: "Back in the 70s, 80s, the music business was awash with money. Everyone was making money. If you signed 5 bands and 4 didn't make it, it didn't matter because the 5th one would make so much money...So basically, it became fashionable to record. McCartney would go out and record on a boat in Australia or something. It became the fashion or the thing to do to be recording in some exotic location. So when everyone in the U.K. and the U.S. heard that George Martin, the Beatles producer, has opened a studio where you could make an album on a paradise island. 'Let's go!' because A. You knew the studio was going to work. It was going to be run professionally. B. Instead of [being in] the middle of Oxford Street in London or Lexington Avenue in NY, raining and whatever, you were going to be in a beautiful location. But the killer was that it was George Martin's."

In 1976, George himself experienced recording at one of the most famous destination studios of the day producing America's "Hideaway" album at Caribou Ranch. The studio was built in a renovated barn on a former Arabian horse ranch outside of Boulder, Colorado. The isolated rural location in the Rocky Mountains provided quite a different experience for artists than most urban modern studios of the day, with its expansive and isolated location, mountain views, high altitude, and rustic activities. In Billboard Magazine in 1979, George said that he had been contemplating the idea of an "environmental studio" after he had recorded at Caribou Ranch.[1]

In 1977, George was seeking a suitable location for his personal destination studio. He considered several options including Canada, Mexico, and islands in the Caribbean.[1] In his search, he found Montserrat with its lush tropical environment, geographical isolation, and relatively modern infrastructure. Dave Harries said that George liked that the island's communications systems and its roads were particularly good compared to other Caribbean islands. It also helped that the island was a British protectorate which would help facilitate many financial and legal facets of the business. One of the most important characteristics of Montserrat, which convinced George that it would be the perfect location for his new studio, was the culture of the island. He said "The reason that I chose Montserrat was that it was the first place I'd come to which seemed to be together as a people. They are warm and friendly which is not typical in the Caribbean because of our pasts and the guilts that we bear [due to slavery] ...The Montserratians are open and friendly, and I fell in love."[1]

The main drawback of building a commercial recording studio in Montserrat was that the island lacked an international airport. This was a major hindrance for a business that relied on regular visitation of artists, producers, and engineers traveling to and from the island, as well as the complex logistics of moving large amounts of sensitive instruments and gear required to make records. Also, the transportation of materials to build and maintain the studio's physical complex would be more difficult in Montserrat than on neighboring islands such as Antigua or Barbados. Dave Harries said that the lack of an international airport was "a pain in the ass. I preferred Antigua for the studio," but since AIR was George's business and this his personal project, Montserrat was chosen to be the location for the new studio.

With Montserrat selected, George needed to find an isolated location on the island that was suitable for building a remote studio, one with privacy for the artists as well as being an ideal distance away from locals so that they would not be disturbed by the loud music regularly coming from the studio. He wanted something that would be a special place, one that would capture the natural beauty of Montserrat and the Caribbean, a true destination studio. The search was on...

1 McCullaugh, J. (1979, December 15). "Martin: Montserrat Has 'Peace Of Mind'". Billboard, p. 41.

THE RIDGE

In Montserrat, George Martin had found the perfect location for the new studio at a property known as 'The Ridge.' Set high on a hill, 370 feet above sea level and facing west overlooking the Belham Valley and Old Road Bay, it offered sweeping views of the island's lush green hills, the Caribbean Sea, and gorgeous sunsets every evening. Set on thirty-six acres away from Montserrat's most populous areas, it offered privacy and seclusion for the famous artists that would be recording there, but prior to George's development of the property, it was simply a family home.

A Sturge Family Picnic On The Lawn Of The Ridge Property
Photo: Julie McNamera

The Sturges

Originally, the property that eventually became the home of AIR Montserrat was part of the sprawling estate of the Hollender family known as The Waterworks. It had been a sugar plantation in colonial days and had remained in the Hollender family for many generations. In the early 1960s, Joseph Edward Sturge and his wife Julie moved to Montserrat from England so that Joe could take a position with the Montserrat Company. The Sturge family had been long associated with the modern history of Montserrat dating back to Joseph Sturge, a Quaker who came to the island in the mid-1800s and helped the newly emancipated slaves gain independence from indentured servitude that they were forced into after slavery. He and his descendants operated the Montserrat Company which was integral in the development of the lime and cotton industries of the island. Joe Edward Sturge had been on the board of the Montserrat Company and was living in England when the company was sold to a Canadian firm in 1961. Because of his knowledge of the family business, The Montserrat Company's new owners hired Joe to work for the new company on the island. Joe and Julie left England and relocated to Montserrat. They moved into a small house in Richmond Yard while searching for a permanent home. They found what they were looking for in a parcel of land that was purchased from the Hollenders which had been part of the Waterworks Estate. They named the property "The Ridge" due to its location on the edge of the hill leading up to the Waterworks Estate.

The Ridge Villa Under Construction
Photo: Julie McNamera

There were no structures on the property at the time, so Joe and Julie worked with local builder Stan Myers to design a villa for the family to be built on the property. The villa included a master bedroom located off the large living room with two smaller bedrooms in a wing perpendicular to the living area of the main house. The bedroom wing was expanded to three bedrooms a few years later. The main living area included a large fireplace, elevated dining area and expansive kitchen. The location of the kitchen across from the bedroom wing formed a courtyard garden behind the villa. The bathrooms were decorated using lavender colored tiles, sinks, and toilets which Julie said "was quite unusual for the time." Two other unique features of this home when compared to other contemporary houses on the island was the design of the foundation and the balcony. The island was prone to volcanic earthquakes which Julie called "the shakes." Stan Meyers decided to build the foundation of the villa on a bed of sand so that the house could move independently of the earth below it. This would help the cinder block walls avoid cracking from the vibrations during a quake. Additionally, off the dining room, a cantilevered balcony was built, a first for a home in Montserrat. It was a small balcony built looking west over the valley and sea below. The villa was completed in 1964.

The Original Cantilevered Patio At The Ridge
Photo: Julie McNamera

The Sturge's family villa was home to many social parties, often hosted on the lawn in front of their home. AIR Montserrat studio manager Yvonne Robinson, who is a native of the island, said that she remembers visiting the Sturges at The Ridge for events when she was a child. Joe grew sweet potatoes on the land below the balcony which would eventually become the location of the studio swimming pool. Joe and Julie raised their two children in the home over the next 10 years, but when the marriage fell apart in the early 1970s, both Joe and Julie moved back to England leaving the property vacant.

It sat unoccupied for several years until George Martin discovered The Ridge when looking for a suitable property for his new island studio. He purchased the property in 1977 from the Sturges for 30,000 English pounds which Julie said was a low price at the time. Interestingly, the studio's architect David Hodd had been in negotiations to purchase the property prior to George's interest but he only wanted to purchase the villa and four of the thirty-six acres of land that comprised the parcel. The Sturges were not particularly interested in selling only part of the property so when George offered to purchase the entire parcel, they jumped at the opportunity.

Now that the property had been purchased in Montserrat, the real challenge began: designing and building an ultra-modern recording studio on a remote Caribbean island, thousands of miles from AIR's home office in London.

STUDIO CONSTRUCTION

With the Ridge property purchased from the Sturge family, George's next step was to hire an architect to design the studio complex's structures. The existing villa on the property would provide the living, dining, and entertainment areas of the facility but the recording studio itself would need to be designed and built from scratch. For the architectural work, George turned to local Montserratian architect David Hodd.

The Architect

David and his wife Maureen, who were British, had moved to Montserrat in 1970 from Africa. They told me that they had only planned on staying on the island for one year but ended up staying for the next fifty. David recalled that George called him in the Fall of 1977 and asked if he had any experience in designing recording studios. David said that although he had not designed a recording studio before, he confidently told George that "I could do it. No problem." Although he was living on a British protectorate, David had not been accredited by British architectural authorities at the time, but given George's ethos of granting people the chance to branch out into new territory within their chosen field, David was hired to design George's newest studio project. To give David some insight into the current state of modern recording studio design, George flew him to London and took him on tours of several of the local studios in the city. David said, "I got a very good idea from that trip." He arrived home in Montserrat telling Maureen, "I've got to design a recording studio and I have nine months to do it." Not only did he have to design the studio building itself, but he also had to make changes to the existing Ridge villa to accommodate George's ideas about how it was going to be used in this "environmental studio" setting. David went to work immediately.

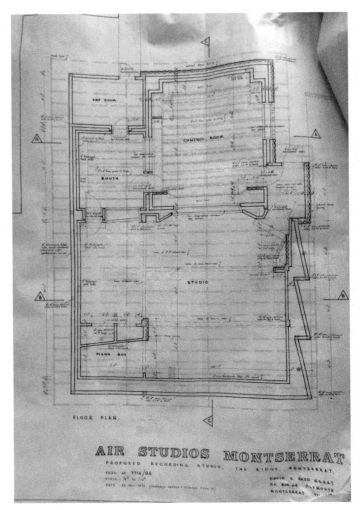

Original Architectrural Plans For The Studio
Courtesy of David Hodd

Finances

On the financial front of the studio's development, AIR worked with the Montserratian government to develop financial incentives for the company in exchange for the economic and promotional benefits that the studio would provide to the island. The deal that was struck was an incentive program approved by the Governor-in-Council in January 1978. This program provided a 15-year tax holiday for AIR's local corporation in Montserrat, AIR Studios Montserrat Limited. It also allowed for duty-free importation of machinery, equipment, and building material to be used in the studio complex. Considering the millions of dollars of imported recording gear and materials needed to build the studio, combined with 15 years without taxes, AIR

Studios was saving a considerable amount of money on both the initial startup costs and future income taxes due to these incentives offered by the government. Malcolm Atkin, former managing director of AIR, estimated that the studio construction costs would have been 30%-40% higher if the import duties would not have been waived. The studio's construction funding was provided by George with financial assistance from AIR, Chrysalis Records, and the Bank of England. In an interview from 1979, George estimated that his investment was about 800,000 pounds.

The Construction Team

Dave Harries, who was the studio manager of AIR at the time, was tapped to lead the construction project and design the acoustics of the studio. Dave started in the recording industry after receiving his degree in electronics while serving in an apprenticeship with the Royal Radar Establishment. In the early 1960s, he went to work for EMI at their aptly named EMI Studios, better known as Abbey Road in later years, where he worked in their research department. His responsibilities at EMI eventually led him to work alongside with George Martin and The Beatles where he made a whopping 50 pence an hour to work on many famous Beatles recordings, starting with Revolver. After George Martin left EMI to start AIR studios in the mid-1960s, Dave stayed with EMI, working with George when he would record at Abbey Road. In 1970, Geoff Emerick gave Dave a tour of AIR's Oxford Circus studios, which were under construction at the time. Dave was concerned that the location was going to be problematic but when some of his ex-EMI engineering cohorts asked him if he would be interested in joining them to work on the new studio, Dave decided to jump ship from EMI to AIR. He said, "It was a real opportunity to go there." After the studio was completed, Dave became chief engineer for AIR and eventually studio manager for company. When it came time to choose a manager for the daunting project of designing and building AIR Montserrat, Dave was the obvious choice for George.

In the earliest stage of the project, as the design and construction details were being hashed out, Dave and George Martin flew to Montserrat to meet with David Hodd and construction manager Des Larkins. Dave remembers sitting at the bar at Olveston House (a local hotel) on the island discussing the specifications for the project with George, Des, and David. Quite an informal location for a serious meeting about a complex endeavor but this was very typical of the culture of both AIR Studios and of Montserrat.

Des Larkins was the manager of Bostleman International Limited, a local construction company. Bostleman Construction, started by Fred Bostleman, had been operating in the U.S. successfully for many years. Fred had left his successful construction business in the hands of his sons during the 1970s after building the company from scratch over the previous decades. He wanted to move on and began looking for a new challenge. Having spent time on the island during holidays, Fred had decided to start a new business venture there, a construction company in Montserrat. Being the only construction firm on the island that could handle a project as complex as a cutting-edge recording studio, his company was chosen as the general contractor for the project with Des Larkins running the company at the local level. Des also had a personal connection with the island: he was Maureen Hodd's stepfather.

As David Hodd developed the plans for the studio's architecture, Dave Harries called upon the expertise of Geoff Emerick to assist with the acoustical design. Geoff was George Martin's engineer during much of the Beatles' recording years. His creativity and incredible sense of sound design led to a number of novel recording innovations that can be heard on Beatles' albums such as Sergeant Pepper's Lonely Hearts Club Band and Revolver. When George started AIR Studios in the late 1960s, Geoff declined to join him, instead choosing to take a position with Apple, the Beatle's record company, as the designer of their new recording studio. Geoff learned much about studio design from that project: acoustical tuning, construction materials, project management, and electrical design. After the studio was complete, he grew disenfranchised with Apple and decided to leave. He considered returning to work with his former partner, George Martin, at AIR but he was not sure if George would have him back after turning down his offer to join AIR several years prior. He rang Dave Harries to see what he thought George's reaction might be to Geoff's request to come aboard. He asked Dave, "Do you think George would have me back?" to which Dave replied, "Of course he would. [What] a silly, silly question!" Geoff moved to AIR from Apple and began working with George again as his engineer as well as producing records of his own and doing sound design for the company. It was a natural fit for Geoff to be involved with the AIR Montserrat project considering his sonic expertise and history with George. Dave Harries recalled a story that illustrated Geoff's clout in the design process of AIR Montserrat. The story involved Geoff, David Hodd and himself during the design process where the 'squareness' of the studio rooms was chosen: "I used to go out there [Montserrat] with Geoff...and sit with Hoddie [David Hodd] and he used to do all of his [architectural] drawings...So he'd be on his drafting board and Geoff would be sitting outside having a cigarette and having a drink or whatever and I 'd be running between the two. 'Geoff, what do you think of this? Could we do this?' [Geoff] 'Nahhh' [Dave] 'Can't we have some angles so it's nice and..' [Geoff] 'Nahhhh. Square. I want it square.' I said 'C'mon. That's boring.' [Geoff] 'No. Square!' So we had it all square. There's a square control room. Well, not square ...it's oblong but the corners are square...You had the [vocal] booth next to it. Same square and the machine room, square. And the studio, more or less square with the corner cut out for the piano booth." Although this made the room a bit more difficult to tune acoustically compared to many modern studios where wall angles are used to help treat frequency response, this decision to eschew anything other than a "box-like" shape is an example of the strong influence Geoff had on the final design of the studio.

Malcolm Atkin

With the architectural and construction personnel in place, Dave had to choose someone to design the technical and electrical specifications of the studio. For this, he turned to Malcolm Atkin who was head engineer for AIR Studios in London. Malcolm had earned a degree in electronic engineering several years prior but unlike most of his engineering cohorts at university, he was focused on music and played in a band. He had started working in the recording industry working as a technician for a record company which he described as "not a cool studio." The sole highlight of the gig for Malcolm was that they had a mobile recording unit. When the studio sold the mobile unit, Malcolm was tasked with delivering it to the new owners. When he arrived at the studio which had purchased the mobile unit, he quickly realized that this was the "cool" environment in which he wanted to be working. He described it as, "Suddenly, I met rock and rollers. This was what I signed up for." He made excuses with his employer in order to stay onsite as long as possible after delivery by claiming that the mobile unit was not working properly. It was there that Malcolm met Dave Harries when Dave stopped by the studio to deliver some tapes. Within a few days of this chance meeting, Malcolm received a call from Dave's assistant inviting him to an interview at AIR and in December of 1974, Malcolm's career at AIR Studios began. For several years, Malcolm was a studio technician caring for the electronics and electrical gear in AIR's studios in London. By the late 70s, he became the "#2 technician" at AIR by "process of elimination" as he described it. Other more experienced techs had moved to other positions within the company or had left AIR, so he came to be the #2 tech by pure happenstance. When Malcolm's boss resigned, Dave said to Malcolm "You can be the head engineer." Malcolm was rather nervous about accepting the position considering his young age, his lack of experience, and the responsibilities of the position. Another employee of AIR, tape operator John Walls, gave Malcolm some good advice: He had to take the position regardless of his inexperience because opportunities like this did not come up often. Malcolm accepted the offer and became AIR's de facto head technical engineer in 1977.

Although he had been with AIR Studios for several years at this point, Malcolm had only limited contact with its owner, George Martin. George was busy producing records and running the business, so he did not have much interaction with employees such as Malcolm who were on the front lines of keeping the studios functional on a day-to-day basis. Malcolm had only been head technical engineer for two weeks when George Martin suddenly appeared and said to him, "I've just been to the Caribbean. I bought 36 acres. I want you to build a studio there." Malcolm was taken aback and said to his boss, "But I've never built a studio before." George replied, "Don't worry about it. Dave [Harries] will show you how it is done." Suddenly, only two weeks into his tenure as head technical engineer, Malcolm was thrust into a project at AIR in which he had little knowledge or expertise. He said, "At the tender age of 26, I get thrown out in the West Indies...I must admit one of my thoughts at the time was 'Well, it is a long, long way away [from London]. Not too many people will see it. I'm bound to make some horrible mistakes.'" Once again, George Martin had demonstrated the AIR ethos of taking chances on people based on their personalities and skills rather than their experience. In London, Malcolm began to work on the technical electronics design of the studio while physical construction began in Montserrat.

As construction began, Dave recalled one problem that caused a delay of the studio construction at its onset. There was a house-sized boulder residing in the exact plot where the recording studio was to be built. Considering the frequent earth tremors from the island's dormant volcano, it would have caused problems with the structure's foundation. It had to be excavated before any work could begin. With the boulder removed, construction of the studio could start.

Villa Changes

To meet George's vision of the studio complex, David Hodd had designed several changes to the existing villa. The small, cantilevered balcony overlooking the ocean was to be extended to more than double its original size with a traditional Caribbean open roof overhead. This would create a large open-air patio to be used for dining or relaxing by artists where they could enjoy spectacular sunsets and cool evening breezes from the comfort of the villa. Immediately below the newly extended balcony, at the pool level, would be a glass enclosed recreation room with a pool table, table tennis, and dart boards. Since the villa was now being used as part of a recording complex and in a capacity far beyond its original intention as a family home, other functional changes were made to accommodate the villa's new role hosting recording artists and AIR staff members. A large capacity walk-in freezer was installed. Much of the lower level of the villa was changed to meet the needs of a working recording studio such as equipping an electronics workshop for AIR technicians, storage for bands' gear and recording media, and power equipment for the studio. Although there were many changes made to the villa, much of it remained the same including the bedrooms, bathrooms, and main living area. Julie Sturge said that when she visited the studio in 1989, many of the furnishings they had left behind when moving to England in the early 1970s were still in use and the same unique lavender tiles were still in the bathroom, 25 years after they built the home.

Included in David's plans was the addition of a 50-foot swimming pool to be installed at ground level below the balcony with a diving board, slide, and surrounding patio. Located only a few steps from the studio control room and the villa, it would provide respite for the artists when they needed to take a break from hours of recording. Below the swimming pool, the land was cleared for a large multi-acre lawn.

Complex Logistics

Although there was an assortment of basic building supplies available locally on the island such as concrete blocks, plywood, and cement, there were a significant number of specialized materials that were not which had to be imported. Items such as the air conditioning system, freezer, certain electrical fittings, and even the spiral staircase for the balcony were brought in from abroad. Transporting the large number of items needed to build the studio to the island took significant planning and time. There were no direct freight flights to Montserrat which meant that there was no expedient method of moving materials from London to Montserrat. Almost everything delivered to the island for the studio's construction had to come in by sea. Back in England, AIR contracted to have large shipping containers located near the local docks and AIR staffers would load materials for the studio into them. Once full, the container would be loaded onto a ship bound for the West Indies. Since Montserrat lacked the facilities to dock large sea liners, when the ship arrived, the containers needed to be moved to a "little boat" which then brought it to the island's small pier. Once the container was on dry land, all materials were unloaded and had to be inspected by the local customs agents before being delivered to the construction site. The complexity of the logistics meant that planning was paramount.

Of course, AIR did take some liberties in transporting items for the studio via passenger flights. Smaller items were brought to the island in luggage or as personal items. This was a much cheaper and expedient way of getting things to Montserrat than shipping them over 4,000 miles on an ocean liner. Steve Culnane, the first technical manager for AIR Montserrat said that "We had a shipping agency...Gander and White. Between Gander and White and ourselves, shall we say, we took liberties with British Airways as far as handling stuff that was going out there to the point where I think...BA, again I might be talking out of turn here, BA was considering banning us because we got away with so much stuff going across at a cheap price." As an example, he told me a story of Dave bringing a frequency generator to Montserrat on a commercial passenger flight. The studio was having issues with its Hammond organ. It was designed to work with a power frequency of 50hz but power in Montserrat is 60hz so the organ was out of tune. The solution was to use a frequency generator which could filter the 60hz power and reduce it to a 50hz frequency. The problem was that this frequency generator was back in the UK and needed to come to Montserrat...and it was extremely heavy. Steve said, "So Dave took it out to Montserrat as hand luggage. We're talking about...a one man lift if you are going about 2 or 3 feet. Anything more it's literally 2 men to carry it. And he managed to [convince British Airways] that it was hand luggage. It sat next to him in the plane on the floor."

The necessity of bringing supplies from overseas occasionally caused issues during the construction of the studio. Since importing items took days and sometimes weeks to be delivered, any delays in arrival or problems with the construction materials themselves could have major repercussions. Malcom said, "One of the most complex problems going in that you had to remember to take with you every last nut and bolt. You had to anticipate. There was nothing on the island but wood and concrete. You had to take everything [with you]." He told me of a materials problem that occurred during the construction that caused a long delay. They were installing electrical conduit junction boxes in the studio and the boxes had to be covered and sealed prior to the roof being installed. Once the roof was put into place, it would have been difficult to reach the boxes so the installation of the roof depended on the completion of the electrical installation. In the process of installing the electrical box covers, they ran out of a particular type of screw that was proprietary to the design of the boxes. There was no substitute for these screws in Montserrat or any of the neighboring islands. An order for these screws had to be placed with a supplier in England and the roof's completion had to be put on hold for two weeks waiting for a single box of 200 screws. Malcolm said that while things like this did not happen often during the construction process, this problem "was a wakeup call" that better planning was needed when it came to materials procurement and logistics. The difficulty of obtaining supplies would be a recurring theme throughout the life of the studio.

Managing Director Harries

Dave had been named managing director of AIR Montserrat for the duration of the project. He said AIR gave him that position so that "I had the power to sign checks and stuff." He remembered: "I had arranged an overdraft with the bank. It was like $2500 dollars or something...Of course, we went over that. So I was trying to avoid the bank manager. One day, I was on the golf course with David Hodd. And the bank manager, I saw him. I was trying to hide from him. We were still playing golf so it was difficult to hide while you're on the course. I couldn't say, 'I'm going to leave this [and] go.' I remember this big booming voice [of the bank manager] across the golf course, 'HARRIES!' [Laughing] I had to phone Terry Connolly, the Chrysalis managing director, and say, 'Terry, we need a bit more money.' [Terry says,] 'Oh yes. How much, Dave? How much do you need? What is it? $2000? What? $5000? What do you need?' I said, '50,000 US?' [Dave laughing again.] There was this terrible silence on the other end of the phone. But we got it."

Running a construction project of this scope on a remote Caribbean island is usually fraught with all types of friction coming from the locals at all levels whether it be government approvals, inspections, importation, or immigration. Dave said that, for the most part, was not the case. He said, "I think because we had the biggest contractor on the island and possibly, although not the best qualified architect, one [that was] very well known. Everybody was freemasons and everybody played golf so all the high up guys in the government and all of the guys playing golf, our contractor, and our architect, and our chairman as well, Mr. Martin (not related to George) were all members of some lodge or other. So I think that's how they smoothed the way. [John] Kelsick was an [AIR Montserrat] director who was the principal lawyer on the island." The other local representative on the AIR Montserrat board of directors was "the biggest land agent on the island."

Arrival Of The Electronics

Malcolm headed out to Montserrat for the first time in May 1978 to meet with David Hodd and discuss what Malcolm referred to as "integration."

Integration is the design of electronics' locations within the studio environment. Malcolm needed to make sure that there was proper placement of conduit ducting and holes in walls for wiring, control panels, etc. so that his design of the electronics of the studio would be feasible. Onsite at the partially built studio, he used ropes to estimate the lengths of wiring between the locations where the planned gear would be installed. After working with David and finalizing the physical specifications needed for his design, Malcolm returned to London where he and AIR staffers began prebuilding as much as possible before shipping parts to Montserrat. Items such as electric panels and wiring looms, which were made to the lengths specified by Malcolm's ropes, were built in London. He said, "I was trying to make it so that when I got to the island, a lot was 'plug-and-play.'"

Interestingly, the air conditioning system that was installed in the void between the walls was designed off-island and shipped to Montserrat as a kit. Malcolm Atkin and Dave Harries, who were not trained in air conditioning system technology, were able to install the bulk of the system themselves. The manufacturer supplied a diagram with each piece of ducting labeled with its location. They had to climb into the loft above the inner building and install the duct work like a puzzle. Dave described working in the loft as miserable with the temperature cresting at 150F with them having to work "stripped to the waist." Included in the system were sound-attenuating fiberglass panels in the duct work so that sounds could not travel easily from room to room while recording.

Contruction Of The Studio Control Room
(Notice The Pool Frame In The Background)
Photo: Dave Harries and Malcolm Atkin

Dave told me of one mishap that caused a bit of friction on the jobsite. During construction of the studio, he would come to the jobsite every evening to inspect the work completed that day. One evening, he came across a major issue. In the studio's plans, there were two stone columns in the control room that were designed to hold speakers. For proper sound reproduction, the speakers needed to be equidistant from the listeners who would be working behind the control desk. The studio's plans had the columns aligned in a single plane in front of where the control desk was to be installed. Dave discovered that the workers had built one of the columns three inches in front of the other which would have a negative effect on the acoustics of the room. They needed to be lined up perfectly. Dave said to the workers, "That's no good. Take [the wall] down and move it." The workers were hesitant to move what they thought was a perfectly fine wall that they had just built. Having no knowledge of studio sound design, it seemed strange to them to tear down the wall they had just spent many hours building. Dave insisted that the wall had to be moved to match the plans. The workers were able to move the wall but only because Dave had caught the problem in time. The cement had not yet set. If he had not come to the jobsite that evening, the cement would have cured, and it would have been a much more difficult endeavor to move the wall the following day.

40

Expertise of many of the tradesmen on the island was not up to the standards that the AIR staff were accustomed to in their native England. This likely had to do with the lack of trade schools for training on the island as well as the tradesmen's lack of exposure to complex technical systems like those required by the studio. There were few if any buildings on the island that had the electrical and refrigeration complexities of the studio. Additionally, AIR staff members said that the "psychology" of the island tradesmen was such that they always gave the impression of confidence that they knew what they were doing, even if they were not. In these situations, it was only after the fact when something went awry and repair expenses were higher than expected that the tradesmen's lack of expertise would be made apparent. One example came from Malcolm Atkin. The compressors in the air conditioning units of the studio were consistently failing which was unusual. The compressors were expensive to replace and had to be shipped to Montserrat from England every time one had failed. To find out what might be going wrong, Malcolm watched the local Montserratian air conditioning repairman as he installed a new compressor. Once the repair was complete, the repairman started filling the system with liquid refrigerant. The amount of refrigerant in an air conditioning unit is extremely critical to its proper functioning. To measure this, a technician uses pressure gauges (known as 'steels' in the UK) while filling a unit with refrigerant to know exactly how much is in the system. If the pressure is too high or low, it can cause problems such as low cooling capacity or the compressor failing. Malcolm was taken aback when the repairman simply attached a bottle of refrigerant to the unit and began filling it with no gauges attached. There was no way for the repairman to know how much pressure or refrigerant was in the system. Malcolm asked where his gauges were and the repairman told him that he did not use them. He told Malcolm "I just know how much. I'm so good at this." To which Malcolm replied, "We keep blowing compressors and you are just [now] telling me now that you don't know how much [refrigerant] is in there?" Malcolm called AIR London and asked them to send a set of gauges to the island. Once they had arrived, Malcolm handed them to the repairman who asked, "Why do I have to use these things?" Malcolm admonished him by saying "You WILL use those and weigh [the refrigerant] properly."

Another problem that occurred during construction was caused by tradesmans' lack of experience. Dave Harries had purchased a walk-in freezer for the studio because there was a need for a large volume of cold storage capacity to accommodate the amount of food needed for the artists, their staff, and entourages when working at the studio. It was built into a room on the lower level of the villa. After installation, the freezer seemed to be working for several weeks but suddenly one day, it caught fire. A freezer such as this works by cooling 23 hours and 45 minutes a day and then heating for 15 minutes to melt any frozen condensation that had accumulated on the cooling coils. The installers had installed a relay backwards and the freezer was actually heating 23 hours a day and cooling for 15 minutes, the opposite cooling cycle that it should have been using which is what caused the unit to burn up. Dave said that it was lucky that the freezer was installed in a concrete walled room or it would have burned the villa down before the studio opened for business. He said "That Foster fridge that we paid thousands for lasted for about four weeks out there. It was our first wakeup call that these guys don't know what they are doing, do they?"

With that said, many workers and craftsmen who worked on the studio construction project were competent and were very hard workers who took to the project with aplomb. The Montserratian stonework in and around the studio was particularly beautiful and attests to the skills of those who built the studio. Dave told me that whatever the workers might have lacked in experience was more than made up for in their enthusiasm and extraordinary efforts to help make George's dream studio a reality, even in this most unlikely of environments. The stories included in this section were told not to disparage the workers in any way. They simply capture the level of difficulty of building such a high-tech facility on an island like Montserrat. Dave's reverence for the Montserratian workers, regardless of the mishaps, was made clear when he said, "They were such nice people. I wouldn't want to upset them [with these stories] because they don't deserve it."

Salty Stones

Another story typifies the difficulties of the studio's unique environment during construction. Before she was officially hired, local Montserratian Minetta Francis, who would become head housekeeper for the studio, was brought to the studio by Dave Harries for a problem that was quite unusual for most contemporary studio construction projects. Three walls in the main performance area and control room were covered in decorative sea stones, installed by the local Montserratian stone workers. This was a commonly used method of wall decoration on the island, using locally sourced sea stones. While these sea stones did not cause problems when installed on the exterior of the studio building, they did present a problem indoors. Because they had come from the ocean, sea salt was leeching from the stone as they dried in the studio. The salt could cause corrosion in the sensitive electronics and instruments that were in use in the studio. Dave was curious if Minetta had any solutions for this problem. She said that she did. She asked a construction worker to give her a hand and they went down the hill below the studio. They returned with sour oranges and lemons harvested from local trees on the property. They began scrubbing the stones with the acidic citrus juices. She returned each day for a month, using the fruit juices on the walls until the salt was no longer leeching from the stones. She says that she believes her efforts and ingenuity were part of the reason for her earning an employment contract with the studio.

Although there were issues during construction, Dave felt as if it went as well as it could have, considering the circumstances. He said, "The construction was fine. There were a few mistakes, but it was all fine. You know, it's the West Indies."

Montserratian Workers Celebrate The 'Topping Out' Of The Studio
Photo: Dave Harries and Malcolm Atkin

STUDIO DETAILS

The AIR Montserrat studio was built to meet the standards of high-end recording studios of the day but with the unique requirements of one built on a tropical volcanic island.

The Structure

The studio structure was, as described by Dave Harries, "a building within a building." It consisted of a smaller concrete structure, which housed the studio, within a larger shell-like building that protected the inner structure from the elements. The inner building was built to be an incredibly strong and soundproof structure. It was so strong in fact that it was designated as an official hurricane shelter for the island. The walls of this inner studio structure were constructed with 6-inch thick hollow concrete blocks that Dave Harries had filled with mortar so that they became solid blocks when set in place. Steel reinforced ring beams were placed every six feet in the walls as was required in an earthquake prone area like Montserrat. The floors in the main room were made from 1-1/2 inches of concrete poured over a six inch steel mesh reinforced concrete slab. The ceiling of the inner building was made of a 6-inch slab of concrete which was reinforced with steel rebar every eight inches. Due to its thick concrete shell, the studio's walls protected the surrounding outdoor area from the high volume of sound that might be present in the studio during a recording session. Although the island was relatively quiet as compared to a large city, the concrete walls were able to stop loud exterior sounds from intruding into a recording session as well. One of the initial concerns about outside sounds impacting recordings were sonic booms from aircraft. A Concorde passenger jet flew between Caracas, Venezuela and Paris, France and it passed over Montserrat in the late afternoon. This supersonic jet flew two times the speed of sound and created a loud sonic boom along its flight path. During construction, David Hodd and Dave Harries went up to the construction site one Friday evening to take in the view and talk about the studio project. As they stood there, the Concorde passed overhead and they heard the sonic boom. David Hodd said that Dave Harries was concerned. Dave said to David, "Oh my God! I wonder if you will hear this in the studio." So, the following evening, Dave grabbed his sound meter and he and David went up to the worksite "with a crate of Heineken" to wait for the Concorde to pass by on its return flight to Paris. As the plane passed overhead, they looked up to the sky and heard the sonic boom. When the plane had left the vicinity, Dave looked down at his sound meter and realized that it did not have a "peak hold." This meant that it did not retain the maximum decibel reading that registered at the peak of the sonic boom. Dave had missed his opportunity to measure the sound levels of the plane passing overhead but he did not fret. He told me, "It wasn't as loud as a thunderstorm so what's the problem?"

Surrounding the inner concrete building was the outer structure which is what was seen when looking at the studio from the outside. Since the studio sat high on a ridge overlooking the boats of Old Road Bay, architect David Hodd said that the studio's outer structure was "designed to look elegant when viewed from the sea." It is larger in all dimensions than the inner building so there is an open void between the two. The only room that had a single wall and no void between it and the outside world was the amp room which housed the amplifiers, power supplies, and other equipment. The walls of the outer structure were made from 8-inch thick concrete blocks but as David explained, if there was an earth tremor, the walls of the outer building could vibrate unlike the inner structure. The void between the inner and outer walls allowed for easy installation and repair of the wiring of the inner structure and for ducting for the air conditioning system.

Due to the possibility of hurricanes in the Caribbean, the roof was designed by a company in Miami that specialized in hurricane-resistant building structures. It was built to be impervious to the high winds present during a hurricane. Dave Harries said that it was purposely overbuilt. "There is a lot of timber in that roof," he said.

Another interesting feature of the studio building was the window in the control room. George Martin thought that it would be great to have a view of the valley and sea from the control room, so David Hodd designed a window on the west side of the room. The window featured double paned glass to keep sound from passing through it and a shade to cover the window in case an artist would prefer the control room to be darkened. In the rest of the control room, the windows between the control room and other rooms had both panes of glass angled slightly towards the floor on each side. This lessened the sound conductivity of the windows.

Contradicting erroneous information found on the internet, the floor of the studio was not "built on ball bearings" or a "layer of oil." The main room floor was simply hardwood flooring over the concrete slab. Perhaps this misinformation was drawn from the fact that the control room did have a floating floor. It consisted of several layers of plywood that floated on joists. This provided some isolation for the equipment in the control room from the ground beneath the studio which could vibrate during earth tremors.

The studio sat on a grade so part of it was suspended over the uneven ground, supported by steel reinforced concrete columns or blocks located at the corners of the rooms and at intervals between them. These columns ran into the earth below and sat on large concrete foundation footers buried below the surface. The entire area below the studio was backfilled after the supports were constructed and a wall built surrounding it so that it had the appearance of being flush with the ground. When looking at the original architectural drawings, the floor and supports look like a pier you might see in a harbor, only the supports were driven deep into the ground rather than into the sea.

45

An interesting feature that David Hodd included in his plans for the outer building was the staggered angled walls on the side of the studio which faced the pool and ocean. He told me that it was purely a cosmetic feature that he added to the exterior design to create triangular shadows on the building when the sun was overhead. Several years later, these walls would be painted white as the black paint was absorbing too much of the sun's heat and causing cooling issues in the studio.

Front of Studio Building With David's Angular Shadows
Photo: David and Maureen Hodd

The Studio

Being a studio "of its time," it was built to sound very "dead" in the main room. The fashion of sound design in the 1970s was to restrict the reflectivity of the recording areas so that there was little sonic ambience. The idea was to record the instruments and vocals with no reverb, echo, or ambience and then add those effects later through various recording equipment. To give you an idea of what this "dead" sound is like, clap your hands in a small closet full of clothing. The lack of echo or reverb in a room filled with fabrics reflects the "dead" sound that was popular during that period. To accomplish this effect in the main recording room, sound absorbing materials were installed into the ceilings to stop sound waves from reflecting towards the floor. Floor-to-ceiling drapes, sewn by Maureen Hodd, were installed on the walls of the main room to reduce the reflectivity of the hard walls of the studio. They could be pulled to the side to allow the walls behind them to be exposed, which helped liven the room's sound if so required. Carpeting was installed along the bottoms of most walls and movable rugs were available to cushion equipment or to further deaden the sound in a specific area of the main room if need be.

Onsite instruments available for use during recording were a Hammond organ, Fender Rhodes electric piano, and a full sized Bosendorfer grand piano.

AMU Student Plays The Piano During Studio Downtime
The Piano Is Fully Inserted Into The Piano Box With The Flap Down
Photo: Frank Oglethorpe

In the corner of the main room was the piano "box." This was a feature unique to AIR Montserrat that Dave Harries is quite proud of. The piano box allowed for the studio piano to be isolated from the rest of the instruments while recording live. This innovative feature stopped the sound of the other instruments from bleeding into the microphones of the piano. The way that it worked was this: First. the piano was rolled out of the box on its casters. Then the engineers would install the microphones into the box while the piano was removed. (The microphones could be placed anywhere they wanted in the box. There were no fixed microphone locations.) The piano's lid would be removed and the piano would then be rolled back into the box. Lastly, a flap was lowered above the keyboard to help seal the sound within the box. With the piano and microphones isolated, the keyboardist could play with their fellow musicians and not have to worry about other instruments'

47

sound bleeding into the piano's microphones as they were recording. It worked so well that Dave said, "You got a nice tight piano sound even with the drummer outside." The only design flaw, which was pointed out to me by Peter Filleul, keyboardist of the Climax Blues Band, was the fact that when the piano was pushed into the box and someone was at the keys, they were looking directly at a stone wall and not able to see their fellow musicians. This made it difficult for communication between the pianist and the other performers. When Dave Harries and Chris Thomas were discussing this problem during my interview with them in late 2019, Dave had an idea of how to fix it 40 years after the studio's design: They could have simply put up a mirror on the wall in front of the keyboardist so they could see the musicians behind them. "Hindsight is 20/20" as they say.

Studio Main Room in 1979
Hammond Organ, The Neve's Cue Mixers, and Movable Gobos, Piano Box In The Background
Photo: David and Maureen Hodd

In the same structure as the piano box were amplifier chimneys. The chimneys had the same purpose as the piano box: To isolate their sound from the main recording area. Unlike the piano box which was designed to keep sound from bleeding into the piano microphones, the chimneys' purpose was to keep the loud volume of guitar amplifiers from spilling out, keeping them sonically isolated from the main room.

To isolate live players and instruments from each other within the main room (called separation in the recording industry), the studio had a number of gobos, which are portable walls that could be placed around and between musicians as they performed. The gobos in use at AIR Montserrat had sound absorbing materials at the top and bottom with windows in between to allow the musicians to see each other when separated by them. They were as tall as the lower ceiling in the main room.

Power

The local power company, Monlec, was modern by Caribbean island standards of the period but the electrical power grid on the island was not as robust as most other recording studio locations which were usually situated in or around major cities. Power outages and fluctuations were more common in Montserrat and any electrical disruptions could have had a major impact on a recording session. To help alleviate any downtime associated with power issues, the studio had a large generator installed on the property grounds. It was located in a shed across the road from the villa. It had the capacity to run the studio's equipment, lighting, and air conditioning for hours at a time. Although it served its intended function over the life of the studio, it was a frequent maintenance headache for the technical managers tasked with its operation, as demonstrated in stories which appear in later chapters. A large constant voltage transformer was installed in the lower level of the villa and fed power to the studio. Malcolm described this transformer as the "size of a small car." Its purpose was to condition the power coming from Monlec. It reduced voltage spikes and electrical noise and protected the studio's equipment from fluctuations in the power supply. Technical manager Geoff Irons told me that when he arrived in Montserrat, the room that the transformer was installed in was quite damp from leaking water supply pipes prior to its installation. Geoff said that the water pipes were not installed very well, but as happenstance would have it, once the large transformer was installed, the constant heat radiating from it kept the room dry.

The studio consumed so much power at a constant rate that when AIR technicians would test the generator and take the studio off the island's power grid, the Monlec's technicians at the island's power plant would see the sharp drop in demand for power and know that the studio was operating on generator power. Studio manager Steve Jackson would always expect a call from the power company to confirm that they were only testing the generator and that there was not a bigger problem with the power grid.

Another quirk with the island's power supply is that it operated at an uncommon standard. The European standard for power is 240 volts operating at 50 hertz. In this context, hertz is how many times a second the current alternated between the maximum and minimum voltage. North American power is supplied at 120 volts (1/2 of the European standard) operating at 60hz (10 more hertz per second than the European standard.) Montserrat's power grid operated at the 240 volts European standard, running at the 60 hertz of the American standard which made it incompatible with either standard. Malcolm believes that the logic behind the decision to operate at an uncommon electrical standard was made so that American appliances could easily be used on the island, requiring only a simple voltage transformer installed in the home to drop the voltage to 120 volts. Unfortunately, artists working at the studio would be bringing instruments, amplifiers, and gear made for either the European power standard, the

American standard, or both. Either way, neither was compatible with the island power so AIR had to have transformers installed onsite to convert power from Monlec into both standards.

Studio Room Dimensions(as specified in the original architectural drawings supplied by studio architect David Hodd)

Main Room- 30 feet by 35 feet (includes piano box and amp chimneys). 13 foot ceiling over the main area. 10 foot ceiling between piano box and vocal booth. Doorways to vestibule and vocal booth.
Vocal Booth- 14 feet by 11.5 feet. 9 foot ceiling. Doorways to main room, amp room, and control room
Control Room- 23.5 feet by 20 feet. 11 foot ceiling. Doorways to vocal booth and vestibule.
Amp Room- 8.5 feet by 11.5 feet. 9 foot ceiling. Doorways to vocal booth and outside.
Vestibule- 10 feet by 6.5 feet. Doorways to outside, control room, and main room.

Studio Control Room In 1979
Photo: David and Maureen Hodd

Control Room Equipment

The control room was stocked with state of the art electronics for use by the artists in the studio. As recording industry trends changed and technology improved during the studio's history, the equipment list changed as well. A few of these equipment changes are so significant to the story of the studio that they are documented separately from the following gear list.

Mixing Desk

The heart of a studio is its mixing board, also known as a "desk" or "console." (These terms are used interchangeably throughout the book.) At AIR Studios Montserrat, this important piece of recording gear was a custom desk built to AIR's specifications by Rupert Neve. The "Montserrat Neve" mixing desk is famous for its rich sound qualities and was an integral part of the sound of AIR Montserrat. The desk has its own complex story and is covered in its own chapter.

Tape Machines

Dave Harries said that he would have liked to have purchased 24-track Studer 800 tape machines for AIR Montserrat but they were in short supply when they were sourcing gear for Montserrat, having been introduced to the recording studio market less than a year before the studio opened. Instead, the original tape decks that were installed in the studio were two MCI JH-16 machines using 2-inch tape. They were purchased from Music Center Incorporated (MCI) whose headquarters were, according to Dave, "just over the water in Miami." The decks could be used independently or linked together for playback and recording using a synchronizer device between the units. According to Malcolm Atkin, these MCI decks were selected to appeal to the American recording market. In retrospect, he thinks that the purchase was a bad decision. He said that they were reasonable tape machines but "with crap American engineering." Two years after the studio opened, MCI swapped out the JH-16 decks for free, replacing them with the "improved" JH-24 model. Malcolm said that this was the worst thing they ever did, describing the new tape machines as "just awful." They had frequent tape alignment issues which caused near constant headaches for engineers and tape operators. This problem stemmed from the fact that the deck plate was made of punched aluminum with a torsion bar underneath to allow for deck alignment. When the tape machine was in operation, the heat from the electronics in the unit would increase the temperature of the deck plate. The aluminum would expand, warp very slightly, and the tape heads would no longer be aligned with the tracks on the tape as it passed over the heads. A technician could realign the heads during a session, but once the machine cooled down, the heads would become misaligned again. During one recording session, a producer threatened to shut down the session and leave the studio due to the tape machine problems. Malcolm had to rent a set of

Otari MTR-90 tape machines and ship them at great expense to the island to placate the producer and salvage the session. Geoff Emerick, John Burgess, and George Martin were all "screaming" at Malcolm to get the MCI tape machines out of the studio before the problems caused the studio to lose clients. Malcolm purchased a secondhand Studer A800 for AIR Montserrat which was a 24-track analog tape machine engineered in Switzerland. It could be synchronized with the remaining MCI tape deck for 48 total tracks. This Studer machine was much more stable and it was in use until the studio closed.

The studio also had three Ampex ATR-102 2-track tape decks which used ½" tape. These were used for rough mixes, final mixes, playback of ½" tapes brought into the studio, as well as other various recording functions.

Speakers

The studio used several different sets of studio monitor speakers to meet the various needs of artists and producers who recorded at the studio.

JBL 4350- These large monitors were installed high in the control on the tops of stone columns on either side of the control room window. Malcolm Atkin says that, like the MCI tape decks, they were purchased to appeal to the American market as they were in use in many prominent recording studios in the United States. Their frequency response was not favored by AIR's U.K. staff. Malcom said that "They sounded awful to our ears."

Tannoy Golds- These speakers, with custom enclosures designed by Dave Harries, were installed in the Montserrat studio as well as AIR's London studios. They were used for monitoring in the control room.

Urei 813C- These monitors had a "bright and hard" sound and were used for in-studio monitoring during recording.

Yamaha NS10 nearfield monitors- Used in the control room.

Auratone 5C Super Sound Cube nearfield monitors.

Outboard Gear

Scamp Rack with various processing modules including two MXR Auto Flanger and Auto Phaser modules.

Two AMS DMX 15-80 Digital Delays- Introduced in 1978, this was the first microprocessor controlled digital delay in the recording industry. AIR Technical Manager Frank Oglethorpe said that they were "horribly unreliable" and that he "wanted to throw them into the pool." Regardless of reliability issues, Dire Straits used them on their "Brothers In Arms" album recorded at the studio to clean up bass tracks utilizing the digital sampling feature of these delay units.

Two AMS DM2.20 Tape Phase Simulators

One Eventide Harmonizer Model H949

Four UREI 1176 Compressor/Limiters- The UREI 1176 was a high-quality compression unit that was considered a standard in professional studios for many years.

Two Universal Audio 1/3 Octave Graphic Equalizers Model 57-A

Two UREI Parametric Equalizers Model 545
Six Dolby A-Type Noise Reduction Units Model 361
Two Fairchild 660 Tube Compressors
DBX 160 Compressor

Other gear was brought into the studio over the course of the studio's decade of operations. Some of the additional equipment was introduced due to the evolution of the recording industry and had an impact on the history of the studio. These significant additions of gear will be mentioned in later chapters as they appear in the chronology of the studio.

THE NEVE

The Montserrat Neve Recording Console
Photo: Frank Oglethorpe

The A4792 (its serial number) Neve recording console that was installed into the AIR Montserrat studio is legendary in the recording industry for its rich high-quality analog sound. It is the first of three custom Neve consoles purchased by AIR Studio for its Montserrat studio as well as its Studio One and Studio Two of their Oxford Circus facility in London. Although these consoles are now heralded by many artists and producers as being the best mixing consoles of all time, Neve was not the first choice of manufacturers for the Montserrat studio's new desk.

Geoff Does Not Want A Neve

By 1977, Geoff Emerick had engineered several Gallagher and Lyle recording sessions with producer David Kirshenbaum that were recorded in studios that used Neve consoles. Geoff was known for his incredible sense of sonic clarity and through his personal experiences of working on Neve consoles, he had the opinion that their current consoles "sounded muddy" and that they "sounded better through the monitor part than through the mix part." Dave Harries said that Geoff told him that "It was like putting a bit of cloth over your speakers." When AIR started the design process for the new Montserrat studio, Geoff was adamant about not using a Neve console in Montserrat. According to Malcolm Atkin, Geoff said "I don't want another Neve. They don't sound very good. I want an MCI." MCI was based in Miami and manufactured high quality mixing desks in the late 1970s (unlike their tape decks that had design flaws.) Geoff thought that one of their desks might be the right choice for the new studio but Dave Harries was not sold on using an American product. Malcolm describes Dave as a "stalwart Brit" and that he preferred to use British made products if possible, so The Neve Company, which was based in the U.K., was Dave's first choice as a supplier for a new console for AIR Montserrat.

Knowing that Geoff had a strong opinion on the subject of using a Neve in Montserrat and that he held huge sway over the decision of which console to purchase, Dave and George Martin told Rupert Neve "We've got a problem here, Rupert." At AIR, a test was devised: A 10khz sonic pulse was sent though the audio processing channel on the existing Neve console installed in Studio Two at AIR London. The results were analyzed on the output section of the desk. This was done to see if the Neve console was altering the sound signal as Geoff claimed it would. Ten signal pulses were sent through the console and only nine measurable pulses were output. Malcolm said the Neve console was "Chopping off all the front end of it." In other words, the circuit design of the board was losing some of the signal from input to output. In Malcolm's opinion, there were too many transformers in the circuit. Once AIR had the results of the test, they sent the results to head engineer and Neve founder, Rupert Neve. Rupert reviewed the results of AIR's testing and replied that he had a new circuit design that would solve the issue they had found. Rupert visited George and Dave and presented some figures on the new design. Dave said that the 3db point of the console was 180hkz which he said was incredible. What this means is that the console could process sound up to 180khz with virtually no drop in signal quality. This is many times greater than the highest frequencies of human hearing. Dave also said that Rupert's figures showed no noise and no distortion. Rupert asked Dave, "Do you think Geoff would like that?" to which Dave replied, "Yes...I think he would!" Rupert then developed the final circuit design for the new AIR consoles.

A Group Effort

This new circuit design became the one used in the Montserrat console. Malcolm said of the new design, "It is completely different than anything else that Neve ever built." Although Rupert Neve was responsible for the unique physical electronic design that provided the foundation for the incredibly rich sound of the Montserrat Neve, it was a group effort that produced the final product. Geoff worked with Neve to develop many of the customizations that would be of use to engineers who would use the console, features such as the dynamics of the compressors, headroom for the mic inputs, the law of the faders, and custom frequency equalization curves which Dave refers to as the "Geoff EQs." Malcom summarized Geoff's contribution to the Neve design: Geoff worked on all the design aspects involved with making the final product "sound good." Malcolm was responsible for the systems design which involved aspects of the console such as number of channels and outputs, monitor facilities, and physical layout. He also worked with Geoff and Rupert, assisting with interpreting Geoff's auditory ideas into engineering concepts that Rupert could work with. The design was a decidedly collaborative effort between the manufacturer (Neve) and its client, AIR Studios.

During the systems design phase of the project, Geoff shocked Malcolm by turning to him and suddenly announcing that the new Neve desks were going to have cue mixers to which Malcolm replied. "What are those?" Geoff said that he wanted eight channel mixers coming off the monitor board which would provide headphone mixes for the artists who were in the studio. These mixers would allow the individual performers to personally customize the mix of volumes of the recorded instruments coming into their headphones while performing. Normally, headphone mixes would be controlled by an engineer in the control room and every performer would hear the same mix in their headphones. The problem for Malcolm was that the desk, at this point in the design process, was not designed to accommodate what Geoff was asking for. Malcolm told Geoff that he could only give him two channels. Geoff claimed that he had requested eight channel cue mixers from the beginning. Malcolm said that "This was my first design embarrassment because I don't know to this day whether...I dropped the ball there or he dropped the ball. But by the time we realized that we weren't on the same page, it was too late. The board had been ordered and on its way." In the end, they ended up with eight channel cue mixers but could only use two channels due the board's design.

A unique design feature of this mixing console design was the location of the microphone preamplifiers (mic preamps.) Traditionally, a microphone is connected to a cable which is run into a mic preamp which converts the extremely low level of signal that is output from a microphone into a higher level that can be used by mixing consoles, effects gear, etc. The length of the cable used is dictated by the location of the microphone and the distance from the preamp receiving its signal. This could be long distance in the case of a studio where the microphone in a performance area is far removed from the control room. These cables often ran through conduit and channels in walls and ceilings and could be of varying quality. Because the signal from a microphone is very weak and cable runs could be long, electrical interference and signal loss could be introduced to the sounds being captured. To counter this, Rupert had the unique idea of placing the preamp as close to the microphones as possible to reduce the microphone cable lengths and the chances of signal degradation. He designed a system for the Montserrat studio where the mic preamps would be placed in the performance rooms of the studio rather than in the control room. This would limit the length of cables between the microphones and preamps. The levels of the preamps were able to be controlled remotely from the control room by a current ladder circuit that Rupert designed for this purpose.

In the end, Dave said that Geoff thought the Montserrat desk sounded fantastic and that, in his opinion, Geoff never liked another mixing console as much as the Neve that they designed for the island studio. A total of three consoles were built for AIR using this design, two of them destined for studios at the Oxford Circus facility. When Dave ordered them, two of the consoles were ordered to provide a view from the desk. The desk destined for Studio Two in Oxford Circus had the producer's table located on the right so that those in the studio could look out the window overlooking the London streets below, while the Montserrat Neve was ordered with the producer's table on the left. This provided the studio patrons with the gorgeous view of the Belham Valley and Caribbean sea from the console though the studio window.

The Long Road From London To Montserrat

The seven-foot long console was assembled and tested in London and had to be transported to Montserrat which caused significant logistical problems. Since there were no freight flights to Antigua from the U.K., they had to find an alternative island in the region that had incoming air freight service. Guadaloupe, 53 miles south of Montserrat, was a territory of France and had regular air freight service via AIR France airlines. The Neve was disassembled, crated, and put on a flight to Guadaloupe on an AIR France flight. With the Neve on its way to Guadaloupe, Dave had to arrange transport of the console to be brought to Montserrat. Knowing that the predominate language of the island was French and being far from fluent in the language, Dave Harries enlisted the assistance of the school-aged daughter of the financial secretary of Montserrat to accompany him to Guadaloupe to pick up the Neve console. She spoke French and could provide translation services for Dave as he worked with the customs department of Guadaloupe. When they arrived, Dave was surprised that they were not allowed into the airport. He spoke to the local airport officials through his school-aged translator and explained that there was a large consignment from England that had arrived and that he was there to claim it. He was simply told "No." Dave tried for several days to get into the freight area of the airport. He said, "Eventually, I got fed up with this bloke saying 'No!' so I went past him through the gates where you're not supposed to and there on the tarmac were two great big boxes covered in polythene sheet. Ours! The bloody idiot didn't even know they were there." Dave contracted a truck to take the crates holding the Neve desk and its components to the local docks. Prior to arriving in Guadaloupe, Dave had found a boat owner in Antigua to pick up the Neve in Guadaloupe and deliver it to Montserrat. He was a treasure seeker who was in the process of building a large cabin cruiser for his business. The cabin cruiser, while seaworthy, was not completely built and thus had an ideal location on the unfinished deck for carrying the Neve desk in its transport crates. Dave was concerned that the ship might not be able to handle the immense weight of the console and asked the boat's owner if it might sink. The owner laughed and said that the boat had four tons of lead in the keel and that, despite the Neve's substantial weight, the boat would only sit about 3 inches lower into the sea when loaded. One mixing console was not going to sink his vessel. It was loaded on the boat and the Neve was finally on the last leg of its long journey to Montserrat, but they had to wait until high tide before they could leave Guadaloupe. It was about one o'clock in the morning and pitch black when they set sail for Montserrat. As they navigated out of the harbor, the boat's owner was hanging over the front of the vessel shining a flashlight into the water, hunting for something. Dave asked, "What are you doing that for then?" He turned to Dave and said, "Well, there's a reef here somewhere but I'm not quite sure where it is!" Dave thought to himself, "Oh yeah...Great! Here we go." Luckily, the trip to Montserrat was quite uneventful.

The Neve Hangs Precariously As It Is Unloaded From The Boat
Photo: Dave Harries and Malcolm Atkin

Once the console reached the shores of Montserrat, it had to be transported to the studio property for installation. Dave said that the only vehicle available that could perform the job were what he called "tipper lorries" which are also known as "dump trucks." The back end is lifted on one end allowing the contents of the truck's bed to empty on the ground below. This is exactly how the large and expensive Neve console was delivered to the studio. The truck bed was lifted up as it would to dump a load of gravel, letting the console (in its crate) slide out until it touched ground. The workers then put oil drums under the end of the crate that was still in the truck, driving away and letting the crate land on the drums, crushing them but providing a somewhat softer landing than if the box, with its sensitive electronics, went crashing to the ground. It was a white-knuckle experience for those who were there to install the console. Dave said that Rupert Neve was onsite when the console was delivered and was "having a fit about it." The console was moved inside the control room and was installed by Malcolm, Rupert, and others who were brought to the island for the electronic systems installation.

The Precious Cargo Arrives At The Studio
Photo: Dave Harries and Malcolm Atkin

For Malcolm, the entire experience of designing, building, and installing the Neve desk was a harrowing and humbling experience. He told me, "In hindsight, here I was, first console that I have ever put in. It's a completely unknown design. It's a one-off [design]. No one else on the planet can help me 'cause I've got the only one here and it's sitting in the middle of nowhere. [Laughs] That was a fun bag of problems. Anyway, we got through it." When reflecting on the project of getting the studio operational, he said, "I made some horrendous mistakes. I found out afterward how to do it. [design a studio] That's what life is all about. It is a constant learning process."

With the Neve console installed and the studio nearing completion in late 1978, some artist was going to have to be the first to test out the new facility and deal with the unforeseen problems that would likely arise during this initial recording session. For that pioneering effort, George Martin reached out to a band who had dealt with this situation before. Enter The Climax Blues Band.

THE GUINEA PIGS

The first real test for the studio was the recording of the album "Reel to Real" by the Climax Blues Band. In 1970, Climax had been the "guinea pigs" for AIR Studios when they were testing their newly built Oxford Circus studios in London. Climax recorded an album while the London studios were still under construction so when George Martin needed someone to stress test AIR Montserrat with a full recording session, he called on them again. He knew that they would be willing to work through the bugs that came with opening a new technically complex state of the art recording studio. Described by CBB keyboardist Peter Filleul, the band was "very well mannered, very 'British', and we did not throw things out of hotel windows. We were not heavy drug takers and were deeply polite." They were a rock band without the outlandish behavior associated with many of their peers. Thus, they were a perfect match for what George had in mind for testing his new studio, considering its location on an island whose citizens were not used to Western rock musicians. Being on the AIR roster of bands and the first artists to record at the studio, they were able to secure a recording session deal with AIR that was, as Peter described, as "a good a deal as they would have at any other studio."

Winter of Discontent

The band arrived in early 1979 during what is often referred to as "The Winter of Discontent" in the UK. Trade unions from many different industries within the UK economy went on strike demanding wage increases. This led to a collective stress for U.K. citizens as trash piled up in the streets and access to basic services such as ambulance response, petrol stations, and even mortuary services were limited. Coupled with the normal cold and dreary British winter, it was from this environment that the members of Climax Blues Band found themselves recording in the relaxed tropical paradise of Montserrat. None of the band members had been to the Caribbean before so the abrupt shift in environment was both jarring and welcome.

Roughing It

When they arrived on January 4th, 1979, the studio building itself was far enough along into the construction process that the band was able to record but the greater studio complex was far from complete. Bassist Darek Holt told me, "It was one of those things where George was building this brand-new studio and it was being built [literally] around us really when we were there." Many of the amenities that were designed to make the studio a great experience for the artists were not finished when the band arrived. One of the most unique features of the studio, the pool, was not complete. When they arrived, the pit for the pool had been dug with a rebar frame built around it but the concrete had yet to be poured. AIR maintenance manager Steve Culnane said that "The studio was 90% there enough for Climax Blues and to record everything. The rest of the facilities were zilch. The kitchen wasn't there. The main areas and the office weren't there so it was a bit like camping out. It was like a modern studio with nothing around it."

Climax Blues Band Arrives
Pool Is Still Not Complete
Photo: Derek Holt

The first evening that the band was on the island, George and Judy Martin hosted a party at a hotel on the island to introduce the band to the local dignitaries and other special guests such as Gary Brooker from the band Procol Harum and the prospective UK Attorney General Michael Havers.

The following day, Tony Brinsley, CCB's manager, went to the studio to assess its readiness and was not pleased. Dave Harries, who was still onsite managing the construction project, said that Tony "gave me so much schtick because the studio wasn't finished." Not able to start recording, Peter said that "They sent us to the beach for a week to start with." While the band worked on their tans, AIR staffers corrected the most pressing issues while studio construction progressed. Peter recalls that the Neve desk had "a small fire" around that time. Another major issue that came to light quickly was a power issue. Since the studio designers had anticipated that they would have artists from around the world recording at AIR Montserrat, they had installed electrical outlets that would meet two of the most common power standards used in the music industry. As stated in a previous chapter, musical gear, such as amplifiers, keyboards, and effects, are designed to use the power standards for the market where the equipment is sold. In the United States, that power standard is 120 volts. In the U.K. and much of Europe, the standard is 240 volts. Each power standard uses a different physical prong layout on its wall plug. Since CBB was from the U.K., their equipment used 240 volts with the British plug standard. When CBB's technical roadie plugged in one of their amplifiers into the appropriate socket, the amplifier did not function properly. "It sort of murmured," Peter said. Something was clearly wrong, so the technician tested the power at the outlet. The 240 volt British socket was only providing 120 volts. He then tested the 120 volt U.S. standard sockets and found that they were providing 240 volts. All the region-specific power outlets in the studio had been wired to the other's voltage standard. All the power outlets in the studio needed to be rewired before the band returned. Luckily, the first band was British instead of American. Plugging 240 volt gear into 120v simply underpowers the equipment with no damage occurring but if it had been the opposite situation, putting 240 volts into equipment expecting 120 volts, the electronics would have likely would have been seriously damaged.

Everyone Was There

When the band returned to continue the recording session, they brought their wives and families with them and stayed in rented villas in the area around the studio. The villas included personal housekeepers that kept the place neat and tidy, but this level of service was new for the group. Peter told me that "none of us was used to having 'help' and I recall we felt quite embarrassed. I insisted on making my own bed." Since the studio's kitchen was not functional at that point, meals were served at the band's villas rather than at the studio as was the custom post-construction. A photo of one of the band's dinners was captured in the inner sleeve of the album recorded at AIR Montserrat, "Real to Reel." AIR staffers Malcolm Atkin, Dave Harries, and Cindy Eid are featured in the foreground of the photo with the band, their families, and crew behind them.

Most of AIR's important managers were onsite during the session, each wanting to see how the studio fared during a proper studio session and to assist in fixing problems as they arose. Being responsible for the studio construction and setup, Malcolm Atkin and Dave Harries had been on the island for quite some time and were onsite for the session. Since this was his pet project, George Martin was also present as well as engineer and producer Geoff Emerick who had helped with the acoustic design of the studio. As CBB bassist Derek Holt described the situation, "It was definitely a work in progress...so everybody was there trying to make this thing work." Additionally, AIR staffer Colin Fairely, the first AIR engineer assigned to work at the new studio, assisted CBB with recording the album. The only major player missing was AIR Montserrat's first studio manager Denny Bridges who had been hired but had not yet arrived on the island.

Derek describes the island and the session: "We were in, no word of a lie, it was paradise. What a beautiful island! The emerald island of the Caribbean they call [it]. To be sort of allowed to be at a place like that. It's such wonderful surroundings, the jungle, the sea, state of the art facility, thousands of miles from anywhere. It was quite strange." He said in an interview from 1979, "When we were recording there, we just lost contact with the rest of the world. I hadn't a clue as to what was going on outside."1

Giving Back

The band enjoyed their time on the island and interacted with locals not just in a social sense but also in a musical one. Band members would head to bars in town after recording and sit in with local bands, soaking up the island's musical flavors. This was to happen quite often over the years the studio operated on the island as artists would seek out local musicians for camaraderie and musical inspiration. The band was asked to perform a benefit concert for a local girl who needed money for overseas medical treatment, which they were happy to do. Derek said that, "thousands of people turned up and there were a few bands on and we were headlining the thing. It was great. A bit of give and take. [We did it] for being so nice to us." Peter remembers: "The venue was called the Paragon - a cavernous building with a corrugated iron roof...Local bands played first and then after us as these events go on 'until', much later than we might expect in Europe or the US. The 'until' deadline covers [locals'] expectations of delayed starts, power outages and general bad organization and is a familiar feature of every show [on the island.]" He continued, "The proceedings were curated by a vociferous MC who harangued the audience between acts. This is standard practice in the Caribbean but [un]usual for us to witness." Dave Harries remembered that, "All of the locals were outside [the club.] They'd hadn't gone in. It was about 11 o'clock at night. Saturday night. They'd heard about the band but they didn't go in. And then [Pete] Haycock started up his guitar in there. [Makes a rock guitar sound] And they all flooded through the gates to go in. 'Oh listen! Let's go!' and in they went." Peter said, "Pete Haycock started the show with a solo exhibition of exuberant guitar playing which left local jaws dropped and which has had a lasting impact on local guitarists to this day."

Power fluctuations were a problem for the band during the session. The studio's lights would go out until the power returned or the generator kicked in. Power surges would affect the amplifiers and cause disruptions in the recording process. The band would stop recording during the frequent rainstorms common in Montserrat to avoid potential issues from power loss and surges. Derek remembers that, "They used to have incredible rain there. Torrential rain. I remember those days...You'd be in the studio. Everything would stop. 'STOP! Switch everything off!' And then power it all up again when the thing had passed."

During the recording, a fellow musician who is well known for his love of the tropics stopped by. Jimmy Buffet sailed into Montserrat to see the studio.

The band showed Jimmy the studio and he had dinner with the band. Very soon, Jimmy would be recording at AIR Montserrat himself.

Asleep On His Feet

During the session, AIR sent Technical Manager Steve Culnane to the studio to relieve an exhausted Malcolm Atkin who had been burning the candle at both ends for months, rushing to get the studio electronics installed and functional before the first recording session. Steve told me that, "Malcolm was literally exhausted. He was asleep on his feet. We'd go out in the evening and literally he was being taken home because he was falling asleep at the table." Malcolm returned to London leaving Steve in charge of the studio's maintenance during the CBB recording session. Steve said "And then he left me on my own. [laughs] It was so frightening, it was unbelievable...I had never been abroad. I'd worked for a big corporation like the BBC, [having] support and all the rest of it. And there I was on my own with the equivalent of a Radio Shack that sold mostly car radios...It was a bit daunting...But we managed to get most of what we would call it in English, 'snagging', which is all of the small little faults that hadn't been resolved...like the record player not working, things like that."

More Cowbell

CBB had a big international hit in late 1976 with the song "Couldn't Get It Right" from the "Gold Plated" album. It featured a near constant cowbell keeping time throughout the song. Thinking that they might recreate that magic on their new album, the band decided to try a cowbell in one of the new songs. To get a fuller sound from the cowbell, someone suggested recording it in the empty pool which had recently been completed during the session. They were hoping the concrete walls of the pool would reflect the sound of the cowbell and create a unique sound not able to be captured in the studio's recording rooms. Running wires from the Neve desk out of the studio door, across the pool deck, and down into the pool, the engineer placed microphones around the pool and recording began. Alas, the cowbell was not to be. The band could not get the sound they were looking for and the cowbell was abandoned but not for a lack of trying.

As much as they loved the island and it's laid-back atmosphere, the recording session was not as efficient as they had hoped. Peter said that the session was "labored." The band had decided not to use an outside producer for the album, self-producing "Real to Reel." Derek said that he thought that the lack of a producer made the process more difficult. "I would say we were a little unprepared and of course, a lack of a producer makes it harder, I think. It's always nice to have some sort of direction. We produced the thing ourselves with [engineer] Colin Fairley...It was always a committee meeting as to when you listen back. Peter said that the band producing the album led to "ten pairs of hands going, 'No! Turn that up there!'" The session had originally been scheduled for a month but started to run over schedule. Peter described the situation as being "The job you are doing expands to fit the time you've got." One month ran into two which then ran into three. Peter: "The management was just getting a bit tired of us being here after 3-1/2 months." They were given a hard date that they had to be finished with the record. Peter told me that they were completing the final mix as the sun rose on the last day they were on the island. With the 'Real To Reel' complete, CBB finished the first official recording session at AIR Montserrat.

Before leaving the island, the band and the technical staff from the session autographed a freshly poured concrete slab behind the villa. The original plan was to have bands who recorded there each have their own autographed slab to mark the session. Unfortunately, only four bands signed slabs over the entire life of the studio. When I asked studio manager Yvonne Robinson (Kelly) why this was the case, she told me that it was often overlooked during the whirlwind of activity of the session. "'We'll do it at the end.' And the next thing you know, you are at the airport," she said. She also said that George Martin's wife Judy did not like the look of the slabs and thought they detracted from the beauty of the villa patio, so much so that she actively discouraged the staff from making the slabs at the end of sessions.

Autographed Slab For Posterity
Photo: Derek Holt

Reflecting on the effect that the island's vibe had on the album, Steve Culnane said that "at the time, it's such a good atmosphere of the whole place you went 'God this is real funky stuff. The tempo is up'...It's only when you actually came back to London and actually realized that it was quite laid back.

Your whole feeling of timing and all the rest of it out there was in parallel with the laid-back feel of the island."

After CBB, the band America used the studio to record vocals for their album "Silent Letter." George Martin had produced all of America's albums from their 1974 album Holiday up until that point in early 1979. The band had started work on "Silent Letter," in Los Angeles, California, using session musicians to record the backing tracks for the songs, leaving the vocals to be recorded elsewhere. George decided to move the vocal recording sessions to AIR Montserrat which was still under construction at the time. Recording vocals is a much simpler endeavor than recording an entire band so the studio space did not have to be complete to accommodate George, engineer Geoff Emerick, and the band which had been reduced to a duo at that point. Although George and Geoff had been present for the CBB session, neither was in the role of producer and engineer, only observing the session and assisting with studio problems. Recording the vocals for America was their first use of the studio in a real recording session.

With these two initial sessions complete and the studio construction nearing completion, a date was set for the official opening of AIR Studios Montserrat in July 1979.

1 Jarvis, Elana. "Band's rock style is fitting for Climax." Colorado Springs Gazette, 9 Aug. 1979, pp. 3E

OPENING DAY

With the facilities fully operational, a date was set for the official opening of the studio: July 28th, 1979. George and Judy Martin, Dave Harries, Malcolm Atkin, and David and Maureen Hodd were to be at the ceremony as well as the Governor of Montserrat, Gwilym Wyn Jones, and his wife. Other local politicians, dignitaries, and church leaders were invited as well. With the studio ready for new clients and the list of important people attending the opening ceremony, one might assume that the opening ceremony would have been a well-planned event with everything in place, ready to go the day of. AIR Technical Manager Geoff Irons tells quite a different story.

Geoff was the second technical manager to be assigned to the new studio, arriving in April of 1979. Prior, he was Malcolm's support technician in London during the studio buildout. One of Geoff's roles during the run up to the opening ceremony was to assist with preparing the studio facilities for the event. This led to several problems for him due to some last-minute decisions by George Martin. Geoff explained, "Dear old George used to leave everything to the last minute. He was a good man when he walked in the door and he had problems to solve. He'd do it there and then. But planning, I don't think was ever one of his fortes."

An Explosive Situation

About a week before the event, George came to Geoff asking if he was going over to Antigua that week. Geoff had plans to hop over to the larger island that weekend so George asked him if he could find some fireworks for the opening ceremony while he was there. George wanted fireworks, like Catherine Wheels and rockets, that could be lit in the evening to create a festive atmosphere. Geoff replied, "Oh yeah. Of course, I can" while thinking to himself "There's nobody making any fireworks in Antigua. No chance." Imagine his surprise when he stumbled across a vendor in Antigua who sold fireworks. Geoff bought "a load of them" based on what George was asking for. With the package of fireworks in hand, he jumped on the return flight back to Montserrat. When he arrived, the customs agent asked what was in the package Geoff had brought back to the island. Geoff answered honestly, "A box of fireworks," naively unaware of the major legal faux pas he had just committed. The customs agent exclaimed "Woah! That's explosives! That's firearms! You can't bring these into the country. They're illegal. You are going to jail!" The situation suddenly got very serious, very quickly. Geoff hastily explained that the fireworks were for the opening ceremony for the new studio. Word of the situation reached George Martin in short order, and he quickly placed a phone call to the Governor, trying to sort out the problem. Meanwhile, back at the airport, Geoff was asking the police if they could wait until George could work something out before hauling him off to jail. They agreed but took the fireworks from him and impounded them. Eventually, a phone call came in from the Governor who told the police to let Geoff go, that he knew why the fireworks were brought to the island. Geoff was immediately released from custody and a few days later, the fireworks were approved for use at the studio with the applicable taxes levied, of course. Geoff went back down to the customs house and picked them up, not realizing that his problems were not over quite yet.

Improvisation

Just before the start of the opening ceremony, George came to Geoff saying, "Geoff, we don't have any [ribbon] to put across the door for the governor to cut...can you think of something?" Knowing that quickly finding an appropriately thick ribbon somewhere on the island would be difficult, Geoff was exasperated saying to himself, "My God! Thanks a bunch, George." He scrambled to find a substitute that might be passable for a ribbon cutting ceremony. Using his ingenuity and grace under fire, he quickly found a ribbon substitute that would be the most appropriate "ribbon" for a recording studio opening in history: two-inch reel to reel recording tape. He wound enough tape onto two reels to give the tape 'ribbon' some support in order to counter the strong winds that day. With no obvious way to place the tape across the walkway, Geoff placed the reels on top of two of the headphone cue mixers from inside the studio and stretched the tape between the two. A perfect solution found in the nick of time. (You can see Geoff's setup in the picture below.)

"Ribbon" Ready To Be Cut At The Studio Opening
Photo: Geoff Irons

At the ceremony, George, dressed in a dapper white suit, gave a speech to those gathered on the pool deck. The governor cut the tape "ribbon" and the studio was officially open for business.

As evening began, everyone was gathered around the pool deck, drinking and socializing. Suddenly, George remembered the fireworks display that he wanted for the opening event. Both he and Geoff had completely forgotten about it and none of the fireworks had been set up to be lit. George asked Geoff, "Can you go around and nail a few on the trees...and light them?" So, in the pitch dark of the studio lawn, Geoff had to set up and light the entire fireworks display in a matter of minutes. Geoff described the moment: "I was running around like a madman, nailing Catherine Wheels to trees and sticking rockets in the ground and setting to light them. So I never actually got to see the fireworks display because I was too busy going around, lighting them all. That was my memories of the opening ceremony."

A local steel band played, local dance groups performed for the guests, and a barbeque was served by studio chef George Morgan. As the official ceremonies winded down, George opened the doors to the local islanders so that they could see the completed studio property. Many brought their families, and a good time was had by all. One of Geoff's memories of the studio open house exemplifies the simple life of the island at that time in the late 1970s. Locals were milling about in the villa's main living area and Geoff had placed a TV in the corner of the room by the bar. He had put on a movie, "Fist Full of Dollars" starring Clint Eastwood. Geoff describes the scene: "The whole area was packed with guests, most of whom had never seen a TV before and they all sat silently enthralled." Of all the anecdotes told to me about life in Montserrat at that time, this one really shows the simplicity and insular nature of the local culture of the island, the culture that convinced George to choose Montserrat for his destination studio project.

With the studio officially open for business, it was time to bring in the studio's first manager, Denny Bridges, and start making records.

George Martin Gives The Opening Day Speech
Monstserrat Governor Gwilym Jones Looks On
Photo: David and Maureen Hodd

A Catherine Wheel Whirls At The Opening Ceremony
Photo: David and Maureen Hodd

DENNY TAKES THE HELM

Denny Bridges Enjoys A Drink After Some Fun In The Sea
Photo: Geoff Irons

Denny Bridges, AIR Montserrat's first studio manager, had worked for AIR as an engineer and interim studio manager prior to arriving to the island. As a recording engineer, he had assisted George Martin on Jeff Beck's landmark "Blow by Blow" album and later, as described by Dave Harries, "looked after" the London studios while Dave and Malcolm Atkin were busy with the Montserrat studio project. Since he had gained some studio management experience with this post, he was then hired as the

Montserrat studio manager. Prior to accepting the position, he came to Montserrat to check out the island and in typical AIR fashion, brought things on the flight that were needed at the studio. He said, "A year before, they sent me out for a couple weeks. Heading down with the latest drawings and a few bits and pieces for installation...I had 2 weeks in Montserrat to have a look around and see if I liked it and whether I felt I could survive there, etc...Looked like something I could do for sure."

He arrived on the island for the studio manager's gig after Climax Blues Band completed their record. Denny brought his wife Meryl with him to Montserrat, and they took up residence in the manager's suite in the studio villa. He said that construction workers were laying the last of the tiles on the pool deck the day he arrived at the studio. With the studio nearly complete, America became the first band to record at the studio once Denny took over as manager. Once clients started arriving, Denny quickly learned that being a manager at AIR Montserrat was much different than in London. 'When I went to Montserrat to actually run the studio, not to go on two-week vacation, it was a steep learning curve to say the least," he said. There was much more involved with running a remote studio, tasks that went far beyond the usual responsibilities of a studio manager. The actual studio operation was not a problem, it was all the ancillary issues that are involved in running a destination studio. He told me, "It wasn't so much involved in the running of the recording studio per se, because that basically runs itself. It was setup [properly.] It was a great studio. Worked perfectly well. But my role was involved much more in management. I was involved in catering. I was involved with accommodation. I was involved in hotel management and all that kind of stuff, none of which I had any experience at all...So I had to learn on the job."

We need to take a step back and take a brief look at the contrast between managing a typical recording studio and AIR Montserrat in order to appreciate the additional level of difficulty that studio managers faced there. When an artist booked a session at AIR Oxford Circus in London or The Power Station in New York City, most of the logistics of the session were handled through someone other than the studio, such as the artist's management or touring companies. Other than scheduling the studio session times and in-house staff for engineering and operations, which the studio manager handled internally, the artists themselves were responsible for most everything else. Gear transportation, accommodations and transport for musicians and their entourages, meals and entertainment, car rentals, etc. were arranged for and paid directly by the artist, their management, or the record company. Contrast that with the responsibilities of the AIR Montserrat's studio manager. From the time the plane arrived in Antigua, everything that the artist needed was procured or arranged for by the studio manager. Getting artists and their equipment through customs and immigration was required. The studio manager arranged for hotels and villas for all guests' accommodations. Meals were provided at the studio and at artists' villas. Transport of all guests and gear to and from the studio was arranged by the studio manager. Car hire was arranged for. Entertainment options were facilitated through the studio. With the small insular, albeit friendly, culture of the island, AIR staff would often help "introduce" the artists to the island's people and businesses. Since the island's supplies were so limited, meeting the artists' wants and needs could often be a problem. Anticipating what they might ask for was paramount because if, for example, they wanted a particular brand of cigarettes or vodka, it could take days for these specialty items to arrive in Montserrat, if they could be procured at all. Any problems that the artists may have with their experiences with food, entertainment, transportation, accommodations, etc. were the responsibility of the studio manager to correct. The manager at AIR Montserrat was much more than a "studio manager" in the traditional sense. They were more like a tour manager that stayed in the same location every night.

A Different Type Of Studio Management

Denny's experience managing the studios in London was quite different than the situation he found himself in when he took over managing AIR Montserrat. He was out of his element and overwhelmed. One of Denny's strategies for dealing with this steep learning curve was to keep a tight grip on the staff. Every staff member had a silo of responsibility and Denny expected each one to stay strictly within that silo. Barman Franklyn Allen described the situation to me: "He was very strict with everything. It's like...I was a bartender. And when you work in a restaurant with staff, staff [members] help one another, [but with Denny]...if I'm a bartender, there's only bartending." One time someone asked Franklyn to get some coffee so he went to pour a cup from the kitchen, which was considered another area of responsibility separate from the bar. He said that when Denny saw that he had done this, Denny said to him, "What is your job description?" Franklyn replied, "My description is to be a bartender." Denny said, "Good. So what I see you do there, don't do it again." Denny expected the food service staff to serve coffee, not the bartenders. When I discussed this with Denny, he explained his reasoning: "It was very much the way that I felt I needed to make it work...To go back to my point about it being a steep learning curve. I needed everyone to...hold their end so I didn't have to worry about that particular element [of responsibility]...I'm pretty much like that anyway. If I allow disorganization, then it's disorganized...To reiterate, if a person just fulfills their role and does that job, then the big picture holds together." While Denny's response to this overwhelming level of responsibility is logical in a sense, as Franklyn said, in a dynamic customer service situation such as a restaurant or, in this case, a destination studio on a small Caribbean island, staff can better serve the customers if they are able to cross job delineations as the situation requires. Bartender Desmond Riley echoed Franklyn's sentiments but ultimately recognized Denny's authority: "Denny. He works like 'to the book'...like precise. He's straight to the book... 'That's your job, you do your job. Don't worry about anyone else's' which I think you must have some flexibility...but that's how he want it, that's how he get it." Efficiency and order were Denny's priorities. To assist Denny, his wife Meryl acted as an intermediary between him and the housekeeping staff allowing

Denny to focus on the more "management" activities like procurement and logistics.

The studio budget was also an issue. When the studio first opened, money was tight for the staff. Steve Culnane, the studio's first technician, told me, "To be honest...we were skimped. The studio was working. The money had been plowed into the studio but there wasn't much [else]. I think there was a Barclay's [Bank] on the island and it took a while to find out that we could actually go down to Barclay's and cash a check. Per diems were non-existent. There wasn't any petty cash...You'd never have milk and breakfast cereal at the same time. You'd have one or the other. It was a bit hand to mouth in some respects but again, the pioneering aspect [of working there.]" Meryl's background in finance helped with the day-to-day tracking of the budget but the lack of financial information flowing from AIR London led to stress for Denny. The studio had its own bank accounts and budget but, according to Denny, that was often "blown" which then had to be augmented with funds from London. The expenses for the studio were paid from the local studio bank accounts but AIR London received the revenue from the artists, so there was no way for Denny to know how the studio was performing financially at any point. He explained that, "The money was going out at our end, but the money would be going in on their end. So it wasn't a question of that we could balance in and out, because we only saw the out. We didn't see any of the in...Car hire was a major bleed, you can well imagine, if you were actually paying for car hire upfront which is what would happen quite often. The client would [eventually] pay for it but there would be a time lag, of course, when they settle up the bill [with AIR London]...So it was weird. It was tight. It was difficult. It was stressful at times to say the least. Trying to balance that."

During the first year of what was truly an experiment in recording studio operations, many facets of running the facilities were still works in progress. The walk-in freezer that had previously caught fire was having problems. Denny explains: "That damned thing never worked. We had people coming up the whole time and replenishing the freon and goodness knows what our carbon footprint was like at the time. It wouldn't keep things cold...So we had a deal with one of these stores in the town to...borrow freezer space...to keep our freezer stuff which is all very well but other people were going into that freezer too. And I'm not suggesting that things were stolen but things would get moved around and we'd lose track of who's was what. What was ours, what was someone else's...That was a real pain."

A recurring theme throughout the life of the studio was keeping stock of items for clients that were not readily available or very expensive to buy on the island. Denny tells a tale of trying to find wine for the studio: "One of the projects I had which was quite time consuming and somewhat difficult and out of my remit was...I had to get some wine in some [significant] quantity. It'd be very expensive to be going down...to the local store and buying a couple bottles of wine every night for the artists...So I got in touch with some people who put me in touch with some other people. Anyway, it ended up with a merchant in Guadaloupe who was importing French wine. So I thought 'That's a good idea' and negotiated to buy quite a few cases, a dozen cases of this wine which I remember was called Blanc de Blanc. [I thought] 'That sounds like a French wine.'...So off I go to Guadaloupe and meet up with this guy and buy this wine and then organize for [transport]. There was a gentleman called Orville Paine who flew a Piper Aztec...I hired him and we loaded up the plane with these dozen [cases] of wine and flew them back to Montserrat and took them up to the studio...[but] what do you do with a dozen boxes of white wine in that sort of temperature? [The studio villa did not have air conditioning.] So we put some in the pool pump room...in concrete and there were some in various different places...I always remember that as being a difficult time. A bit too much to expect for a recording engineer to do really." Finding specialty items like wine was an occasional problem, but shortages of staples that were in daily use could be a big problem for the studio manager and their budget. Denny explains: "At times, things weren't available...And one of the things that went through my year's experience [in Montserrat] was that there was always shortages of something. Something wasn't available. You couldn't get...not that it matters so much to me, but sometimes the island had no cigarettes and wouldn't get cigarettes...and the boat didn't necessarily come over regularly. And sometimes you couldn't get fresh produce...So all sorts of things like that you had to deal with and sometimes you had to go to heroic measures to deal with that by having a crate of tomatoes flown down from Puerto Rico. It was an expensive way of doing it, for sure...It wasn't an ideal situation to be throwing money at problems frequently...When it was a regular occurrence, you could decimate the bank account quite quickly."

Unlike later studio managers, Denny and Meryl chose to live in the studio villa in the manager's quarters. This was originally the master bedroom of the Sturges who built the property, but it had been updated to provide additional functionality needed by a studio manager living on premises. What Denny quickly found was that there was a downside to being onsite 24/7. He said that people would be knocking on the door quite often and that the job could "be getting up to 18 hours [a day] dealing with stuff." Later managers utilized the manager's quarters as an office but recognized that having some private space away from the studio was healthy for their lives, especially when the studio was in session so they rented homes away from the studio.

Part of the job of the studio manager was to socialize with the movers and shakers on the island. Denny said that he was a representative for AIR "to a degree [but] I wasn't actively promoting AIR Studios...I was socialized with a lot of people around....part of the job really was to keep in contact with local people. I would be invited to the Governor's dinner parties. It would be 'Here's a curiosity. Here's a...manager of a recording studio that we've got on our island.'" When George and Judy Martin would come to the island, Danny and Meryl would be tapped for assistance. "If George and Judy would be having dinner with someone on the island, you'd have the kids."

The Boat, Lost At Sea

George Martin imported a speed boat to Montserrat for personal and studio use. Geoff Irons, having sailing experience and an interest in all things boating recalls quite a few details about the vessel. He says that George had named the boat "Solitaire" claiming that "George bought it on the money he made from the Bond film." [Solitaire is James Bonds' love interest in the 1973 film "Live and Let Die." George wrote the film score for the movie.] Geoff continued, "It was a day-boat and it had a big canvas canopy that you could put up over the back to keep the sun off. It had a Volvo Penta...engine on it. It was quite a good boat. You could ski off the back of it." Many an AIR staffer and client would water ski behind the Solitaire over the years. Denny said that if there was no client in session, they would go water-skiing almost every afternoon. Geoff's experience maintaining boats came in handy as the Caribbean seas can be rough on boats. He told me, "Everything out there decays and rusts unless you look after it. Because I had a lot of small boat experience, I knew the shortcomings of boating out there. So I used to have a bucket of tools that I took with me every time I went out because there's no rescue, none whatsoever." Malcolm Atkin, who used the boat for waterskiing himself echoed Geoff's sentiments about the boat's reliability: "Ran like a bat out of hell...when it was in good condition."

The boat's reliability would come to haunt poor Denny one day, in another story from Geoff Irons. Geoff told me that Denny and Meryl went out on the boat for some recreation on the open sea. They set off drifting along the shoreline without using the engine. Far from shore, they tried starting up the engine which promptly failed to start. Without any propulsion, over the horizon they drifted without any way to signal anyone on shore. Eventually, someone noticed that they were missing. Geoff Emerick, who was on the island at the time, quickly phoned up a local charter pilot to hire a plane to go on an air search mission to find Denny and Meryl, but they were losing light as it was late in the day. The search mission would have to wait until the next morning. Geoff Irons, concerned that Denny and Meryl would be desperate for food and water being at sea for so long, decided to build a container to drop from the plane to the boat when it was found. To test its ability to withstand the shock of hitting the ocean at speed, Geoff climbed up onto the roof of the studio buildings and tossed the container into the pool. While his efforts to help were well appreciated, Geoff Emerick pointed out to Geoff that the wind speed of the plane would not allow them to open the door to toss supplies to Denny. The mission to find Denny and Meryl was that much more critical now. The next morning the plane took off and searched over the areas where the boat would likely be found. Luckily, the Solitaire was located and a local fishing boat headed out to pull it back to shore. Geoff recalled the scene when the pair arrived back on the island: "It was a bit embarrassing because when [they] got back, Meryl said to me 'You're the sailor, what would you have done?' And I said 'Well I would have started the engine before I cast off.' She said 'Yeah but what would you have done if the engine had broken down?' And I said 'I would have just chucked the anchor over the side.' And Meryl, I can still see her clear as a bell, she just walked straight back to Denny and started shouting at him about 'Why didn't you chuck the anchor over the side?' But, I'd the set of skills. I knew what was necessary to safeguard yourself out there." This story personifies the pioneering nature of AIR Montserrat and the attitude of AIR management. An ocean faring boat was available for use by staff and clients and yet, with all of the dangers associated with sailing in the Caribbean Sea, no one on staff was properly trained for sailing or repair of the boat, the exception of Geoff Irons who simply happened to have prior boating experience. With the crisis averted, Geoff knew that there needed to be a way to signal for help if the boat broke down again while at sea, so he contacted AIR London who responded in typical AIR fashion. Geoff again: "I said 'Listen. We need some flares for the boat in case we get stuck out to sea. So they just put them on a plane and sent them out...explosive flares in the hull of a jumbo jet. Nobody batted an eye. Nobody gave it a thought."

Early Non-Problems

During the first year, some problems with the studio construction took time before they would be discovered. Another story from technician Geoff Irons: "The other thing I learned which was quite odd was [this]...I went out there I think in April and this is a story about the hot water. You just used the hot water. Come October, the staff said to me. 'Geoff, the hot water's run out and it's run cold.' I thought 'There must be an immersion heater somewhere. I bet that's popped its clogs. [slang: died] When I finally went down and I managed to scramble over the top of the tank and had a look with a mirror. The immersion heater had not even been connected! The wires were in there dangling loose. The whole studio had been running off of solar panel heat all that time. We had a solar panel on the studio and there was enough heat generated from the sun that the water never ever went cold until October when the days got cooler."

As it turns out, not all "problems" were actually problems. One day, David Hodd stopped by the studio to see Geoff. The studio's architect was a bit panicked. He was worried that there might be a problem with his design. "He came up one day with a very worried expression on his face," Geoff told me. "He said 'I don't know what the problem is but [it] looks like we're losing a bit of water out of the pool. I hope to God it's not cracked somewhere.'...because it's very volcanic. The ground could move." After inspecting the pool for cracks or leaks, nothing was found. It took some additional research with the staff members to find out what was causing the water loss. Geoff again: "It turned out that what happened was that there was a drain pipe out the back and the gardeners were using this to fill their buckets to go off and water the garden." Crisis averted.

During Denny's tenure as manager at the studio, he was present for sessions from some big acts, as well as some not so well-known ones. America, Jimmy Buffet, UFO, Lou Reed, John Townley, Roger Daltrey, and Private Lightning all recorded at AIR Montserrat during the first year of operations. Denny even stepped behind the desk to engineer and produce an

78

album by the Caribbean Heet Waves (spelled correctly) who hailed from the neighboring island of St. Kitts.

Gerry

While Denny's day-to-day management of studio operations was competent, his soft skills would be tested greatly with an extremely difficult session with Gerry Rafferty. By 1980, when AIR Montserrat was chosen as the studio for his "Snakes and Ladders" album, Gerry was heading down the path into alcoholism and was known to be quite volatile. Peter Filleul from the Climax Blues Band told me that he thought that even before Gerry arrived, "he got it in his head that he was not going to enjoy it." From the time he set foot in Montserrat, the situation started to unravel. Denny said that the band arrived late at night with their producer sporting an ankle injury. Denny had to scramble to find a doctor who could help him at that hour. He eventually found a retired physician to lend a hand. Once the producer was patched up, Denny found that the studio chef, George Morgan, had "gone AWOL" so there was no one to make dinner for Gerry and his crew. Scrambling again, he called a local hotel restaurant that said that they had no available tables. He was able to convince them to squeeze the party of ten in. The problems were just starting.

Once the session had started, there were issues with the piano. Denny spins the tale: "The recording started going and there isn't a problem but for some reason, they insisted on having the studio door open when they were working which meant that the temperature rose which meant the piano kept going out of tune...Now the piano was [normally] tuned once a week or twice a week, by special request, by a guy who traveled around the islands tuning the pianos of all of the churches and stuff like that. So the band would come to me or whoever and say 'The piano's out of tune. We need the piano tuned.' So I had to locate this guy and who knows where he was. I remember a couple of times, fortunately, he was at the airport, not on the plane yet...So he would come tune the piano. The same thing would happen the next day. I have to find the guy [again]...This went on and I had to explain things to the band. 'We can't keep bringing this guy back.' We were very lucky like that. He was able to get to the studio in a matter of hours. I had to be quite emphatic. I said 'This guy has a family. He has his own life. I can't be having him going back and forth. And every time we do that, we have to pay him and it had to stop. Feelings were hurt, should we say." Things were not going well.

Gerry was having a hard time on the island. Geoff Irons said, "I think Gerry Rafferty in all fairness to him was having a nervous breakdown when he was there. He was so obnoxious to all of the staff. He really was... We found out after he left that he was having the servants, whenever they came up to serve him, he was making them click their heels." According to John Silcott, who was working at the studio as a wine steward, Gerry fired all the studio hospitality staff...except John. Once everyone was fired, Gerry hired a local chef and his staff from a restaurant he'd been frequenting to take AIR staffs' place, but without a wine steward of his own, John was kept on at the studio. John was not happy with the situation. No one was.

Steve Lipson was engineering the session for Gerry and was not used to using the Neve recording console that AIR had installed in Montserrat. He preferred using the consoles made by the up-and-coming console manufacturer, Solid State Logic. According to Dave Harries, his frustrations also added to the negative tone of the session.

Additionally, power issues at the studio were contributing to Gerry's mood and the negative vibe at the studio. Session bassist Mo Foster was part of Gerry's recording band at the time and explained the situation: "The island power supply was intermittent. And the studio was only 6 months old and they hadn't gotten an agreement with the authorities. They had a generator but they weren't allowed to leave it on. It could only kick in after the power supply had cut out. So you'd be in the middle of a take and suddenly everything goes dead. The whole island goes black. Then the generator starts by which time you've blown transistors and things. That was the problem. Something Dave [Harries] and Malcolm [Atkin] had no control over. And it just upset Gerry enormously and so he took it out on them which is unfair." Not to mention Denny.

Mr. Jackson

Malcolm Atkin said that Gerry and Denny were both "screaming back to London" so he and John Burgess were sent out to try to iron out the situation and please their client. Meanwhile, Gerry's keyboardist Billy Livesy knew of a good instrument technician back in London who might be able to help deal with the technical issues they were having. His name was Steve Jackson. Steve, a great raconteur, told me the story of the call: "He called me up and he said, 'We've got some problems with the keyboards here.' I said, 'Where are you?' He said, 'At AIR Studios.' So I said, 'O.K. I'll be up in about a half an hour' and he said, 'No. We're in Montserrat.'" Steve did not believe him and said, "Yeah, fuck off!" and hung up. Billy rings Steve back and says to Steve, "Don't hang up! I really am in Montserrat." Steve had no idea where Montserrat was located although he had heard of AIR Montserrat through his connections in the industry. Billy asked if he would be willing to come out and lend a hand. Steve agreed and prepped his gear. He got a call from AIR London asking if he was truly willing to head out to Montserrat. Steve was agreeable if they made all arrangements for the trip. He still did not believe that it was going to happen. He said to his wife Jan, "When I get the ticket in my hand, then I will know that they are for real." That afternoon, the ticket was delivered and the next day he was on a flight to Antigua.

Steve had never been to the tropics before. He said that when he landed in Antigua, his reaction to the unfamiliar surroundings was "Where the fuck is this?" He was approached by two guys who turned out to be Dave Harries and John Burgess. "Are you Steve Jackson?" They told him that they had chartered a plane to take them to Montserrat. John Burgess told Steve, "You realize that you don't actually have to fix anything here." Steve, who wanted to earn his pay said, "Well I will. I'm good at what I do." John replied, "All we need to do is show that we are doing everything possible to make this session happen." AIR had brought Steve from London to Montserrat, a trip of over

4000 miles, to give the appearance of trying to save the session, not necessarily to actually repair anything since Gerry's problems were more personal than technical.

Steve arrived at the studio and the tension was palpable. He said that John and Dave seemed nervous about going into the studio because of all the animosity of a session gone "horrible bad" so he, John, and Dave were having cocktails rather than stepping into the den of angry musicians. Eventually, Steve said, "C'mon! Let's go into the studio. I've got work to do." Steve entered the studio first and after surveying the room said, "You fucking miserable bastards. What are you complaining about? You are on this beautiful island!" The musicians instantly started pelting him with sandwiches. Steve reached in his bag and started throwing things back at them...but it was all in good fun. It turned out that Steve had a good relationship with many of the guys in the studio through his years in the music business. He said it gave him license to be like, "I'll fix your gear but I can behave like a total prick." Steve set about fixing the gear and got the problems sorted out. Gerry and the musicians are happy with the results although, as they let the island, mooned Dave Harries as they left the studio on their way to the airport.

Steve was ready to head home so he wanted to catch the last daily flight back to Antigua and get a seat on the midnight flight back to London. Dave Harries approached him and said, "Just stick around a little bit. We like you being here." Little did he know what machinations were in motion behind the scenes.

With Denny's one year contract as studio manager expiring and the disaster of the Rafferty session still present in everyone's minds, management at AIR had decided that they wanted to go a different direction at AIR Montserrat. Denny was on his way out. Malcolm Atkin said that the simple fact was that Denny did not have the right personality for the job of studio manager. "Dealing with islanders and everything else [involved with that] and the stars wasn't his bag...I think that [he] was a bit too interested in minding the 'Ps and Qs' and the money rather than keeping the client happy." Denny did not recognize that managing the studio in Montserrat was as much a customer service and public relations position as it was facilities management. Geoff Irons put it this way: "[The studio] needed somebody resourceful...none of that had ever been done before so it needed somebody that could think on their feet as it were and have ideas...Denny was very much [fine] if you gave him a plan, he would see it through come hell or high water but of course, out there, there was no plan." Granted, it was not clear that this was in the "job description" before Denny found himself in Montserrat and knee deep into the day-to-day operations of running such a unique studio.

Minetta Francis Gives Denny A Peck Goodbye As He Leaves Montserrat
Photo: Minetta Francis

When I interviewed Denny, he told me that he had not thought about AIR Montserrat in many years. I asked him if he felt fondly of his time in Montserrat despite the problems, he said, "Yeah, pretty much. Yes, I do. It was a good experience and Montserrat is lovely and the people were great. Yeah, I had some good times." Asked how he thought about the experience in retrospect, he told me, "I have thought that I just should have stayed in the studio as a recording engineer and producer and not gone over to administration, but it did lead to many other things [and] provided me with an interesting life." He returned to the U.K. and managed traditional studios for several years before returning to his roots as a freelance recording engineer. Later, Denny's experiences at the studio helped him manage band touring. These days, Denny and his current wife Jackie live on a solar powered farm out in the countryside, far from the music industry that was once was his livelihood.

With Denny and Meryl returning to London, the studio needed a new manager...He was already on the island.

THE JACKSONS

Steve And Jan Jackson
AIR Studios Publicity Photo For AIR Montserrat
Photo: Steve Jackson

When Dave Harries asked Steve Jackson to stay for a bit in Montserrat rather than return to London, Steve agreed to hang back on the island. The Rafferty session was not over so his calming effect was still needed. As he told me, "The musicians were all bummed out...They were all just moaning and groaning." Steve wanted to have some fun since he was on this beautiful island, goading the musicians by saying, "Let's have some fun. Go downtown and chase after the women. Do all sorts of things. Let's get stoned." He arranged a trip to the island's famous waterfall for the band. He ended up staying for a week. His wife Jan told me that, "He called me every day. 'I'm sorry...another day.' I said that you better not come home with a suntan." It was October and poor Jan was stuck in England which was "cold and horrible."

When Billy Livsey was getting on the plane to leave the island, Steve told the AIR directors that he too was heading home since there was no reason for him to stay. "The keyboard player is going and that's why I'm here," Steve told them. When Steve got home, he promptly sent AIR the bill for his services, but Montserrat was still on his mind. He had fallen in love with the island and had a prediction for Jan, "We're going to be living there in six months."

Steve got a call from AIR London, asking him to come into their offices. He was expecting them to give him grief about the bill: "I was good but I was expensive." When he arrived at AIR London, he said, "I guess this is about the check?" The AIR representative hands him the check and says that they were grateful for his help and that the price for his services was reasonable. They tell him that George Martin wants to personally meet with Steve and Jan. Steve was confused. He said that he was thinking to himself, "What the fuck is going on?"

A few days before Christmas 1980, AIR called again and asked Steve and Jan to come into London to meet with George. Steve told me that he was ecstatic. His heroes in the recording industry were not the musicians but the production and technical luminaries behind the scenes, so an invitation by George Martin was a very exciting prospect for him. "I'm meeting the ultimate superstar producer." When they arrived, George was out shopping for Christmas gifts, so Jan and Steve had to wait for him. While they waited, AIR staffers start serving them straight brandy. Jan said, "It was like ten o'clock in the morning and by the time George gets back, we're drunk." George made some small talk with the couple and Steve's thought was that George was going to ask him to be the maintenance tech at AIR Montserrat, which Steve thought would be great opportunity. Being a bit tipsy, Steve remembered: "And then he said 'Blah, blah, blah...general manager.'" Steve was taken aback and said to George, "With all due respect, I've never run a studio in England, in a city. Least of all on a tropical island." Steve said that George replied, "Well, we took a chance with four musicians a few years ago and we were moderately successful with them. So I will take a chance with you." When Steve told me this in the interview, he smiled at me and said, "How can you turn a line like that down?"

Two months later, on Valentine's Day 1981, Steve and Jan were on a plane to Montserrat with two children, one of which was only a year old. Steve was to become the second general manager of AIR Studios Montserrat. He told me, "I was just in the right place at the right time."

Steve had some background with tour management, so he hit the ground with the attitude of "the client is golden" as he described it. His management style was quite different than previous manager Denny Bridges. Geoff Irons was the technician at the studio at the time of the transition from Denny to Steve and described the difference between the two as "Chalk and Cheese" which for us non-Brits means that they were total opposites. Geoff said that they were, "Absolutely different. I don't think that Denny Bridges ever had it in him to be a manager. He was not what I call a people person. I can say this easily because I'm not a people person. People persons go down the pub with everybody and they just get on and make a really good host...Denny never did any of that. He just ran it efficiently." He continued, "[Steve] was really sociable. He could mix with people. He could quite happily...For instance, Denny had to be told that it might be a good idea to take all of the staff down to the Vue Point and have BBQ down there once a week or something, just to get us out of the place. The only time we ever did any beach BBQs was when George [Martin] turned up and he said 'C'mon. Let's go to the beach and do a BBQ.' Denny could never organize anything like that AT ALL. George would rally round and he'd get some locals there with their boats and ship everyone out to the white sand beach on the north end of the island. We'd have a great time...I think Steve Jackson was the other end of that." Steve was a "people person", very social with the staff at the studio, locals from the Governor to beachcombers, and with the artists, adept at keeping everyone happy. Dave Harries said of Steve: "He was a good bloke. He was a lovely guy. And he was great with clients...superb with clients...If you can work with somebody like Gerry Rafferty and his mates, then you must be good."

Steve and Jan arrived as Cheap Trick were finishing up their session with George Martin and Geoff Emerick. He was curious as to who was on the schedule for the upcoming months and when he asked, the schedule looked a little thin. Earth, Wind, and Fire had been booked for a session but had cancelled at the last minute. They had made the trip all the way to Antigua but backed out when they saw the tiny size of the plane they had to board to get to Montserrat. Steve had a personal relationship with the group, working with them recently on the "I Am" tour. He rang them up and said "I will get you a bigger plane. Change of plans. You are coming down." Steve chartered a "great, big Piper Chieftain" for the trip between the islands and EWF made the trip back down to Antigua and on to Montserrat. Steve's philosophy of "the client is golden" was able to convince a reluctant client to come back to Montserrat. AIR Studio driver Llyod Francis said that, "Steve totally was an action man. Anything to keep the client happy, Steve would do it. That's him."

Having a family, Steve and Jan decided that they needed a place of their own rather than stay in the manager's quarters in the studio villa like Denny and Meryl had. When the studio had clients in session, Jan said that "You have to get away from it." AIR rented them a villa outside of Plymouth in the Richmond Hill area. Steve commuted to the studio from home although some more demanding clients needed a more "hands-on" approach. For those clients, Steve would stay at the studio when required. EWF was one of those clients.

Nazareth Lends A Hand To The Island

Guitarist Jeff Baxter, of The Doobie Brothers and Steely Dan, came with the band Nazareth to produce their new album at AIR Montserrat. One of the local musicians, Onyon, guitarist for the Soca band "The Burning Flames", was hanging with the band at the studio for an impromptu jam session. Jeff was watching Onyon play and had a question for him: "Is that how you get that Caribbean sound?" Onyon was confused by the question. Jeff said, "Well, I noticed you only use five strings [instead of the normal six]." Onyon replied, "That's because I can't get the sixth string. There aren't any on the island." Getting basic supplies for musicians like guitar strings was quite difficult in Montserrat. Seeing the need of their fellow musicians, Nazareth were willing to lend a hand. In the music industry, famous bands such as Nazareth are often endorsed by equipment companies in order to get exposure for their products. This means that the bands get free gear in exchange for using these companies' products on their records and during concerts. Seeing the lack of local availability of basic gear for local island musicians, Nazareth opened their equipment coffers and donated cases of guitar and bass strings, drumheads, and sticks to the musicians that had been given to them by their sponsors.

Montserratian AIR staff member John Silcott's mother was very ill and needed expensive treatment for her ailment. No having the means to quickly earn the money needed for her treatment, he was attempting to sell his belongings to raise the money. Nazareth were in the studio at the time recording their album "The Fool Circle." When the band heard that John was having trouble paying for his mother's health care, they asked Steve if there was anything they could do to help. Together they decided to help raise money for John and his mother by hosting the "the biggest concert the island had ever seen." Steve went around the island to all the local bands asking to borrow their gear for the concert since Nazareth had only brought equipment to record, not to play live. Steve said to the bands, "I want to borrow your [equipment]. I'm not going to pay for it. The only guarantee is you'll get it back in better condition [than before]." By offering to repair the island bands' equipment in exchange for its use, Steve was using both his strong personal connections in the community and his technical expertise to secure free gear for the show. He said that they used some of the outboard gear from the studio to supplement the borrowed equipment and were able to put together a great live show for the island featuring Nazareth, who were more than happy to lend a hand. "It was a benefit for a friend. We raised too much friggin money, it was ridiculous", Steve said. Excess money was given to a local boys home. Steve thought of the studio as being integrated with the community. Steve put it this way: "We were part of the island. We were AIR studios. It was [also] their AIR Studios. It was Montserrat's AIR Studios."

Thief In The Night (For A Good Cause)

As he starts weaving this tale, Steve prefaces this story with the statement, "They can't come after me now." Knowing Steve's brash personality, this comment let me know that what follows is going to be a good story. George Martin was in the studio producing The Little River Band for their "Time Exposure" album. "You've always you have to be on your Ps and Qs [with George there.]" LRB was working very hard, putting in long hours in the studio. It was mid-April 1981 and the band's session was running up against the Easter holiday. Everything on the island was going to be shutting down

86

for the holiday. Since much of the island would be closed, the local electric company planned on doing preventative maintenance on the power system on Good Friday, two days before Easter. It was known in the community to expect power outages that day.

That evening, AIR's maintenance tech went to check the generator to make sure that it was in working condition so that the session could continue irrespective of what the power company would be doing. Steve asked if there was sufficient fuel in the generator's tanks and the technician said that he thought that the tank was full. Just to be sure, Steve headed to the fuel tank and tapped the fuel level meter to make sure it was not stuck. Ping! "Oh Fuck!" The needle dropped precipitously to indicate that there was not much fuel available. Steve hoped it is enough to tie them over until they can buy some diesel fuel, but when the power dropped at midnight, the generator only ran briefly before running out of fuel. With the client in mid-session, Steve had to come up with some way to procure fuel in the middle of the night. With the island shut down, this was not going to be an easy feat. At this point in the story, Steve said to me, "I'm going to get arrested for this story if you fucking print this, but anyway..." after which we all laughed loudly. Continuing on, Steve said that with no other options, he grabbed a few empty 55-gallon diesel fuel drums and loaded them into the studio truck. They drove down to the power station which was still quite noisy at that hour with lots of activity going on but it was locked up. The gate to the station was on a slope so there was enough of a gap that a person could slip under it. Steve climbed under the gate and headed over to the security guard station where he found the guard sound asleep. Steve looked around the guard box, found the front gate key, and knicked it. "In we go...we drive up to where all their fuel is...and we start filling up with diesel from Monlec's pump...We just finished, put the pump back, and [were] about to get in the truck to turn around, when out comes somebody from the power station. I went, 'Don't worry about it. Everything is fine. Just go back and pretend we weren't here.' This guy turned around and walked off the other direction." Feeling that they were in the clear, they headed back to the studio.

They filled the generator's tank and tried firing up the generator. "We're safe!", he thought...but not quite yet. The generator would not start. Steve did not realize that when you run out of fuel with a diesel motor, you needed to bleed the motor's injectors which, even if he had known, he had no idea how to do. It was now about one o'clock in the morning and Steve was still in a major bind with a client wanting to record but having no power to do so. He had no choice but get help from the chief engineer of Monlec, the company that he had just stolen diesel fuel from. As it turned out, the chief engineer was ill at home which is why he was not at the power station where Steve had just come from. Steve drove down to his house and when he arrived at his home, the engineer's wife refused to rouse him. Steve tried impressing on her how dire the situation was. Eventually after much negotiation, the Monlec technician finally came out to greet Steve and went with him to the studio to lend a hand. They bled the system, got the generator running, and LRB was finally able to continue their session.

About eight in the morning, George Martin arrived at the studio to find the AIR staff, as Steve described, "Covered in diesel, totally knackered." He comes up and he says, 'Everything alright, Steve?' [Steve replies in a low voice] 'Yeah, peachy. Yeah.'" On the following Tuesday morning, Steve went to Monlec headquarters to pay for the diesel he had "borrowed." He said, "Um...Don't ask how but I got three drum loads of fuel" to which the Monlec representative said, "Who served you? How did you get it? Who did you sign with?" Steve said, "I didn't sign anything. I've got three 55-gallon drums of diesel. How much do I owe you?" The rep just shook his head and said, "I've never known a thief to come back and pay." "Well, I'm the first," said Steve.

A Pair of Truck Stories

As I mentioned in the chapter about the Neve console, Dave Harries was a 'stalwart Brit' who wanted AIR to purchase and utilize as many British-made products as possible. Two of the AIR Montserrat's staff vehicles were British-produced Ford autos. A Ford transit van for picking up people from the airport and a Ford Escort Estate which was for the studio manager's personal use. Steve said that the manager's car was always breaking down and parts were extremely difficult to come by in the Caribbean. He said, "My car had 16 variations of the brakes in that one [model] year. So no matter what you send for...remember, it takes forever to get to you, it was always wrong. Eventually, the thing gave up the ghost for good." Steve decided to buy a new vehicle that had a reputation for reliability, a Toyota truck. Purchasing a Toyota also had a huge advantage for a business vehicle on a remote Caribbean island. "Anywhere in the world, you can get the parts," Steve said. Dave Harries was not happy. Steve said, "Oh man, did I get shit for that. I broke a lot of rules."

As Steve starts telling me this next story, he and Jan are giggling. Steve was at the studio with AIR engineer Steve Crane and keyboardist John Locke who had played with the bands Spirit and, most-recently, Nazareth. Steve recalls that they were in the studio recording a song called "On The Rock." ("The Rock" is a nickname that locals have for Montserrat.) Tropical rains had been pounding the island. Steve said, "We had 12 inches of rain in less than 24 hours. It was 'hammering it down.'" Steve Crane went to get a drink from the villa and came back into the studio wide-eyed saying, "Have you seen it out there?" They ran back to the villa and saw "a waterfall coming down from the patio down into the dining room." The Jacksons were supposed to be hosting a dinner event at their home in Richmond Hill, so Steve decided that they had all better leave and head back home in case the rain continued and the roads became too treacherous. He and his guests jumped into the studio's pickup truck and headed down the studio drive. Almost immediately, they ran into trouble. At the end of the steep studio drive, you have to take a sharp left to head across the Belham Valley towards Plymouth. Steve said, "As we're going down the hill [from the studio], I said, 'Hey guys, I hope I can make the bend at the bottom because I can't stop. We're going with the water." The river of rainwater was so deep that the truck was being swept along. Steve continues: "We get to the bottom. The Belham River Bridge...you couldn't see the bridge. It was all water. So we didn't even know if the bridge was there." Steve was not sure if they were going to make it. He said, "Listen guys. There may not be a bridge here. Keep your fingers crossed." Luckily for them, the bridge was intact somewhere under the torrent. As they climbed up the road away from the river towards Cork hill, the truck's front wheels started coming off the ground and then slamming down when Steve would let off the accelerator. This happened a few times and everyone was perplexed until they realized the problem. It was raining so hard that the entire bed of the pickup had filled with water and was weighing the back of the truck down. The water weight was counterbalancing the weight of the front of the truck so the truck's front end was lighter than the rear when climbing the grade. Taking it slow, they finally arrived at the house, soaking wet, in shock, but safe.

As they settled in, there's a pounding at the door. They opened the door to greet a frantic Errol Eid, a local musician, begging for help. "My pickup is stuck down by Sturge Park!" Steve jumped back into the studio truck and they headed back out into the monsoon to where Errol's truck was trapped in the mud. Sturge Park was the lowest point in Plymouth before the island hits the sea so all the water from town was rushing directly through the park. They quickly tied a rope to Errol's truck but realized that there was the potential for a bigger problem. Hundreds of tons of slick heavy mud had now gathered against the wall of Sturge Park. If the wall collapsed, there would be a great mudslide that would wash Steve, Errol, and his truck into the sea. With Errol's truck tethered to the studio's truck, they furiously tried to pull it to safety, but the slick mud was not allowing for any traction. Knowing the gravity of the situation, Steve got an idea. "We need to go up to public works and get one of those big vehicles." He was referring to a large earth mover used for excavation. They headed up to the public works facilities and once again, Steve Jackson, manager of AIR Montserrat, broke into a government facility in an emergency situation. Steve found the keys to the earth mover and stole it "for a good cause." Steve drove the large vehicle down to Sturge Park and was able to pull Errol's truck out before it could be washed out to sea. Steve said that on his way returning the earth mover, he was able to pull a few other people to safety. When it rains, it pours. (Pun intended.)

A number of smash hit records were recorded at AIR Montserrat during Steve's tenure there. Several memorable stories from these sessions follow in the next few chapters.

The Jacksons Move On

The studio needed some help with administration, so Steve hired a personal assistant to help him with the day-to-day operations of the studio. Her name was Yvonne Kelly and she had been the owner of a local restaurant in Montserrat. She was attractive, young, and ambitious but had no experience in the music or recording industry. She had wanted to start a career at AIR Studios and this was her opportunity.

When I interviewed Steve for this book, I was the first journalist that he had ever spoken to about his time working at the studio. He said that at the end of his time working for AIR Montserrat, there were some negative events that led to his departure from the studio which left him with a "bone of contention" about the experience. For almost 40 years, this made him reluctant to talk about his experience of working for AIR, which was understandable. Almost everyone that I spoke to about Steve was complimentary regarding him as a person but anyone in the know about the situation leading to his departure, including Steve, were reticent to talk on the record about what had happened. Regardless, Steve had made many AIR clients, local people, and the staff at the studio very happy but changes were in the wind. Steve and Jan left the island by the end of 1982 and a new manager stepped into their shoes.

YVONNE

Yvonne Kelly At An AIR Holiday Party
Photo: Frank Oglethorpe

Yvonne Kelly, AIR Montserrat's third and final studio manager, had a history with the island long before she was hired by AIR in 1982. Her father was a musician who was Montserratian while Yvonne's mother was English. Although she lived in the U.K. much of her life, Yvonne had spent time as a child on the island, attending school at Montserrat's secondary school along with Desmond Riley who would later work with her as AIR Montserrat's famed bartender. She had family members spread across both England and Montserrat, so she had always felt that she had "two homes." She was working in the accounting field in England when she read about George Martin's new recording studio being opened in Montserrat. She had recently travelled to the island for her honeymoon and was excited to hear about such a prestigious recording studio opening in Montserrat. In a 2016 interview, she said, "I decided right then and there that I'd leave my job and move to Montserrat to work at his studios. I had spent some time there when I was younger, so I knew the island."[1] To have the best chance of getting a foot in the door at AIR, she decided that she needed to be in close proximity to the studio, so she and her husband Malcolm decided to preemptively move to Montserrat from Doncaster, England in 1980. Needing a source of income while Yvonne worked on her plan to become an employee of AIR, they purchased an established restaurant named Cynthie's on Harney Street in Plymouth. The restaurant's specialties were lobster and "Mountain Chicken" although as a working restaurant they served breakfast, lunch and evening meals.

Yvonne got her big break after Paul McCartney's "Tug of War" session in early 1981. She said, "When Paul McCartney was recording, he and his entourage came to the restaurant frequently. Dave Harries and John Burgess came and asked me to meet George and I was hired to assist Steve [Jackson] with the running of the studio." She was suddenly thrust into the position of personal assistant of the manager of AIR Montserrat! She had met her initial goal of working at George Martin's studio in short time, but Yvonne's ambitions did not stop at simply assisting the manager of the studio. She had set her eyes on being the studio manager herself. Within a year, Steve and his wife Jan were off the island and living in Antigua and Yvonne had reached her goal of managing AIR Montserrat.

Like I said in a previous chapter, no one I interviewed wanted to go on the record as to the reason why Steve Jackson left his position at AIR Montserrat, including Steve. The best way to describe the situation was that Yvonne was very ambitious and that Steve, while being very good at keeping the clients happy and interfacing well with the locals, had encountered difficulties managing a complex business venture like AIR Studios Montserrat, so far removed from AIR's home office in England. Yvonne's ambitions had put her in the right place and time to move into the position of manager when the opportunity arose.

Being the first studio manager to be hired without prior experience in the music industry, Yvonne was sent to England to get some basic training on using the recording gear. Although she never had the opportunity to use the studio's equipment, she said that it helped her understand what they were doing during the sessions. She said, "If you know how to do it [yourself], then you...understand what they are doing [in the studio.]"

Like the Jacksons, Yvonne and Malcolm chose to live away from studio property although there was a manager's suite onsite. She rented a house at the Hollenders' Waterworks Estate a short walk up the hill from AIR Studios. She was not kind in describing the manager's area in the villa: "Really, it was awful...To be honest, I wouldn't live there, so I didn't." She continued, "If you were going to live [there], yes, I know there was pool [and other amenities], but there was nowhere for you to go that's 'just yours'...So at least I had that little bit of distance if I could go up to my house."

When I asked the AIR staff members about their time working with Yvonne as their manager, everyone said that she ran the studio very well. Chef Franklyn Allen said, "She knew how to get along with people. She knew what she was doing. It was like she was trained for that." Matt Butler said of working with her at the studio: "It's great camaraderie and Montserrat was wonderful for that chiefly because of Yvonne's very clever skillful dealing with people. She really ran that place like clockwork." Engineer Stuart Breed, who like some of the other young AIR staffers from England were a bit wild on the island, said this of Yvonne: "Honestly, I loved Yvonne. Yvonne and I got on really, really well...She was the perfect person to be around when we were down there. She didn't have any easy time with us 'kids,' especially me. I pulled some stunts and she would roll her eyes at me and I'd be told off about certain things. I guess I pissed her off at times with my shenanigans. In hindsight, she always had your back." When dealing with the staff and their shenanigans, she said, "I rarely lose my temper if I do, then you are going to see a different side of me [but] it wasn't even temper. I was [just] so disappointed." She said that all she had to do was to simply let them know how she took care of them in ways they weren't aware of and the staffers would understand. "I think that's probably when they...suddenly realized that I was on their side and [they] hadn't seen it from my perspective."

Managers Did Not Just Cater To The Stars.
Yvonne Washes Bosun While Husband Malcolm
and Daughter Ruth Look On
Photo: Frank Oglethorpe

Bonding

Bartender Desmond Riley and driver Lloyd Francis ("X") told me a story where the studio "family" grew closer through adversity. One night, a band was supposed to be flying in for a session, so the staff had taken the time to prepare everything for their arrival as usual. The flight had been delayed so with some time to kill before the client would arrive, Desmond and X headed down to the Vue Point Hotel to have a drink. Desmond said, "So Irene, the lady that helps out in the kitchen, we told her, 'Listen, when you see the lights coming down Cork Hill, give us a ring.'" Yvonne would be driving the clients from the airport to the studio in the dark. Her headlights would clearly be seen as they were getting close to the studio property, alerting the staff that it was almost "showtime." Desmond simply wanted a call from Irene, who was working in the studio villa, to let him and X know that they had to head back to the studio to be present when the artist arrived. X said, "You could see a car coming from at least a couple hundred yards away. From the Vue Point, it is about the same distance [from the studio.]" Desmond continued, "Everything is done. Everything is ready. I don't know if Irene forgot." X thinks he knows why she forgot to call: "She was on the phone. She loved the phone." No call came to the Vue Point...except one from Yvonne. Desmond told me, "So what happened now. We are at the bar in the Vue Point at the bar drinking. Phone rang. One of the ladies...come down and said 'The phone is for you.' [I think] 'Ahhhh! Who knows I'm here?' It was Yvonne and she was MAD!" X said they left quickly and, "We hustle up there, man!" Desmond said that Yvonne was livid: "Yvonne say...'We gonna sack everyone tonight.'" She was quite upset with X since he was responsible for getting Desmond and himself back to the studio in time. Both X and Desmond knew they had neglected their responsibilities. "We were wrong. We were totally in the wrong." X told Yvonne that she should fire him but when he did this, Desmond also said that he should be fired as well. Other Montserratian staffers were quite upset with Yvonne, knowing that all the preparation had been completed prior to the clients' arrival and that, other than Desmond and X's absence, the arrival had been very smooth. In solidarity, Franklyn and others said if X and Desmond were fired, they would leave too. Yvonne left the studio upset and went home. "But we could understand [why] she was upset. I would have been upset," Desmond said. She came back later and delivered a heart-felt apology to the staff. X said, "And from that day, we live together like brothers and sisters...That incident make us come more closer. We were like her two brothers." Desmond continued, "We never had no problems [again]. But then everybody knew what they had to do." X: "And she had confidence in us. Yeah?" Desmond: "A lot of confidence, really."

Yvonne's approach to managing the studio was to provide the clients an environment where "nothing is too much bother." Engineer Ken Blair explained: "The way that Yvonne made us feel, the way we had to behave towards the clients, because it was a question of trying to make them feel as if nothing is too much bother, as if they're there to be creative and have a completely free space." He continued, "Sometimes we would be ready at 8-9 in the morning for people showing up and sometimes they wouldn't show up until 3 in the afternoon, at their whim. We weren't allowed to call up and say, 'When are you coming?' because that was too much the sense...it went against the 'mañana' kind of mentality of making people feel they were free to be creative when they wanted to be creative. So there was never any sense, certainly in the night, of saying 'OK. It's time up guys. We need to go to bed.' It was they want to work until 3 or 4 in the morning." But Yvonne did not just look after the clients, she looked after the staff as well. Ken said, "Yvonne looked after us so that if we were having long hours...she'd make sure we got a break somewhere even if it was at the end of a session...If we had a session where we'd be working really hard when [the clients] all left, she would then charter a boat and we'd all go and just party on a boat. They'd just sail around a little bit around. They'd stick to the coast but somebody would kick up some chicken on board and people were drinking rum and just having a good time. Nice...Yvonne actually paid for us to go to Guadaloupe for the day to give us a day off...Gave us a treat after we'd been working." Ken told me that,

"For that year that I was there, she was my boss. But ever since, she's been a friend."

Yvonne also used the hot Caribbean tourism market to lure clients to the island. She said, "At that time...Antigua was a real holiday destination for a lot of the 80s bands...They would always come and look at the studio which was always great because then it was like 'Brian Ferry's been over.' Bowie came over...I'd go over [to Antigua] and I'd meet them just [to say] 'If you fancy coming to the studio...'"

When I asked Yvonne which artists she remembers fondly, she said, "It's more who I didn't enjoy because we just had fun. Who wouldn't? For me, I love music, you're on a Caribbean island, I love the sun. Elton is really close to my heart because we did 3 albums with him so you get to know everybody and you welcome people back...[like] Midge Ure. Because...with Ultravox we had a great time with them but then he came as a solo artist, bought a house in Montserrat, our kids played together, and he's still a friend...I don't think I can say that there was a favorite [artist] because my job was just my favorite time. I was just having my favorite time."

The Studio Was A Family Affair.
Yvonne And Ruth Enjoy A Swim In The Studio Pool
Photo: Frank Oglethorpe

[1]Fottrell, Stephen. "Sir George Martin's Caribbean legacy: AIR Studios Montserrat." BBC News, 9 Mar. 2016, https://www.bbc.com/news/entertainment-arts-35761728

THE ISLAND STAFF

The Monstserratian Staff Of AIR Studios
Photo: Frank Oglethorpe

The Montserratian staff was integral to the experience of recording at AIR Montserrat. The culture of the island, which was personified within the staffers at AIR, created a sense of relaxation and privacy for the clients of the studio. The staff worked hard, played hard, and went the extra mile for the artists. Yvonne Kelly said that "There's something about Montserrat. You know when people say...you shouldn't overestimate what people'll do for you? That's not how it is in Montserrat. That's not how it was with the staff. They would do almost anything for you." Steve Culnane echoed those sentiments by saying, "They were all fantastic. What was great about them was that they were unfazed...They just fit in so well...It's hard to explain it. Just perfect. They really worked together. There wasn't any underlying 'us and them' situation. It would be very hard to have an us and them situation in Montserrat because it's such a happy place."

For Montserratians who were hired to work at AIR Montserrat, it was considered a prestigious gig. Pay was very good compared to most similar positions on the island and the mystique of the secluded location, the advanced technologies of the studio, and the famous clientele only added to the air of prestige. High in the hills above Old Bay with only one narrow driveway to get there, there was both a physical as well as cultural separation between the studio and the islanders. Minetta Francis, head housekeeper, said that when she went there for the first time, "my eyes were 'wide open'...This was another world." When I asked Lloyd "X" Francis, maintenance worker and driver for the studio, what it was like working there, he replied, "It was great working there. When I used to work there, to me, [it was] like I was on a different planet. At AIR Studios in Montserrat, it was like it was a different country in the same country. AIR Studios was like a different place [from Montserrat.] You understand?...Everything there going so fast and smooth." Unlike the rest of Montserrat, the laid-back vibe of "island time" was replaced with an urgency and precision to meet the needs of the clients who were used to the high level of service they received back home. Working at the studio provided a culture shock for many Montserratians employed there but they quickly adapted and became an integral part of the experience of recording at AIR Montserrat.

Daytime Chef And Barman Franklyn Allen
Photo: Frank Oglethorpe

Many of the staff members that were hired at the studio were either currently working for or had been previously employed by The Vue Point

Hotel or The Coconut Hill Hotel, the two modern hotels on the island. Owned by the Osbourne family, The Vue Point was a hub for dining, entertainment, and lodging for the well-to-do visitors of Montserrat. When it opened in 1961, Minetta said that, "The Vue Point was the first excitement in Montserrat. It was jobs for everybody...That hotel fed a lot of Montserratians." Since its staff was known for its high level of service, many staff members were poached directly from The Vue Point. Franklyn Allen, barman and daytime chef, said that, "All of us worked at The Vue Point. We were trained before we got the job [at AIR] so we know how to go around people and so on. How to treat them nice, how to answer questions and all that." Franklyn said that he had received a letter out of the blue from AIR soliciting him to come work at the studio as a bartender. Like many other Montserratians, he had no idea that they were building a recording studio on the island. Two names had come up for the position: his and John Silcott. When he asked his manager for permission to pursue the job at AIR, he was given his blessing to "move on." Although trained professional employees were few and far between in Montserrat, it seemed that the managers at the Osbourne's properties were open to letting their employees take advantage of this amazing new opportunity of working at AIR Montserrat, often allowing them to return to the hotels' employment without repercussions if things did not work out.

As time went on, the studio managers would solicit recommendations for positions from the locals who worked at the studio so hiring was done "word of mouth" as Yvonne Kelly put it. She said that she wanted to know that the person would "fit in" with the other staff members so having them recommend someone directly was an effective way in finding those potential hires who already had some sort of relationship with the current staff. Others were hired because their skills were demonstrated in their work around the island. Lloyd "X" Francis was originally hired to build a fence at Olveston House which was owned by George Martin and John Burgess. Studio manager Steve Jackson needed some maintenance work done on the studio property and when he saw X's handiwork at Olveston House, he hired him as a freelance maintenance worker for the studio. After some time working for the studio as a contractor, Steve offered X a permanent position as a studio employee. Eventually, X's friendly and welcoming personality allowed him to move into the driver's position at the studio where he would be working directly with the artists on a daily basis.

Staff Car Pool
George Morgan, Desmond Riley, And Others Get A Ride Home From Work
Photo: Frank Oglethorpe

The Montserratian staff were hired under contract with the studio and were paid a salary whether there was a client in the studio or not. While this could be viewed as a quite generous arrangement considering the amount of downtime the studio might have throughout the year, the demands on the staff were extremely high when an artist was onsite. Meeting artists' demands could be difficult to do. Staff members would have to be on call or stay late if the artists needed service after hours. This could be especially hard on staff members that interacted directly with clients such as the bartenders and drivers. The housekeepers would not only keep the property's buildings spic and span but often, they were drafted into babysitting the children of the artists while they worked long hours in the studio. X said that when artists were on the island, he had to be available "24-7, like a policeman on duty." His routine could be quite lengthy. In the morning, he would take Minetta shopping in Plymouth for the food supplies needed for meals that would be prepared that day. He would then pick up many of the staff members for work whose homes were spread around the island. Then, he was required to be available to take the artists to whatever destinations they wanted to go throughout the day and evening. After dinner, he would drive staff members home and return to the studio to wait for the artists to finish for the day. If they decided to record until 3AM, Desmond "Micey" Riley, the bartender, and X would have to remain onsite until then. Often, at the end of a day of recording, the artists would want to go out and visit a local bar to unwind so Desmond and X would often be asked to hang out with them which they were happy to oblige since, as Steve Jackson said, "The client is golden." After the artists would get their fill of post-recording pub time, X would drive them back to their villas to rest and he would finally be able to head home for some sleep. The next morning, X would have to start the routine over again having only had a few hours of sleep himself. He said, "Sometimes, you get no rest." Regardless of the intense demands of their jobs, X and Micey always seemed to have a good time. Ken Blair remembered: "[Desmond] had a brilliant attitude because he was so modest and obliging and...gently friendly...If I had to go upstairs from the studio for anything, often Desmond would be behind the bar and Lloyd would be sat in the chair waiting by the bar for something to do. These guys were obviously having a lot of laughs together. So the atmosphere up there by the bar was always one of laughter...these two guys obviously hit it off. They had a lot of banter together." To this day, X and Micey remain very close and see each other often in London where they live today.

LLoyd "X" Francis and Desmond "Micey" Riley
Notice the Elton John T-Shirt. The shirt has the original title of the "Jump Up" Album: Restless
Photo: Frank Oglethorpe

During the down times, many staff members worked other jobs when the studio was empty. Desmond would often tend bar at establishments around Montserrat for extra cash. X cared for the pool at Midge Ure's house. Others would work part time doing everything from cleaning vacation villas to babysitting for tourists to selling BBQ downtown in Plymouth. These side hustles allowed them to earn some extra income when the studio was quiet.

The staff worked hard and long hours during booked sessions, so when it was suggested that they be dropped to half pay while the studio was to be empty during Yvonne's pregnancy in 1984, she balked at the idea. "We had a situation one time when we hadn't got many bands in, mainly because I think they were trying to 'run things down' because I was expecting. John and George came up with this idea that they would put everybody on half pay. I said, 'Well, in that case, come here and deliver that note to them.

Because only I know and they know how hard they work. They work twice as hard...when we've got bands in so I don't think it's fair.'...We expected an awful lot of them...They would do almost anything for you. So it did seem like so disrespectful to even think they would go on half pay when there's no band in because they'd given so much." Quickly, the plan was abandoned.

This Is 'Us'

Due to the island culture and the high-pressure nature of working at the studio, the staff bonded strongly. There was a sense of teamwork, camaraderie, and of family. Minetta said, "All the people I worked with were very nice people. We worked together, we moved together. We were 'homies.' [Lauging] If we were upset with one another, right away, we jumped together again. It's nothing to keep fixation with each other. It was very good working together." Steve Culnane said, "They were all fantastic. What was great about them was that they were unfazed." If someone needed help, others would lend a hand. Yvonne told me a story of how this all came together for her: "One time, when Elton John was recording, I drove up the studio hill and I could smell this dreadful smell. The staff was there but none of the artists were there [yet]...I have a very sensitive nose so I walked around to see what this smell is. And I get near the pool and I look over the side into the pool room, where they keep all of the workings, and it's this deep in water. And it stunk absolutely awful...I said, 'I can't have Elton John sitting on the [deck], it's going to blow [up there.] So I went and got a bucket, rolled up my dungarees, took my shoes off, and started doing this. [Bailing water] And X was the first one [to notice.] He said, 'What are you doing, manager?' I said, 'I'm getting rid of this water.' He said, 'You shouldn't be doing that!' I said, 'Elton John is coming in a minute. We can't have this smell.' Where as before, I don't think anybody would have helped me, he came and eventually there was a line of us doing it...That was my moment where I felt, 'This is my staff now. This is, actually, not my staff. This is 'US', we're doing this together.'...I didn't expect anybody to come help me. I just knew that I wasn't going to have Elton John come and smell this dreadful smell...For me, that's when I felt, 'Ah, we're all doing this together.'"

Desmond, Stephanie, and Franklyn In The Villa Kitchen
Photo: Frank Oglehtorpe

Downtime at the studio allowed the staff to keep up with maintenance issues that were not part of the daily routine like cleaning all of the windows, repairing furniture, or other tasks like building the famed bar in the studio villa where the artists sipped libations served up by Desmond. X remembered fixing the steps that ran from the pool deck up to the patio above the game room. They were quite slippery at times so he needed to figure out how to make them tacky so that someone like Eric Clapton would not tumble down the stairs on his way to dinner. Holding true to the island's creed of improvised and creative solutions, he came up with a plan. X went to the beach, scooped up some of the island's black sand, mixed it with varnish, and applied it to the stairs. The rough texture of the sand in the varnish made the steps safe again. He said, "When you are at AIR Studios, you have to invent things."

Most staff members truly valued their jobs and took great pride working at AIR. It was rare that the staff would steal from AIR but on occasion, as it does at most every business, theft would happen. Some would be indirect like a driver using the studio's minibus to run a taxi service on the side. Sometimes it was more direct theft like allowing family members to fill up their cars with petrol on AIR's account or taking home food stuffs to feed the village. The bonds that the staff had with the managers meant that smaller infractions were usually dealt with internally with only the most egregious infractions leading to dismissal.

The Red Light

The studio building was sacrosanct for the Montserratian staff. They did not enter the studio if artists were working inside. An exception was Franklyn who, napkin draped over his arm, would offer pina coladas to the artists at midday as a treat but only if they were not recording. He said that "If the red [recording] light was on, do not go into the studio." The housekeepers, who did not interact with the clients as much, were even more hesitant to go inside, even to clean. Steve Jackson remembered one time where housekeepers Ruby and Irma ran to him panicked. "Manager! Manager! Man in the studio!" (An aside...Montserratians, whether employed by the studio or not, called the studio managers "Manager Manager," not by their given names. Yes, the title was repeated twice when addressing them.) Although the client was not currently recording, they were afraid to go into the studio. Their fear of upsetting the artists was so great that finding a man sleeping on the couch in the studio caused them to panic and run to Steve for help. Occasionally, staffers would be asked into the studio to hear a completed track for feedback and not wanting to upset the artist would answer with something like "You have a million-dollar hit there!"

Interacting With The Stars

When I asked staff members if there were any specific rules that they had to follow when interacting with clients of the studio, they said no. When I asked Desmond if they were instructed not to impose on the artists for things like autographs or photos, he said, "Not really rules but [we knew] it just wasn't right, if you know what I mean. It was like you were infringing on the people...So within ourselves [we] said 'Boy, I don't think this is a good idea'...It not like the bosses said 'Don't do it" if you know what I mean. Just within us we think 'It wouldn't be right.'...There was no rules like that but within ourselves we think [that] it wouldn't be nice...They'll think that we are harassing them already and they hadn't been out on the street yet." The staff did not ask for autographs nor pictures of the artists or would they fawn over them. The exception being chef George Morgan who basked in the glory of being "chef to the stars" and would get photos with them to put on the wall at his restaurant. Another exception was a story that Stephanie told me how she wanted an autograph from Eric Clapton: "[The artists fame] didn't matter. Otherwise, I would probably have a whole bunch of autographs. I only got one [autograph] and that's from Eric Clapton. At the time, I think I had like a little crush on him kind of thing. That he was kind of cute looking. [I was] a teenager. I asked my mom, 'Can you ask him for an autograph for me?' And he took a picture and gave me an autograph and I keep it. But I don't even [try] speaking to him other than if he passes, you say hello. That was it. I thought he looked cute...I don't think it was him being a star. He was just cute."

AIR allowed the staff to set their own boundaries with artists knowing that the culture of the island played a big part in how the staffers behaved around the clientele. X described the attitude native Montserratians had with the famous artists with the statement: "I am a human being. You are a human being. That's it." Stephanie said, "We didn't bother one bit. All we knew [was] that they were people like us. They came to do something and we [were] going to provide a service and we provide that service with a smile, laugh. Make them feel comfortable and that was all it was about." Clients found this both refreshing and freeing, far away from fans, cameras, and interviews. X recalled having a very personal conversation with Paul McCartney where they discussed his arrest in Japan for marijuana possession. Paul was very candid with X, talking with him as if he was a lifelong friend. This personal moment was indicative of the connection that many artists formed with the Montserratian staff. Many told me that the staff felt like family during their sessions at the studio. The staff members were so integral to the experience of AIR Montserrat that many of them ended up in the credits of albums over the years. Others were immortalized in songs. Desmond, serving his terrific margaritas every day at 5 o'clock during Status Quo's session at the studio, inspired the song "Margarita Time" on their "Back To Back" album. Studio driver known as Blues used the phrase "Let Me Talk!" when trying to make his point in conversations which was immortalized by Earth Wind and Fire in a song of the same name on their "Faces" album.

Artists would often give staff members t-shirts that they brought to the island or had made specifically for the session. These t-shirts could be seen being worn around the island for years. Some of the bigger artists would tip the staff several thousand U.S. dollars for their services at the end of the sessions, others like Elton John would give gifts to the staff like jackets, sunglasses, and jewelry.

The positive attitude of the staff is captured in a story about a broken floor polisher. Early in the days of the studio, the floor of the studio villa was waxed rather than varnished which meant that it needed to be polished regularly to keep a bright shine. One day, the floor polisher went on the fritz and, it being Montserrat, there were no replacement parts readily available. So what to do? Geoff Irons recalled the story...Someone came up with an idea: "'Oh I know, we'll get the staff cloths and we'll put some music on and they can dance around to that.' And that's what they did. Reggae music [was] on and they danced around for a couple of hours in the studio and polished the floor... in the house."

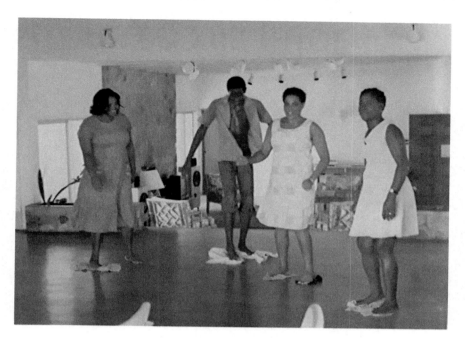
AIR Staff Dances Their Way To A Perfect Shine
Photo: Geoff Irons

The Montserratians that made up the hospitality staff of the studio were the backbone of the experience of recording at AIR Montserrat. While the U.K. staff members came and went during their rotations to Montserrat, the local islanders who worked at the studio were there year after year, some working from the studio's opening to its closing. Paul Rushbrooke summed up their contribution by saying, "They were a very loyal bunch. They were hard working guys...They were really actually the constant when you think about it...They were the one constant in the studio...they were the thing that really defined the...character of the studio...probably more than the people who came and went."

JOHN SILCOTT

The story of John Silcott's life is an inspiring one. His time at AIR Studios Montserrat was the springboard for the success he would enjoy later in life. John is a local Montserratian who worked at the studio during the first few years of its operation. Unlike other locals who were working at the studio, John saw it as an opportunity to grow beyond his station in life and took full advantage. His is an inspiring story.

Like many of the Montserratian staff members, John was working in the hospitality industry on the island prior to working at AIR Montserrat. John was in his late teens, working at the Vue Point Hotel in Montserrat as a waiter and wine steward when a good friend, Hugh Mitchell, asked him if he had heard about the new studio being built. Hugh said that they would be looking for a good wine steward and that John should consider working at AIR Montserrat. Hugh had met with Dave Harries during his time on the island and had recommended John for the job. John was not sure he wanted to leave the Vue Point for this new unknown venture, but he headed up to the studio and met with studio manager Denny Bridges. Since there was no formal hiring process for the studio at the time (and there never was one created from what I understand), Denny told John to write up a job application of his own and submit it to him, which John did. Denny liked what he saw and hired him, but since the studio had just opened and did not currently have a client working at the facility, John had to wait to start working for AIR. A band had booked a session that was starting soon and John was expected to begin his employment then. About a month later, Denny called John and said that there was "going to be nothing to do for a while" since the band had cancelled their session. Although John had been offered this great new opportunity, having been hired but not actually working, he was not willing to wait. He returned to the Vue Point Hotel who welcomed him back.

A Learning Experience

Once bands started coming to the studio regularly, Denny brought John in to serve the artists during sessions but John still split his time between the hotel and studio so that he would have work when the studio was unoccupied. During this period, Judy Martin, George's wife, worked with John to improve his English. As was the laid-back vibe of the island, most of the Montserratians around John were happy with their employment and their lot in life but John had bigger plans for himself. He did not want to remain a waiter and saw the studio as a possible opportunity to grow beyond serving wine to the well-to-do clients at the Vue Point and the studio. He had a curiosity about the electronics he saw the engineers and artists using in their respective trades. One day, technical engineer Geoff Irons, was working on the Neve console in the studio when he noticed that John might have an interest in what he was doing. Geoff told me that "It started off...we were in the control room one day. I've got the console in bits, doing something on it and he showed an interest. He said to me 'Do you have to take this apart at the end of every session?' And that kind of broke the ice. I asked him if he had any interest in it and he said 'Well, yeah. A bit.' So I started to teach him. I started off by teaching him the fundamentals of electronics, Ohm's Law, and stuff like that." Unfortunately, Montserratian culture had the tendency of keeping people locked within their socio-economic strata. Those who were perceived as wanting to move "up in the world" are pressured to accept their lot in life or face being ostracized for their efforts. This is what happened to John. Geoff remembers, "He came to me one day a couple of months later because it had got to the stage where Denny [Bridges] had said 'If you want an assistant, we can do that.' And I said 'That would be great' But [John] came to me a few weeks later and he said 'I can't do this' and when I asked him why he said 'All the local people are saying this is White Man's Magic. Don't get involved in it.' And that was the end of that." This was John's situation when Geoff left the island in 1980, returning to the U.K. after his rotation was over at AIR Montserrat. The story that follows was unknown to Geoff until I interviewed him forty years later and told him about John's life journey beyond the studio. When I told him of John's life post-AIR, he was very surprised by the path that life took for John, only knowing that he left John dejected after deciding to pass on the opportunity to learn from him.

John, being the motivated self-starter that he is, was still not satisfied with remaining a barman at the studio so he approached new studio manager Steve Jackson and told him that he wanted to quit. Steve convinced John to stay with AIR saying "There's got to be something here that you can do." Steve recognized John's potential and wanted to help him move into the electronics field so, working with Malcolm Atkin, they set about teaching John what he needed to succeed. Malcolm said that "We were minded to help these islanders" and this gave him the opportunity to follow through on that mandate. He continued, saying that "John was clearly a bright kid. He was clearly bored with being the barman...So he became my assistant. That was his new title, Technical Assistant." Malcolm took him under his wing and taught him some basic electronics and coached him through passing his math exams which were critical to learning the electronics trade. Steve had taught an electronics class at college so John started going to Steve's house for one on one instruction. John said of Malcolm and Steve: "They...propelled me into thinking that I could do this." For John, the pay was not as important to him, it was the learning of the new technology that was his main motivation...at least at the beginning.

Once again, the ugly specter of the island's cultural classism came to the surface in John's relationships with Montserratian staff members at the studio. "The local staff alienated me at the time. I couldn't even get food to eat [at the studio.] It was tough, really, really tough because they saw me as one of them and all of a sudden, I'm one of the others. So I went through a lot of feelings, pressure at AIR Studios."

As John became more knowledgeable and skilled with electronics, he began to take on more difficult tasks that were usually done by more senior technicians. He said that Malcolm was "a very positive person" and encouraged him to challenge himself. For example, there was a major modification that needed to be performed on each of the 48 channels in the Neve desk. Malcolm pulled the first channel module from the desk, took it to the workshop, and performed the modification while John observed. He turned to John and said, "Now you have to do the rest." The Neve was the nerve center of a recording session at the studio so it needed to work perfectly. Tasking a rookie technician work on such a critical piece of studio gear was a sign of Malcolm's trust in John's abilities. John pulled another module, modified it according to Malcolm's instructions, and left both modules for Malcolm to inspect later. When Malcolm returned and looked at the modules, he could not tell which one was his and which one John modified. John had passed another engineering milestone.

Over the next few years John progressed as a technical engineer becoming quite adept at maintaining studio gear and wiring. He would work with the AIR staffers that were sent from the U.K. to keep the studio in working order. While working on the electronics side of the industry, he began to learn recording techniques as well from recording engineers such as AIR's Mike Stavrou and producer Ron Nevison who recorded UFO's "No Place To Run" album at the studio. With an exposure to recording, John said that he quickly learned that he preferred the technical aspects of recording to sound engineering because the latter required "crazy hours, around the clock." Along with his technical responsibilities, he would be asked to perform other duties such as picking up Stevie Wonder from the airport at George Martin's behest. John said that working in the studio with incredible artists such as Stevie and Elton John was "elevating, to say the least."

Moving On

After working for AIR Montserrat for almost five years, John was at a point where he could be trusted maintaining the studio's gear with minimal supervision. At the time, he was working with AIR technician Frank Oglethorpe, whom John said he got along very well with and who trusted him to get the repairs done. It was as if they were technical engineering peers working shifts maintaining the studio, he said. The problem for John was that he was still being paid as if he was one of the hospitality staff which was considerably less than what AIR's U.K. based technicians were making at the time. Anytime John would ask for a pay increase, he was told "Anyone would give an arm and a leg to work here." At the time, John's wife was concerned about how much effort he was putting into the studio in exchange for the meager wages he was bringing home. Eventually, John had had enough and went to studio management to argue about his pay. He made the point that he was as much a part of the studio staff as was any other U.K.-based AIR staffer. In retrospect, John thinks that Frank had overheard this heated conversation because afterward he told John that "With your knowledge, you can get a job anywhere." John said that "I had to have something better in terms of finances." John had worked a side job while working at AIR setting up a small radio station studio for a new Caribbean communications company. Eventually, he was offered a full-time job working for this company, making almost four times the salary he was making at AIR. Being the self-starter John was, he insisted that the company also pay for some formal engineering education after working for them for two years, which they agreed to. Regardless of the education offer, John saved money for engineering school over the next two years just in case the company reneged on their agreement. When the time came for him to start engineering school, the company did not mention funding his education so John went to the United States to look for an engineering school that he would pay for himself. When the company's owner caught wind of John's trip, he called John to ask him why he was looking for schools. John reminded him of the original agreement and the owner said that he would honor his commitment to John's education. By the summer of 1986, John was pursuing his engineering degree at the University of Wisconsin in Milwaukee.

Over the following years, John built over forty radio stations, located all over the Caribbean and beyond, from the United States to Grand Cayman to Trinidad. Eventually, John started his own communications companies installing and maintaining mobile phone and Internet communications systems around the Caribbean. He also owns several radio stations on the island of Antigua. One of his daughters followed in his footsteps, earning a degree in engineering and is now working in the field of communications and electronics herself.

Starting from his meager beginnings as a barman at the studio, his self-starting attitude led to much greater things after AIR Montserrat. John says that, "Working at AIR Studios...propelled me into thinking I could do this" and he gives thanks and credit to those at AIR Montserrat who gave him the chance to achieve the success he has been enjoying in life. John and Steve Jackson have stayed in touch over the decades following their time at the studio and John still remains friends with several of the artists that he worked with at AIR such as Jimmy Buffet and Bankie Banx.

TAPPY MORGAN

George "Tappy" Morgan was the executive dinner chef at AIR Montserrat, preparing evening meals for the artists when recording at the studio. Dinner was always a focal point of the artist experience with many artists raving about Tappy's food and the experience of dining at the studio villa. In fact, George's name graced many album liner notes in tribute to his amazing culinary skills. He was known for his large stature and imposing presence. Phrases that I heard over and over again to describe George were "larger than life", "big personality", and "what a character." Studio manager Steve Jackson said, "He was the personality of that studio...George was the man."

George came from Montserratian culinary "royalty." His mother was renowned for her famous "goat water," a local goat stew, served at her restaurant, with many people agreeing that it was the best recipe on the island. George started in the hospitality industry in 1964 at the age of 15, working at Montserrat's Vue Point Hotel as a dishwasher. He worked his way up through the kitchen ranks, eventually becoming a chef. To expand his culinary knowledge, the Osbourne family, who owned the Vue Point, sent Tappy to hospitality school for two years at the Hilton Hotel in Trinidad. He also spent time working at the Rockefeller Resort in the Virgin Islands, honing his culinary skills. When he returned to Montserrat following his education, he worked at several restaurants owned by the Osbornes including The Vue Point Hotel, The Emerald Hotel, and the Coconut Hill Hotel, the latter being integral to his hiring at the studio.

In the early days of the studio, management was looking for a talented chef to cater to the artists as part of the destination studio experience. Midge Ure said this regarding meals at the studio: "The food was major...Whether you are in the studio working and focusing...or you're sitting around the swimming pool, the highlight of the day is lunch and dinner. [It's] incredibly important." AIR management needed someone with extraordinary skills to not only wow the clients with incredible culinary delights but to be flexible and improvisational in order to meet the various palettes and dietary requirements of the artists and their entourages. It was a much different gig than a restaurant that had a static menu that varied little from day to day. The studio needed a skilled culinary genius and at the time, someone had told Dave Harries that George Morgan was known as "the best chef on the island." While the studio was under construction, Dave and Geoff Emerick stayed at The Coconut Hill Hotel often. One day, they found themselves at the hotel's restaurant for a meal. The soup of the day was Pumpkin Soup, one of Tappy's signature dishes, which Dave said was "fantastic." Geoff thought so as well, so much so that he passed on an entrée and proceeded to eat eight bowls of Tappy's pumpkin soup in one sitting. Dave and Geoff were convinced. George Morgan was going to be AIR Montserrat's evening chef and they proceeded to hire him away from the Osbournes.

Tappy's cooking was very improvisational. Part of this was due to the transient nature of the food supply on the island. Between growing seasons of local produce, varying quality of local meats, and the sporadic availability of imported culinary supplies, Tappy had to create spectacular meals with what was at hand on the island at any particular time. George explained the difficulty: "Ram's supermarket was the main supermarket...Some of the time, you can't get stuff. Then my head hurts because you want to cook the food and make them [the artists] happy. Some of the people don't eat wheat...Some don't eat this. Some don't eat that. So Yvonne would come to me, or Steve Jackson [and say] 'You need to make this different this or different that.' So sometimes I make [special meals] for one or two people but then the others want it too! So it was a big challenge for me."

The other part of the improvisational nature of the AIR Montserrat kitchen was due to Tappy's style, talent, and culinary expertise. He would cook "off the cuff." Geoff Irons said to me, "George was great. He would just walk around the [studio] gardens and pick a few leaves from plants from here and there and cook them. It would be stunning. He was a really talented chef, I must say." Daytime chef and barman Franklyn Allen said that George could be told that he needed to have a meal for 20 people an hour before serving time and that he would have everything ready without effort. When I mentioned Franklyn's bold observation about Tappy's culinary genius under pressure, Stephanie Francis, who worked part-time in the kitchen with George, said, "Definitely. Definitely! He just come in, all guns blazing and 'Bop, bop, bop' and everything was [done.] He was very serious with his cooking. He didn't mess about with it and the food always come out like [kissing sound.] Always! I don't remember him measuring teaspoons. Everything was like [she makes a pouring motion.] He didn't go about measuring per teaspoon for this to measure. Everything was just added in. It was all about his passion for food. His passion that he had came out." Geoff Irons said that, "He used to just make things as if it was no effort at all. It just used to happen...in a relaxed manner....no fuss, no bother." Studio manager Steve Jackson said that George would ace any modern Chopped or Top Chef type cooking show. "Give him any ingredients and he could cook anything!", he said.

Steve said that Tappy would quietly watch the guests from the kitchen door each evening, surveying their reaction to the dishes served. "He would just watch and then he'd go back into the kitchen and write something down. What he was doing was seeing who liked what...and he was checking everybody out. Next evening, he would blow their minds." George would adapt his ingredients and flavor profiles based on his observations of the guests' reactions to his cooking.

Physically, Tappy was a big man with an imposing presence. Well over six feet tall with broad shoulders and a gruff appearance, Geoff Irons described him as "a big bloke. He had a presence when he walked into a room." Steve

Jackson joked that he looked like someone who had just gotten out of prison. George was known to travel with a meat cleaver in hand, adding to his already tough outward appearance. Managers Yvonne Kelly and Steve Jackson both recalled times when Tappy would have conversations with them, bringing a huge sharp knife with him into the room. Others have told stories of him riding in cars around the island, cleaver in hand. Engineer Ken Blair recalls that "sometimes he stood there...I think he was just kind of having a laugh, but sometimes he stood at the top of the steps on the balcony with a cleaver in his hand, kind of trying to make the point that 'It's dinner time everybody!'" Underlying the gruff exterior was kindness and George had a heart for his guests. Steve told me this story: "There was this one guy who was stoned when he got off the plane. He was even more stoned when he sat down to dinner...He was in a bit of a bad way and he just didn't eat his dinner. He got up and he went over to [Tappy] and he went, 'I'm awfully sorry man. It's not your cooking. I just can't eat anything'...And George just put his arms around him and he said [in a sympathetic tone], 'That's alright. Tomorrow' I will do something special, just for you.'" Ken Blair said that "George was a real character because he was larger than life...He would do that thing where you go in and say something to him and he, like so many chefs, he'd pull a really serious face and say something and you'd think, 'Oh God, I've made a big mistake. I've upset the guy.' And then his face would light up into a big laugh. He'd do that thing where he just kind of wind you up a bit the whole time." Stephanie said that his humor was a big part of his personality. "He like to laugh, make jokes with everyone. To me, he was the biggest character at AIR Studio. Among all of us, he just make you laugh. There was always something to make you laugh at...He can be very serious but he'd make you laugh."

Tappy's presence was central to the dinner experience at the studio. Yvonne said this about Tappy: "George didn't just cook. He performed. He made you know he'd done all this. If you were...at the Vue Point, you never see the chef. But the [studio's] kitchen was very much in the middle of everything... He would be the one who'd say 'I can do all this, you know' and he'd make sure he had a photograph taken [with the artists.]" AIR Technician Paul Rushbrook described Tappy and his evening meals: "He was always a really popular guy with the bands. It was a real focal point...the evening meal particularly. It always was a really good social event because he was basically orchestrating the whole thing. He was a real character. He was central...I would say that he's an important character to the studio [experience.] George was a bit larger than life.... He was fantastic." Tappy was not intimidated by the star power around the studio dining room as recalled by AIR Technician Steve Culnane: "He really was superb. Mad as a march hare but such a great chef. Unfazed by all. He would sit there regardless of who was talking to him whether it was Eric Clapton or Elton John...he wasn't afraid of anybody."

So what did Tappy serve his guests? Many dishes were Western Caribbean or adaptations of English and American foods with a Caribbean twist. Soup might be his famous pumpkin soup or calilou soup, made from the large "elephant ear" leaves of the local taro plants. The entrée might be local lobster or kingfish, or beef, turkey, chicken imported from other islands since the local meats tended not to be up the standards that the artists were used to. If someone wanted a taste of England, they might get fish and chips, roast beef, or Yorkshire pudding. George said he would do this, "To make them happy. So you try to make everyone happy so they don't miss [home]." Quite often, artists were treated to beach barbeques in Little Bay where there would be grilled chicken served with George's famous BBQ sauce. Desserts might be pineapple upside down cake, cheesecake, apple, lime, or cherry pie or pastries. George told me that, "I used to make all them thing by myself you know...from scratch. Not buy them in the store. Because you could not get them in the store to buy. Everything had to be homemade."

Luther Vandross arrived in Montserrat with a personal chef. Luther was on a strict diet at the time and thought that he could use help in preparing healthier meals while recording on the island. Desmond Riley said that "[Luther] brought the chef with him and he sent him back in three days. When he tasted George's food...man...He just tell him 'We don't really need you here.'" Lloyd Francis continued: "George said, 'He put his pots away!'" with a load of laughter following from Desmond and Lloyd, remembering this. George Morgan's food was so good that Luther forgot all about his diet within days of arriving at the studio.

In many cases, George's incredible food also dictated the artist's recording schedule which often started conforming around the serving of dinner. Engineer Matt Butler explains, "We were very ruled by the kitchen. Physically, because George is a big guy and basically took no prisoners. He had very bluff way about him. [But] he is an absolutely wonderful guy. And he was a fantastic cook. If George wanted you to be at the table at 7 o'clock, you were at the table at 7 o'clock. Plenty of artists, I can see them now, came and said 'Well, we will have dinner when we are ready' basically saying 'We are going to tell you when we are going to eat' After the first night, they realized that a. they had to be there at 7 and b. they wanted to be there at 7. Halfway through the afternoon was like 'What time is dinner?' because it was such a wonderful occasion. It's not to be underestimated how much that means to our day."

Since goat water was the unofficial national dish, artists would often want to try this local delicacy while on the island. For this, George would take the artists to his mother's restaurant since she was known to have the best goat water around, but if you wanted to drink, you had to serve yourself. He said, "My mother's place. It wasn't fancy...They put the bottle of rum on the table. They help themselves. That's how they do it on the island. You helped yourself to the alcohol."

Beyond providing terrific meals at the studio, George also procured other "goods and services" for the artists, things that were not part of the hospitality accoutrements provided by AIR Studios. In his interview, he told me multiple times that he could get anything that the artists would want, legal or not. This included finding companionship for band members and marijuana. He said, "I make them happy...Take them to town and I tell my friends at the bar that I'm going to bring the group. They wanted girlfriends...I get them the girls. So I was like more than just cooking. Anything they wanted." Along these lines, Malcolm Atkin told me a funny story about a time when George was tasked with finding some marijuana for the band Nazareth. He started the story describing George: "Tappy got me in all sorts of scrapes. Hilarious fun. A real character. If there was any scamming going on, Tappy was fairly near the bottom of all of it." It was early in the studio's operations and Malcolm was still staying at the studio while the band was recording. On the second day after their arrival, the band's roadie came to Malcolm to complain. Nazareth were a rough and tumble band from Scotland, so the roadie did not mince words. He said, "You tell that [explicative] chef of yours, if our weed does not appear first thing in the morning, he's history." Malcolm continues the story: "So I go to Tappy in the kitchen [and say], 'Tappy, I don't want to know but have you taken any money off that band?' [Tappy grumbles under his breath] and I say 'How much?' [He replied], '200 US dollars.' 'And what did you agree to get them?' 'Get some marijuana for them.' I said, 'Well, I know nothing but if you don't deliver it by tomorrow, you are in serious trouble. I don't want to know anymore. Just deal with it.'" The next morning at 5AM, Malcolm woke up in the studio villa to "the most amazing aroma of marijuana over the whole site." Malcolm continues: "Bleary eyed, I stumble into the kitchen from the bedroom...Before I get to the kitchen there's like a row of a half a dozen marijuana plants the size of Christmas trees...I go into the kitchen and he's slashing them up with a meat cleaver and he's putting them into the big industrial sized cooking pans. And he's putting them all in the oven to dry them out. And of course, all of the aroma goes straight out the chimney. And he ended up with a bin liner full of it. I said, 'They wanted a little bag like this.' [indicates a baggie size] [George says,] 'Well, that's 200 dollars worth.' Because it was cheap as chips down there. 'So where did you get it?' He said, 'I took it off the Rastas and don't tell anybody or else they'll kill me. You don't know where I got this from.' [So I said], 'So you've not only upset the band, you also upset the Rastas. You've knicked their crop!' [laughing] He got away with it. I didn't hear any more about it."

Between his amazing cooking and big presence, George 'Tappy' Morgan was an integral part of the AIR Montserrat studio experience. Steve Jackson summarized Tappy's place in the history of the studio; "He was the personality of that studio. I don't care what we think we put into it. George was the man. They all loved George."

Chef George "Tappy" Morgan
Photo: Frank Oglethorpe

BOSUN

Y ou cannot talk about the staff of AIR Studios Montserrat without including Bosun, the studio's dog. He was a constant fixture at the studio from beginning to end and was a big part of the experience of working there. So many people had stories about Bosun that it quickly became apparent that he needed a chapter of his own.

Bosun
Photo: Frank Oglethorpe

Back in the U.K., George Martin had an Alsatian, also commonly known as a German Shepherd, and was quite fond of the breed. When the studio opened, he decided that the studio needed a dog for both companionship and security. He purchased another German Shepherd from the U.S. breeder from whom he bought his own shepherd, Smuggler. When choosing a name for the new pup, George settled on a nautical theme, naming the dog Bosun. Malcolm Atkin explained that a bosun is a person who was "the go-between between the deck [workers] and the [ship] officers." In the case of the studio, Bosun was "the go-between for the staff and clients...and he did that beautifully." Bosun was described to me by many people as very intelligent, protective, loyal, and although quite fierce looking, was as described by Malcolm, "an absolute sweetheart." He had been trained to be a family pet, not as a guard dog although he looked the part and anyone who was staying at the studio became his best friend (and vice versa.)

Dave Harries remembered that his introduction to Bosun came with a pun. George said to Dave, "Dave, this is Bosun" to which Dave replied, "Oh, what a nice doggie, George. Did you choose his name?" "Yes," George said, "He chews everything he can get ahold of."

Like any other staff member, Bosun travelled to Montserrat via plane, coming through Antigua. Studio manager Denny Bridges flew to Antigua to pick up the new studio puppy. Technician Geoff Irons remembers his arrival: "When Bosun turned up, he was barely alive. He'd been flown out by British Airways and he'd been shut in this container I think with no water...for the whole flight, 9 hour flight. It was only because he was such a young dog, I think, that he survived." Denny remembered that "[I] didn't get a wink of sleep that night. He just howled the whole time."

Shortly after arrival, Denny and Geoff started training Bosun to be a good companion for the studio staff and guests. Malcolm said that since Geoff, who was a facilities technician, initially trained him, Bosun regarded anyone in the technician workshop as his master. Malcolm remembered walking into the workshop while Geoff was away and Bosun looked at Malcolm with a look that said, "Well, I guess you are the boss now." Since Bosun was allowed in and around the studio villa, he needed to be trained to stay out of areas that might be problematic for staff and guests. First, Denny trained him to stay out of the kitchen. Bosun would stop in his tracks at the kitchen threshold. In his interview, Denny said, "He would lay outside the kitchen threshold door and he would be watching and sometimes his paw would go over the threshold" at which point Denny snapped his fingers and made a motion of Bosun pulling his paw back. Geoff trained him to stay out of the studio pool. Clients would not appreciate the large hairy guy jumping in the water when they were trying to cool off during a session. Frank Oglethorpe remembers that on the occasion when Bosun would accidentally fall into the pool, he would get himself out as quickly as possible because he knew he was not allowed in, looking sheepish as he pulled himself out of the water. Ken Blair remembers in the later years that Bosun would seek relief from the tropical heat in the pool: "He was the wrong dog in the wrong country because he was a German Shepherd. He wasn't really designed for hot weather...He'd come round really slowly around the pool and he would step down a couple of steps in the pool and then just lower himself down and as he lowered himself there was just this "Ahhhhhh!" came out of him as if he was hugely relieved to have himself in this cool water."

Bosun Plays By The Studio Pool With AIR Engineer Steve Jackson
Photo: Frank Oglethorpe

Bosun was also taught a unique trick early on. A producer came to the island to have AIR Engineer Mike Stavrou assist him with mixing a record by Dutch singer, Rob de Nijs. During the session, he revealed to Mike that he had previously been a dog trainer and gave Mike some pointers on how to train Bosun. Mike said that there were always doors that were left "annoyingly open" in the studio villa so he had an idea. He used the training method that the producer gave him to train Bosun to close doors on command. Mike said that it only took about twenty minutes to train him to do this. From that point forward, Mike would only have to say, "Bosun, close the door" and Bosun would instantly look for an open door and slam it shut.

Despite being banned from the pool, Bosun loved to swim. AIR staffers would take him to the beach often. Malcolm said that once they hit the beach, Bosun would be in the ocean "within milliseconds" and that he and Malcolm would take ½ mile swims every day when he was on the island. Mike also spent a lot of time swimming with Bosun. Bosun loved to retrieve sticks from the ocean so one day, Mike tossed in a branch and swam out with Bosun to get it. Mike grabbed the stick and Bosun pulled him to shore. Knowing how strong of a swimmer Bosun was, Mike was left wondering what Bosun might do if there was an offshore emergency. The following week, he swam out about 75 meters from shore, leaving Bosun running back and forth on the shoreline. Mike laid floating on his back motionless for a few minutes to see what Bosun might do. Bosun swam out to see what was going on and Mike remained motionless, not greeting Bosun as he normally would, pretending that he was unconscious. Bosun circled Mike a few times, whimpering. Suddenly, he grabs Mike's wrist in his mouth and begins dragging him to shore. Bosun did not stop until Mike was safely on the beach. Bosun was not trained to rescue people from drowning, so it was pure instinct within him to save Mike from peril. Mike's reaction? "One hell of a dog!"

While Bosun was loved by the AIR staff and clients, there was not much affection for him outside of the studio family. At the time, Montserratians did not like large dogs. Dogs on the island tended to be smaller and less ferocious (looking) than Bosun so having him in public places around locals tended to lead to dirty looks and negative comments. Considering Bosun's calm demeanor and status as an AIR "family member," new staffers would want to take him along with them when they would take runs into Plymouth. This would usually lead to a story like one that Malcolm told me: "I do remember once taking Bosun downtown...He was on a lead. He was right next to me. [A local says to Malcolm] "You don't bring this dog downtown. Why you do that?" Every other person on the street was like, "What do you think you are doing?" [So I said] "I'm sorry Bosun, but you aren't coming downtown again." Despite Bosun's friendly personality, locals' fear of his formidable size kept public appearances to a minimum.

When George had the studio built, he cleared the land below the studio for a beautiful, manicured lawn which played a big part in the ambiance of the view of the sea. Many local farmers were accustomed to letting their cows and goats run free on the island, grazing where they pleased so problems arose from local livestock using the studio lawn as grazing land. Considering that he was an Alsatian, a working breed focusing on herding, Bosun was more than willing to keep the fields clear of bovine invaders when the occasion arose. He would go bounding across the lawn, nipping at the heels of the cows as they quickly fled the property. AIR staff would have to chase down Bosun and bring him back to the studio. Needless to say, farmers were not happy with Bosun and his chasing of their livestock and this only reinforced the local misconception of him as an aggressive and dangerous canine.

Since Bosun was such a terrific companion, he was bred with another Alsatian with the hope that the offspring would inherit his personality and demeanor. Unfortunately, that was not the case. Yvonne said that the puppies "were crackers." The studio had adopted one of the puppies and named him Max. He never developed into the dog that Bosun was and died of poisoning early on.

Even though he was not intended to be a guard dog, Bosun's presence was appreciated at times, considering the isolation of the studio property and the potential for fans encroaching on the privacy of the clients. Paul Rushbrooke said that when he was alone at the studio, Bosun helped him feel safe. He said, "If you were there on your own in the middle of nowhere on top of a hill, it was great to know he was just there because if anybody came around, he'd start barking his head off. They'd soon clear off." Yvonne Kelly said that he knew the engine sounds of the studio vehicles so when someone approached who was not from AIR, he would let her know prior to their arrival. Yvonne also said that "He was actually [my daughter] Ruth's nanny for the first two years of her life. Literally, I would put her in the lounge and he would sit by her push chair. If she stirred, he would come and tell me."

121

Yvonne recalled a story where Bosun's innate intuition for protection helped her deal with a high-stake situation. A client was on the island who was known to have a drug habit and some dealers had arrived on the island, smuggling illegal substances into the country with the intention of selling them to the client. They showed up at the studio, saying that the client owed them money for drugs. Yvonne let them into the villa and sat with Bosun at her side. She said to Bosun, within earshot of the drug dealers, "Bosun, just listen to what these people are saying." She then turned to the dealers and said, "So what you are saying is that you went out with somebody, an adult, out somewhere and you [give them] drugs but you didn't have [them] pay for it and now you are walking in here and think I'm going to pay for them? Tell you what I'm going to do…" She uses the trick that Mike had trained Bosun to do several years prior. She instructs Bosun to close the front door, sealing the dealers in the room with him. She says to them, "I'm going to ring the police now and tell them that you've been supplying drugs. The thing is that they will be here in 15 minutes. So now you are in here. Sit down and make yourself comfortable and discuss it." The dealers were sitting on a low sofa with Bosun glaring at them at eye level. They said to Yvonne, "You're holding us against our will!" Yvonne replies, "Get up if you like" knowing how threatening Bosun looked at that moment. They tentatively got up and asked, "What will he do?" Yvonne replied, "I don't know because I've never seen him like this before but I think he's being a bit protective because my voice is a little bit shrill. So I don't really know what he'll do. So what I will do…I'll call him back here and you get into your car and if I were you, I would go straight back to your villa…and pack. I will give you as much time as I know it could take for you to get to the airport and there will be a flight because I'm going to call the police anyway and tell them that you are dealing drugs." As the drug dealers left the villa, Bosun let them go without incident but followed them to their car. Yvonne told me, "I never saw them again…It was all Bosun. He was a great dog."

Bosun was a companion, protector, client liaison, and was absolutely integral to the experience of AIR Montserrat. Paul Rushbrooke said that he was as much a staff member as any of the human staff at the studio. AIR engineer Richard Moakes said it best when he said, "Every studio needs a dog."

A Young Bosun With Malcolm Atkin
On The Villa Balcony
Photo: Malcolm Atkin

A UNIQUE OPPORTUNITY

For AIR staff members sent to the Montserrat studio to work, it was a blessing, curse, and everything in between. For many, it was a highlight in their careers but much of their perception of their time spent on the island is based on how well they adapted to the slow pace and routine of life on "The Rock."

Rotation

Originally, AIR management had the intention of creating a rotation schedule for sending staffers such as assistant recording engineers and maintenance engineers (also known as technical managers) to Montserrat. The hope was to have a regular rotation of staff sent from the London studios to Montserrat so that any staff members who wanted to work on the island would have the opportunity, since it was seen as a prestigious gig by many. This rotation schedule meant different time frames for the staffers depending on their differing job responsibilities. Maintenance engineers (also known as technical managers) were responsible for keeping the facilities and studio running regardless of whether a client had a session at the studio or not, thus one technical manager was required to be at the studio at all times. Their rotations tended to be longer periods than the assistant engineers (and tape operators) who were only required to be at the studio when a client was recording. Assistant engineers could come in for a few recording sessions and then leave once they were complete, although many would remain at the studio between those sessions. Originally, rotations had been expected to be anywhere from six weeks to three months but as time went by, this intention went out the window.

Malcolm Atkin said, "You would have thought it would have been easy to find people who would want to come to the Caribbean for three months" but what became apparent over the first few years was that it took a special type of person to thrive in Montserrat. AIR engineer Richard Moakes said, "Being out on Montserrat, it suited [a special] kind of personality that did really well there. For a maintenance engineer, it would be someone who is quite independent, happy to tinker away in a room with a couple of desk strips, despite it being a full-on Caribbean summer. It would be a sort of chap that would like to [sit] inside a room and happy to be working with a soldering iron, ready to get the call of 'Can you come and fix this for us?'" The gig appealed mainly to the single staffers since accommodations for them in Montserrat consisted of only a single bedroom in the studio villa. Those with families or significant others tended to want to stay back in London, close to their loved ones and families. A trip to Montserrat for a few months had the potential for upending a family's routine. Another issue was that staffers had to leave whatever housing arrangements they had back in the U.K. This made the return to London more difficult, especially if they had to break a lease to work in Montserrat. Maintenance engineers Paul Rushbrook and Frank Oglethorpe worked out a clever strategy for housing while they traded places in Montserrat and London. Paul said, "One of the big problems about working in Montserrat was you never had anywhere to live when you came back. So me and Frank ended up [together]...both lived in the same house...When one of us wasn't there, the other person [lived in the London flat]." Another problem for AIR staffers sent to Montserrat was a concern for their careers. The Montserrat studio did not receive the same attention and focus from AIR management as the London studios, and this was also reflected in the recording industry as well. The world of AIR and its reputation within the industry rotated around the Oxford Circus studios in London. Carol Weston described AIR as, "It was really run on the side of things rather than our main thing." AIR employees' careers were built in London so going to Montserrat could be seen as detrimental. Paul describes the situation: "I'll say...you start thinking about how your position in London was and you had to...think about your career. Your subconscious thought [is] 'Well, I'm missing out on what's going on in London because there's a lot going on in London as well', because there's obviously four studios there. You had to...balance out the thing of 'I want to go to Montserrat because it's a really special place but I might be doing one session there and then a week off...or it could be London...where there could be 4 things going on [at once]...which could really keep you busy and occupied. That was always the tradeoff." The London facility with its multiple studios working nearly around the clock gave the AIR staff many more and varied opportunities to work and to also network with those in the industry as compared to the solitary nature of AIR Montserrat.

Culture Shock

Living and working in Montserrat, immersed in a completely different culture, AIR staff would often find themselves in circumstances that they never would have imagined. Dave said, "I had a band there and they wanted to have a roast pig on the beach. Now, would you get in your car, go over to the other side of the island, buy a live pig, tie his feet together, put it in the boot of the car and take it back? No, you wouldn't even dream of it, would you? But you do that in Montserrat without thinking twice. That's what it's like. It's completely different." He continued this motif in another story about how the island changed him. During the winter, he had to travel from Montserrat for an industry trade show in New York City where the temperatures were below freezing. Having succumbed to the vibe of the tropics, he jumped on a plane in t-shirt, shorts, and flip-flops, not cognizant of the blustery city that awaited him on the other end of the flight. When he arrived in NYC, reality set in quickly when the airline informed him that they had lost his luggage and he realized he had no appropriate attire. He said the dire situation was compounded by another issue caused by him being on "island time." He said, "For some reason, I hadn't even bothered to book a hotel. That's what you're like out there. Your mindset completely changes. If you were in England and you were going to America, you'd prepare...you'd have a schedule, you know what you are doing exactly...It [the Caribbean] changes you completely."

As time went by, it became less of a scheduled staff rotation and more a case of who was willing to leave London and go work in Montserrat. Carol explained, "I think that as it went along, as the years went by, it was much more directed at who could cope with being out there and [whether] it was a good personality and things...I don't know if any of them ever felt like they didn't want to go out there. I think most of them would like to go out there but I don't think they wanted to go out there for too long. [It was] a bit disruptive to their own career really, in a way." Dave Harries thought that for many AIR staffers, the island's slow pace and isolation amplified their personalities, often in negative ways. He said, "When you are on an island like that, if you've got any quirks in your character, they seemed to be squared. You know, if you go there and you like a drink, you'll become an alcoholic. If you like women and sex, then you become a sex maniac. It gets hold of your personality and trebles it. It's really funny and I don't know why."

Dave gave me an example of this. When they were building the studio, John Burgess and George sent a young piano technician out to the island to setup the Bosendorfer piano. Little did the technician know, John and George had decided that since he was out there, they wanted him to become the first tape operator for the studio. Dave said, "The guy knew nothing...He didn't even know that he was expected to be an assistant at the studio. They never told him! They wanted me to tell him. But, of course, he wasn't trained in any way, shape, or form, to do with studios." Dave tried convincing him to do the job and to train him, but it was hopeless. While he was there, the piano tech started to lose it. "He ended up drawing, in The White House, one of the big villas we rented for Climax [Blues Band]. He drew a massive montage of Montserrat all over the walls with mountains, and palm trees. It was a fantastic picture! But he'd obviously gone off his rocker! We had to send him home and then we had to paint over it before the owners saw it. He sort of went mad."

For those for whom island life suited them well, they tended to be sent out for long periods and for several "tours of duty." Frank Oglethorpe loved living and working in Montserrat, so John Burgess was more than happy to send him out to the island. Frank spent eighteen months on the island over three different periods during the mid-1980s. Geoff Irons liked working in Montserrat as well. He told me of his introduction to island life and how he schemed to delay his trip back to England: "They said to me 'We're looking for people [to go to Montserrat].' And they were reluctant [when they asked.] It's almost as if they thought if they asked me, I was just going to say 'No!' And I said 'Why not? I don't mind. I'll go out there.' Because they said it would only be for 6 weeks and I said 'Right-O.' So, I think the second day I got out there, I thought 'This is paradise. Now all I have to do is shut the door and I'm out here for weeks.' So I got my [return] airplane ticket and I tore it up and threw it in the bin. Now this is pre-internet days. The only place you could get an air ticket reissued was where you'd had it issued in the first place and this was a ticket that was issued by British Airways in London. I knew there was nothing that the locals could do about it. And I knew it would take between 2 and 6 weeks to get me another ticket so I waited until they said, 'It's almost time for you to go back.' I just said 'Well, I can't because I've lost my air ticket...They said 'Well, you will have to stay.' Oh, such a shame...I said, 'Why don't you leave the ticket [until] when I really have to go back. We can get another one.'"

Like many of the assistant engineers at AIR, Richard Moakes ended up in Montserrat, not because of the rotation schedule, but because he was sent there for a particular session. Richard had a working relationship with producer Bob Clearmountain and when Bob was heading to Montserrat to mix Midge Ure's album "Answers to Nothing," he requested Richard be sent to the island to assist. Little did he know, it would lead to a "rotation by proxy." Richard recalled the situation: "Bob would always work with the same assistant so when you built up a relationship with the engineer...I was really lucky because I got that gig. So Bob had the offer to go out to Montserrat and he said, 'Well, you know who I want to work with.' The pressure was on, really...John Burgess controlled who went out to Montserrat. That was the deal...Bob asked me to go out there and then they said 'If you are going out then you might as well stay on and do these [other Montserrat sessions.]' That's the way it worked. So I went out for Bob Clearmountain. I did The Fixx. I worked on a gig with John Punter." He also worked with Keith Richards on his solo record that he recorded in Montserrat. Since he had been Bob Clearwater's choice of engineer for Midge Ure's single session, he ended up staying in Montserrat for six months. A similar situation happened for engineer Stuart Breed. He went out to the island to assist Geoff Emerick with an Art Garfunkel Christmas album and when the session ended and the next client cancelled, Stuart simply stayed in Montserrat for several months, helping with whatever was needed, which turned out was not much more than painting the walls and helping local artist Arrow in the studio a few times.

By the mid-1980s, it became more difficult to find AIR staffers who were willing to go out to the island for any length of time. The reputation of Montserrat being so different from London combined with the negative career consequences of leaving Oxford Circus caused many AIR staffers to pass on the opportunity to work on the island.

Getting Technical

Maintenance engineers kept the studio and its facilities in working order, 24 hours a day, seven days a week. The hours could get very long for them when the studio had an artist recording as they needed to be available to fix anything that broke in the studio immediately. This meant not only working as long as the artist was using the studio, but often afterward, repairing things that had to wait until the studio was unoccupied. Paul Rushbooke said, "You worked a lot of hours. A lot of antisocial hours. If you [were] a technical engineer, you probably start working after everybody else had finished. You'd only really fix anything when they...finished. You'd be working overnight. During the day, you'd just be doing bits and pieces. You would be sort of on call really." Unlike their recording engineering brethren, they were not required to be physically in the studio, just available. Often this meant spending down time in the technical workshop which was located on the lower floor of the studio villa. The workshop was a place of refuge for the tech guys and even the assistant engineers, as recalled by Matt Butler: "The workshop was a 'retreat.' And for some of us guys...we liked to go into the workshop and just have 5 minutes to ...dissipate any kind of feelings. Not necessarily stress, could be happiness as well. We'd go into the workshop and just level ourselves out. I called the workshop the 'Growlery' [after a Dickens novel.] I think Paul Rushbrooke called it the 'Screaming Room.' where he would just go in there and go 'Ahhhh!' and get it all out."

The Studio Workshop
Note The Champagne Bottles Among The Gear
Photo: Frank Oglethorpe

During downtime, the maintenance engineers would test the recording equipment in the studio looking for faults, giving them time to proactively correct any problems before they arose in the next session. Unlike their cohorts' positions in the London studios, their responsibilities were not restricted to the recording electronics. Facilities maintenance was a large part of the position as well in Montserrat. Keeping the air conditioning systems running was a constant battle. There were four separate A/C condensing units located at the rear of the studio building for keeping the building cool, but the hot and humid environment was tough on the equipment and they were quite unreliable. Since the huge, hot-running recording console was powered up constantly regardless of whether it was in use or not, a minimum of two of the A/C units needed to be working at all times. (The thought being that turning the gear on and off repeatedly over time might cause problems.) If a band was in, a minimum of three A/C units were required. Frank says with pride that he thinks that he was the first maintenance engineer to have all four units operational at the same time.

The facility's power generator was also a focal point for the maintenance engineers. It was a critical piece of the redundancy plans for the studio, needing to be 100% functional at a moment's notice. With the island's power being less reliable than in most locations where you would find high end recording studios located, the studio's reputation was reliant on being able to operate regardless of the state of the local power supply. Since London maintenance engineers tended to be focused on the electronics in the studio rather than facilities maintenance, many came to the island without the knowledge or experience in repairing industrial systems like generators. Steve Culnane told me, "We had our own generator which...was a major scare to me because I couldn't even fix a lawn mower, let alone a generator. I'm looking at this bunkhouse with a generator...I'm sitting there going 'I have no idea if something went wrong how I'd even begin to try to fix it.'" Geoff Irons remembers trying to be considerate of locals' feelings during power outages: "I do remember some evenings when the generator used to come on. We used to go around and turn off the lights in the garden to save upsetting the locals because they'd all be in darkness and we'd be blazing away up there with lights everywhere." Keeping the generator available was paramount and as such, was a focal point for the maintenance engineers, so much so that Frank asked me to check on the generator building for him when I took a trip to Montserrat in 2019. He wanted to know how it was faring 35 years later. (Unfortunately, it had been consumed by the jungle, but I was told that the generator was still located there.)

Beyond the important systems like power and environment controls, the simplest problems would end up in the maintenance engineers' laps: things like changing out light bulbs, tinkering with broken hair dryers, adjusting the TV antenna, or replacing a studio car's carburetor. If there was any sort of problem with a need for mechanical, electrical, or technical expertise, the maintenance engineers at AIR Montserrat were there to lend a hand. Frank said that he was even tasked with fixing the inflatable pool toys.

A major benefit for the maintenance engineers in Montserrat, as opposed to working at Oxford Circus, was their level of interaction with the artists. In London, the recording engineers and tape operators got the opportunity to work closely with the clients while the maintenance engineers did not unless there was a problem in the studio while the client was in session. In Montserrat, the maintenance engineers lived in the studio villa and were in close proximity to artists on a daily basis as both were working at an arm's length from each other. Passing each other by the pool, hanging out on the patio, or simply going about their daily routine, the intimate isolated location gave the technicians the opportunity to get to know the clients in a way that was simply not possible in London.

Feeding The Family

Coming from London, the quality of the food in Montserrat was not what AIR staff was used to. Artists who came to the island for a session, with their custom catered meals and high-quality food products imported specifically for them, had a different culinary experience than the AIR staff did. When the artists were in the studio, the AIR staff were often invited to dine with them but when the studio was vacant, the staff was on their own. Studio chefs George Morgan and Franklyn Allen did not work at the studio when a client was not in session so the AIR staffers who were living at the studio villa had to "fend for themselves." Engineer Ken Blair told me that, "The thing was that...I never asked and it was never made clear how we were supposed to deal with [food] and so there was stuff in the freezer and there no sense that we weren't allowed to use that stuff but we were all young guys and none of us had great experience in the kitchen...We usually went for whatever was easiest which meant our diet was probably a little strange when we were on our own...I can remember a whole lot of times just cooking up some frozen fries or something like that and having those with ketchup and that's it." Frank said that he "ate hundreds of Thomas' English muffins with 'plastic cheese'" and "lived on Andy's [Village Place] chicken and rum." Others said it was nothing but cereal and sandwiches or whatever was available in the studio's cold storage. They often went to the few restaurants or bars on the island for some variety, but those meals were paid for by the staffers themselves. Occasionally, when an artist was not in, Yvonne Kelly said that the staff would head into town to go to Harry's, a restaurant run by an English couple. Yvonne told me that "All of us would say 'Meet you down at Harry's. We're gonna go and have an English breakfast.'" This meant that they were going to enjoy some ordinary English food together. After spending weeks eating George Morgan's rich, extravagant recipes with the artists or dining at the Caribbean restaurants around the island, the staff wanted to eat a normal English meal, something familiar...comfort food. Yvonne said, "Every night you were sitting down to George's food. Fabulous, but sometimes you just want egg and chips. It was like we were on holiday, but you didn't have to pack."

Top Management Visits

To fully understand the experience of AIR staff working in Montserrat, we need to first talk about the management style of AIR and what it was like working for the company. Carol Weston described AIR as a "family-orientated company." She said, "You were like a family but you worked hard and you played hard as well. It all seemed to work. I think that's just it. When anybody'd work with us in AIR, even from the early days, they all got this feeling as if they belonged to a family. We kept in touch with people even when they left. A lot of people didn't want to leave...I think some of them had to because they got better offers and better jobs but they never wanted to leave. It wasn't the money at all. Very basic salaries. But it was just that fact that that it was just such a lovely atmosphere and a lovely company to work with." In other words, the pay was not great for the staff, but AIR offered a fantastic work environment. A quick aside about the wages at AIR: Assistant engineer Richard Moakes said, "Assistants were paid very, very little generally at that time (Mid to late 1980s) and I remember that my wage was 100 pounds a week. (which is 270 English pounds in 2019, or $344 U.S. dollars) Normally, assistants would be given $25 US dollars as a sort of pin money for the week for drink money if we use it. I...saved mine because I wasn't much of a drinker." What offset the low pay was the unique experience that AIR staff had in working there. Steve Culnane described the difference between AIR and other studios of the day: "I left the BBC and went to work for AIR Studios but two close friends went to work for Virgin Townhouse Studio. And it was 'Chalk and Cheese'[opposites], the difference between the two studios. Virgin thought they were so hip and wonderful and all the rest of it. [My friends said] 'Well, you're just working for another BBC.' And I'm going 'No. It's not. You just don't understand it.' The camaraderie, the teamwork that AIR instilled. There wasn't any petty 'That's not fair' and the rest of it. Everybody put in together because it was such a unique place and George was such a unique man. That carried on when he built Montserrat...The camaraderie at AIR was amazing." Richard Moakes continued the sentiment: "It was very much a family. Everyone got along. Everyone was quite different and yet you knew very much...that you were still part of the same family. Even though it's a very tight space, there was enough room, architecturally in terms of personalities, to be able to find your own particular niche." People were allowed to try and fail, would readily share knowledge with each other, and the atmosphere was quite relaxed. This was quite different from many of the ego-driven studio environments prevalent at the time.

Producer Chris Thomas described the management style of the heads of AIR, George Martin and John Burgess, as this: "To a large extent, George and John were sort of 'outside the bricks'" with Dave Harries adding, "But they had ahold of the reins." In other words, they had control of the business and creative sides of the company but were not generally involved with the day-to-day activities at the studio facilities. The AIR ethos of trusting everyone to perform their jobs without constant supervision was prevalent throughout the company. With Montserrat four thousand miles away and not a daily focal point of the business like Oxford Circus was, it was even more "hands-off" at the island studio. Yvonne Robinson said that she did not feel like she had a direct supervisor, that John Burgess was "sort of" her manager and that he was the person back in London that she discussed issues with when she needed advice or help. She said, "If they felt that you could do it [your job], they would leave you to do it. You would handle most situations and that you [would] know when to ask somebody else for some advice." She said that the attitude from London was, "I'm going to leave you to it. I'm sure you're ok." She continued, "George would never look for somebody to have a [formal] qualification to do something, he would just think 'If they can do that, they can do it,'" This played itself out over and over again throughout the history of AIR.

When the studio in Montserrat first opened, top management from AIR London came to the island frequently to assist with the launch of the new endeavor but as time went on and the stability of the facilities became the norm, they would visit less and less.

George Martin produced several records there during the first few years of operation for clients like Cheap Trick, UFO, and Ultravox but by the end of 1982, he had stopped using the studio for new recording projects. After this time, George's trips to the island were primarily for holidays or hobnobbing with high-end clients who appreciated his presence when they were recording at AIR Montserrat. In the early 1980s, George started a tradition of coming to the island in January with his family for his birthday holiday, a tradition which his wife Judy continues to this day. Frank remembers Judy bringing some Pierre Cardin pool furniture with them on the plane when coming to the island for holiday. It can be seen in many of the photos of the pool that were taken over the years.

John Burgess, on the other hand, was managing director of AIR Montserrat so he was far more involved with the operations of the island studio than George. He and his secretary Carol Weston were responsible for the logistics of getting clients and staff to and from the island. John was the "money man" for the company so the financial management of AIR Montserrat was his responsibility as well. As previously mentioned, he was also keeping the studio staffed on the technical side of things with the staffs' rotation schedule from London. With the studio so far away and communications limited to expensive long-distance calls and Telex (a very primitive text-based long distance communications system), John felt the need to visit Montserrat with far greater frequency than George. Carol explained John's need to travel to the island: "I think it was necessary sometimes because a certain amount of management [needed to be done.] Even I could see that when I went out there. There were a certain amount of things allowed to happen with certain staff taking a bit [of] advantage. You had to sometimes be on the spot and sort things out. It's a bit like running a shop...if you let the staff just do [it] and you don't ever visit the shop, you can get taken for a ride. So I think sometimes he had to sort of have a bit of an eye on things." Of course, John loved the Caribbean so a trip to check up on the studio staff also allowed for a bit of a holiday for the hard-working Managing Director of the company.

AIR Engineer Matt Butler In The Studio
Photo: Frank Oglethorpe

AIR engineer Matt Butler recalled one of those occasions when "the boss" visited the island: "One event I remember when Paul Rushbrooke was there with me was [that] we knew our time alone was coming to an end because John Burgess was coming out and he was bringing his family and that's quite a big occasion. John Burgess was an absolutely terrifically lovely guy. He was really a super bloke...we revered John a great deal. He used to visit [Oxford Circus] and people always looked busy...I could tell John was in because people were looking busy. And for John to come to Montserrat at down time was 'Oh. The boss is coming!' sort of thing. We never felt we had a boss but you know, we were looking forward to it. We had the place spic and span and that afternoon, Rushes, as I call him, Paul Rushbrooke and I were on the beach having one last hurrah before [he was to leave]. We saw this yacht just moor in the bay. These two bikini clad girls swimming...obviously a bit of a party vibe and I say 'Come on Paul. We're professionals. We better get back to the studio now and prepare for John coming back' which is exactly what we did. I was in the shower, I remember, and I heard this 'Hello? Hello?' and the people on the boat had decided to come and visit the studio so they were a 'walking party.' They were still in bikinis, these girls. And it was like 'Well, yeah, we hope you won't mind us seeing the place.' 'Of course!' We were always very welcoming. [They said to us] 'We're having a party tonight. You fancy coming?' 'Yeah! Alright!' and of course we totally forgot that John Burgess was due. And I hope Paul doesn't sue me if I reveal to you that Paul got horrendously drunk. John, of course, and [his] party had arrived. In fact, John's son came to the party so that's how we knew he was there. We all had a great time but dear old Rushes, I had to...We had a little Volkswagen Beetle to get around in and I had to carry Paul out of the back of the Volkswagen Beetle which is almost impossible to carry somebody that drunk into the bed and Paul was shouting at the top of his voice, 'You look marvelous, darling. You look marvelous' and 'J.B. sends hugs...' They were all in-jokes for us guys and I thought 'He's going to be fired.' But the next morning, there everybody was and, of course, nothing was mentioned...There was all the temptation to enjoy yourself too much."

Life on "The Rock"

How did AIR staffers feel about working in Montserrat? It depended on the personality of the individual and their particular life experiences prior to coming to Montserrat. For example, Yvonne Kelly's father was Montserratian and she spent some of her childhood on the island so she had a social network established on the island long before she worked for AIR. At one time during her time at AIR, her brother and father lived on the island as well as other relatives who were permanent residents of Montserrat. It was home for her. Most of the other AIR staffers had never been to the Caribbean so there was a significant amount of culture shock for them. Matt Butler recalled arriving on the island and the first thing that he saw was completely out of his wheelhouse coming from London: "The first thing I ever saw on Montserrat was coming out of the airport with Yvonne and her husband Malcolm was this guy hurtling down a hill on a donkey. He looked completely out of control and I thought 'Wow! I've just arrived from Oxford Circus!' This is quite a shock. But this was the guy's donkey. This is what it's all about and he didn't care how it was. He was going pell mell down that hill. I realized straight away that this is a different culture." He continued, "Frank would always to take me to Andy's Chicken Shack...And you can literally look behind the shack because it wasn't very big and see all of the chickens running around and I swear, there was one fewer chicken running around after you ordered a fried chicken...It was culture shock for many of us coming from London. We had to realize that we're on an island that has its own culture and is very much able to look after itself." Engineer Stuart Breed recalled coming to Montserrat for the first time, landing at night and being taken completely off-guard: "The first impression I had when we got to Montserrat was that I was in a rush...I was on this little plane. Wow! And I went to Montserrat and it was night when I landed so I didn't see the airport. Drive up to the studio. Didn't really notice much. It was sort of a whirlwind. I'm leaving the plane, get my luggage, be in the studio. I walked down to the deck of the studio and there was the noise of the tree frogs. And I just thought, 'How the fuck am I going to take nine months of this bullshit?' And I'd come out of the east end of London. I was 'concrete, bricks, and mortar.' That was me. The only view I'd had was that of a brick wall. So the next morning I woke up, sleep in my eyes, left my room. I didn't think I'd gotten much sleep. I was kind of nervous. I'd not seen anything yet. It [had been] pitch black. Got up. Walked out on the deck and just saw the view and I think it took me three days before Frank finally went, 'Do you want to leave the studio? Don't you want to look around the island at all?' It was mind blowing to be one minute in London, this big industrial thing, and then suddenly 'What the fuck am I looking at?' It was a major, major culture shock for me." Steve Culnane said of his experience on the island, "Looking back on it, it's probably the most weirdest time of my life in fact. It was literally like jumping out of a plane in a parachute and being in the middle of somewhere that you have no idea what's going on."

Some of the staff adapted to the slow-paced island lifestyle while others struggled. For someone like Frank Oglethorpe, island life suited him well and he was able to go out to the island for a total of 18 months without many issues...other than it taking a few days to adjust to working in a big studio again when he returned to London. Stuart Breed laughed as he remembered one of the times Frank came back from Montserrat: "He loved the island, so he was down there for a big chunk of time. [When he returned] back to AIR Studios in London, he was completely useless for about a week or two because he was on 'island time.' We had 4 [busy] studios in Oxford Circus. [They had to keep calling] 'Frank, Frank, Frank!!!'" Richard Moakes echoed the sentiment: "To be able to go on a beach at 9 o'clock in the morning and take a swim and be in this sort of fantastic place, it's idyllic. You can get very familiar with that..lifestyle. I don't think anyone that went came back the same." Both Dave Harries and Malcolm Atkin said that in general, the longer staff members stayed there, the more the island tended to bring out neurotic parts of their personalities. Some would become workaholics, others sex addicts, alcoholics, and drug abusers. At a minimum, they would get used to the slow pace of Montserrat and have trouble readjusting to city life and working in a big, busy studio again. Malcolm said that "nobody came out of that place completely unscathed if they were there for more than 4 or 5 months." Even Frank, who seemed well adjusted to many at AIR, said, "It is a magical place. No doubt about it but in the interim periods [between sessions], you go kind of stir crazy. It's small. Everyone knows everybody. Everyone is friendly but I did end up drinking. Rum and Coke was my poison and I drank tons of it. Not good and it's probably why a lot of my memories [of the time] are a bit vague."

Maintenance Engineer Frank Oglethorpe In His Element
Photo: Frank Oglethorpe

As Frank mentioned, the interim periods between sessions could be brutal due to the lack of entertainment on the island. Since the studio was well-designed and built, there was not a lot of maintenance to be done when the place was empty. The staff would have to find things to do to occupy the time, often leaving the island. Paul said, "It was a nice place to live [but] you could get island fever, that's for sure. You could be there for a certain amount of time and you really had to sort of go somewhere and do something else really because it's quite a small place. There's very little to do. You could go to the beach. You could go swimming. You could go to the bars. You can only do that so many times...You could probably go a bit stir crazy if you're there too long particularly if you weren't working and didn't have much to do. We used to go...to Antigua or Martinique or Guadaloupe. I went to the [United] states once. If I had a week off, I'd go and do something else rather than hang around...For me, 6 weeks of time was a good length of time to be there...That was just about right really." Richard Moakes found the downtime at the studio invigorating: "If the bands weren't in, there were very little studio duties [so] I'd go horse riding. I learned lots of things to do. I learned to water ski. Ride a horse. Play tennis. You just think, 'Wow. Gee. What can I do today? I'm not in the studio.' In London, I'd be so busy that to be in a place where, all of a sudden, rather than four studios, you've just got one studio and if that's not working, you think, 'Well. What am I going [to do?] Ok. I'll find something to do.'"

Unlike Richard, the isolation of the island and the lack of entertainment options had a negative effect on many of the AIR staffers that came from London. Maintenance engineer Geoff Irons, who worked at the island studio for over a year, summed up his experience: "Everybody's got this image of

136

white sand beaches and palm trees and blue skies and that's how it was [visually]. The expression that we had out there was that we'd wake up in the morning and look out the window and say 'Well, another shitty day in paradise, boys' and that's really how it was." For Dave Harries, he said that, "I would have hated to have been there for any longer than I was. As soon as I finished and didn't have anything to do...I was off. I couldn't stay any longer." This sentiment may seem harsh considering that many of the AIR staffers had amazing experiences there and made lifelong friendships while in Montserrat. While many of them think fondly of their time on the island, the impression that I got from most of them was that the experience of working in such a different culture and environment from what they were familiar with provided a counterbalance to what many people would consider an "island paradise." As idyllic as one might think working at a high-end recording studio on a beautiful Caribbean island might be, like many of life experiences, there were negatives that came with the positives of living in Montserrat. Still, most seem to consider their tenure at AIR Montserrat as a special time in their lives and think fondly of their experiences on the island.

Yacht [at the] "Rock"

Because there was a world famous recording studio on the island, the rich and famous would occasionally visit AIR Montserrat, often arriving via their yachts. Neil Young stopped by with his entourage as did Mike Batt (famous for his musical version of The Wombles.) Bob Dylan parked his yacht offshore for three days with the intention of coming to the studio but sailed away without ever stepping a foot on Montserrat. Ken Blair told me of his experience with hanging out on Robert Stigwood's (manager of the Bee Gees and famous film producer) massive yacht in 1986: "Yvonne's husband Malcolm and Frank, the maintenance guy, and myself we went down and they took us across from the harbor in...a big motor cruiser that was tugged along by his big ship. We went on there and he just plied us with champagne for hours and fed us and we just sat there...Actually, the game we played one of these nights...was 'If we were going to have a coup on Montserrat, how would we do it?' That was the game that we played. But we could leap off his boat and swim in the sea. It was a real fun time. He must have had a good time because he came back for a second visit...He didn't seem to make any commercial approach. There was no idea that 'I'm coming to check this out for a project.' He just came by because he knew it was a famous studio and it was there. That was the impression that I got."

Malcolm Kelly, Frank Oglethorpe, Ken Blair On Robert Stigwood's Yacht
With Yacht Staff Member On Right
Photo: Ken Blair

Making Due

Dave and Malcolm had done a spectacular job of planning for all manner of possible technical problems, stocking the studio workshop with everything that they thought maintenance engineers would need to keep the studio running during a session. Combined with the skills of the staff members sent to Montserrat, most problems could be solved quickly with the spare electronic parts the engineers had at hand. Being days from the arrival of replacement parts, repairing gear at the studio could lead to difficulties if time was of the essence and the workshop did not have the parts the maintenance engineers needed to correct the problem. That was not always the case though and novel solutions had to be improvised on the fly. Malcolm remembers being tasked with fixing a Leslie organ during what he thinks was Paul McCartney's session at the studio. A Leslie is a speaker whose sound is sent through a spinning baffle, rotated by an electric motor, that gives the instrument playing through it a warbling, shimmering sound effect. He was in the studio workshop and someone wheeled the Leslie into the room and asked if he "could make it work a bit better?" He recalled the story of the repair: "So I took [the motor] out and thought, 'I'll just run the motor up on the [work]bench.' And so I put it up on the bench, plugged it in and it went 'BANG!' And I was just like, 'You silly sot!'" Again, this was a power matching issue. He had forgotten that the Leslie was wired for the American market, which used 110 volts, and plugged it directly into a 240 volt socket. "I plugged it into the wall and it exploded on me! They wanted it back in the studio in an hour and I've just blown it up! [laughing.] How do I get out of this? I know what I'll do." He took a sample of the winding wire from the motor and headed into Plymouth to a local store. "I said, 'Do you have any old transformers out in the back? Can I have a look through?'" Malcolm dug through boxes of old transformers until he found one with wiring similar in size as the Leslie motor. He bought the old transformer for $10EC and rushed back to the studio. He unwound the wire from the old transformer, unwound the Leslie motor carefully counting the exact number of windings, and then rewound the Leslie motor by hand "must have been about 500, 600 turns." He said, "I put it back in and IT WORKED! [laughing] But that's the kind of thing you HAVE to do because someone is waiting. They can't wait three days...Yeah, I blew it up but I fixed it. It's not something you would entertain doing anywhere else...It's that kind of 'fix and make do' mentality still there in Montserrat."

Stuart recalled a time they were having an issue with a tape machine during a session where Frank came up with a novel solution on the fly: "The machine screwed up one night so we had to stop work and we thought 'Oh no. We'll get another machine sent in from America or England or wherever it was...But Frank took the machine to pieces and found out the problem lay within one of the spindles. And he took a Philips screwdriver and worked through the night. He had a grinding wheel and a Philips screwdriver which he cut and made a new spindle out of the screwdriver...and it worked." Improvisation was sometimes a requirement at AIR Montserrat when parts were days away from arriving.

Angry Art

Stuart Breed and Frank Oglethorpe told me about a session they had with Art Garfunkle where there were multiple equipment issues. Art was a moody guy at the time and was described as "hard to keep happy." Art and Geoff Emerick, the album's co-producer, wanted to record digitally so AIR rented a Sony PCM 3324 24-track digital tape machine and had it shipped to Montserrat. The newfangled piece of recording technology worked properly initially but then one day, it stopped working. The tape feed motors were moving at an inconsistent speed during one third of each rotation of the reel. Frank said that they had sent the maintenance manuals with the tape deck, so he had the information he needed to start troubleshooting the issue. "But this was the first time I had seen one of these machines. This was...bleeding edge technology...I'm pretty clueless [with this tape deck] but I worked out that the take up motor was not functioning properly." It turns out that the tape reel motor was a three-phase motor and one of the phase wirings had gone bad, hence it not turning properly during 1/3 of each rotation. "It was unfixable from my standpoint," Frank said, knowing that there were no spare parts within several thousand miles of the island. Aware of the possible volatility of Art's reaction to the situation, Frank went to Stuart, who was AIR's assigned assistant engineer for the session, and said, "Um...Stuart, it's fucked. You tell [Art.]" Stuart said back to Frank, "No. No. No. YOU tell him." Frank fired back, "No. You tell him." They go back and forth, both trying to avoid telling Art that his session was about to be put on hold for the time being due to an equipment malfunction. Eventually, Frank gave in and told Art, "We are very sorry but the tape machine is broken. There is nothing I can do. We don't have any spares. We are going to have to get another one in." Frank says that Art surprisingly replied, "Ok. Fine." He had taken the bad news very well. Crisis averted. Frank tells Art that they can have a replacement tape machine delivered in four days. At the time, there were only two British Airways flights from the UK to Antigua a week which is why the replacement Sony Dash would take so long to arrive. In the meantime, there was a nice long weekend ahead with a party in Old Town. Frank, knowing full well that Art would say no, invited him to the party. Much to Frank's surprise, Art says, "Oh! That would be fun. Great!" Frank is thinking to himself, "You've got to be kidding me." Frank continues the story: "So a couple of days later, the party rolls around. So I go and pick up Art and Stuart and of course, word had spread like wildfire that Art was going to be at this party...I don't know how but obviously, everybody knew. So we turn up at the house and we're starting to walk up the steps. The music suddenly fades out and on comes a reggae version of 'Bridge Over Troubled Waters.' And Stuart takes one look at me and says, 'I'm out of here' and leaves me with Art." Having worked with Art and knowing his volatility, Stuart was afraid of how Art might react to this Caribbean remake of one of his signature songs and did not want to be there if he got upset. Frank said, "Art, fortunately, says, 'This is cool' and starts bopping and up into the party we go." Another crisis averted but there was trouble on the horizon.

Frank continues the story: "The next day, I get a call from Malcolm [Atkin] saying something along the lines of, 'We missed the flight for the tape machine.' [I'm like] 'You've got to be kidding me!...How on earth can you miss a fight? You got at least two days to get it the bloody thing to the airport!'...So then I had to go tell Art that 'I'm really sorry but the tape machine didn't make the flight. It's going to be another three days.' Art turned around to me and said, 'Frank, you lied to me!' 'I didn't lie to you, Art. I was told...' Art says, 'No. You lied to me.' I said, 'It is out of my hands. Nothing that I can do.' [Art again says.] 'You lied to me.' He was livid." Frank told me that he does not remember what he did to defuse the situation, but it must have been acceptable for Art because, during our interview, Frank's wife Catherine was quick to point out that Art sent Frank 'nice Christmas cards' for years after the session.

AIR Engineer Stuart Breed
Sitting On Old Machinery At An Abandoned Sugar Plantation
Photo: Frank Oglethorpe

Ken Blair- AIR Montserrat's First and Only Intern

Ken Blair, who worked at AIR Montserrat in the mid-80s, found himself working at the studio via an unconventional path. Ken was studying sound recording at the University of Surrey with a "Plan B" of becoming a lawyer. One of his years at university was to be spent working in the recording industry to obtain some real-world experience. He decided that if he was going to work for a studio, he would combine it with some travelling, so he wrote a letter asking if there was any interest in hiring an intern and sent it to 50 studios around the world. Ken told me, "I remember having the letter to AIR Montserrat in my hand in the mouth of the post box, and I almost never let it go because I thought 'What a waste of time. Why are you even trying this?'" Of those 50 letters, he received three replies, all rejections, but to his surprise, a few days later, Ken said that "a postcard hit the doormat with a picture of the studio and the pool on the front and a handwritten letter from Yvonne saying 'I've sent your details to London. They'll be contacting you and you will go for an interview.'"

Ken gets called to an interview with John Burgess in London. Because of his upbringing and instruction from his professors at the university, Ken showed up to the interview in a suit and tie. As he enters the office, he saw that John was wearing a casual open necked shirt. John asked why Ken was wearing a suit. Ken said, "They always say to wear a suit to an interview." John replied, "But that's not how you dress to work, is it?" Ken told me that "I almost failed on the...sartorial dress front." Ken told John that "I'm...keen to do this. I'll pay my own way there. I'll work for nothing. I'm just going to be delighted to be there." Regardless of his overdressing for the interview, John approved Ken's internship in Montserrat and soon enough, Ken was on his way to the island with AIR providing him room and board. Little did he know how much his time at AIR Montserrat was to influence and accelerate his career. He told me the following story:

Ken was "extra" to the normal pool of engineering and technical staff at the studio. He was not sent to replace anyone in the normal rotation of AIR staffers. His role was to be learning the trade and filling in where needed. Partway through the year things changed drastically for Ken, for the better. Black Sabbath had come to AIR Montserrat to record their "The Eternal Idol" album. George Martin had recently negotiated a deal with Mitsubishi for a pair of X850 digital 32 track tape machines. Being that these were both a new product and not in use at any other AIR studio, no one in Montserrat had any experience with them. Ken remembered that for Frank Oglethorpe, it was a bit of a scary moment because it was his responsibility to set them up and support them during the session. Frank got everything up and running and the session was going great until...

AIR's engineer, Carl, was supporting the main engineer, Jeff Glixman, from the back of the control room, acting as a tape operator for the session. The band had been working through some arrangements and decided to commit a take of the song to tape. Carl started the tape decks recording and the band played the song. When the band came into the control room to listen to the take that they just had recorded, there was a complete audio dropout about halfway through the song. Everyone was worried that it was an issue with the new-fangled tape decks. The session was stopped and Frank spent some time performing a diagnostic test on the equipment. The recording gear seemed to be fine but with several hours lost, the session was set to reconvene the next morning.

That morning, Ken was in his bedroom in the studio villa when there was a knock at the door. When he opened the door, Yvonne was there with a question: "Do you think you can handle the session because Carl is not going to be there." Ken was a bit confused. He was only an intern. Why would he be asked to act as an engineer for the Black Sabbath session? What Ken had found out later was that Carl had accidentally hit the button on the tape deck that switched its mode from record to playback when he picked up a pencil that he had resting on the tape deck's control panel. This happened in the middle of the take that had the audio drop out. The problem was that Carl did not admit his culpability in the moment. A situation that could have been solved with a simple apology was allowed to fester for hours while the problem was presented as a technical issue rather than simple human error. Carl finally admitted his error hours later after much time and effort had been wasted. Black Sabbath and their production team had decided that they wanted someone else from AIR to take over the position of assistant engineer. With experienced staff several days of travel away from Montserrat, Yvonne had decided to take a chance on Ken and see if he would be willing to step into the role and get the session back on track. Ken was willing to take on the responsibility but had to convince John Burgess. John said to him, "What if this all goes wrong?" knowing that the session was already on thin ice. Ken was not expecting this question but said to John, "You can have someone here in a couple of days, surely." John agreed and Ken became AIR's assistant engineer for the session. He did such a great job in the position that he became the permanent second engineer for the rest of his year internship at AIR Montserrat.

Gaining a significant amount of experience in Montserrat, Ken returned to university and finished his degree, continuing to post graduate studies. After graduation, Ken used his knowledge from both university and AIR Montserrat to start his own recording company, which is still recording classical music to this day, decades later and half a world away from where he got his start at AIR.

Ken Blair
Photo: Frank Oglethorpe

Recording The Local Sounds

Arrow, the Montserratian Soca artist known around the world for his early 1980s hit 'Hot, Hot, Hot', would stop in from time to time to use the studio for quick overdubbing or mixing sessions, utilizing whatever AIR staff was on hand to man the studio. Paul Rushbrooke remembers: "I think everybody did Arrow. Arrow would pop in and out...You'd probably find if there was a spare couple of hours, a spare evening. If it was cheaper than [normal]...he would always ask Yvonne 'Can I come in and do some mixing?' He would do a...recording in New York...particularly with the brass section but they would come over [to Montserrat] and mix." Matt Butler remembers Arrow giving him a token of his appreciation. He told me, "Arrow was a very direct kind of guy...A heart of gold...He ran a [clothing] shop in the island as well. He said 'Matt, you've done such a good job. You come to my shop and you can have anything you want. And I've still got the rather brazen Hawaiian shirt that I chose. Very proud to have it."

Other local Montserratian artists recorded at the studio as well. Local choirs and bands utilized all of AIR's world class recording gear and staff at little or no cost which was provided as a service to the island community.

Yvonne Kelly said, "I can't remember charging any of it." Ken Blair remembered a tradition of local bands making records at the studio around the Christmas holidays: "I think from Yvonne's point of view, this was about PR and the community. So, she would offer us, the studio, to local bands at Christmas time to come and do something when they were quiet. And there did seem to be a tradition that bands would bring out a record at Christmas time. It wouldn't usually be a Christmas record but it would be the time of year when people brought a disc out. It seemed to be that you'd get the recording made and then somebody would go to Jamaica where there was a pressing plant. Get it all pressed up and come back and then the next thing is, you'd be driving through town and you'd hear these records in all of the rum shops all around town. And that was quite cool having worked on a couple of those records to drive to town and hear your recording coming out of a rum shop sound system."

Ambassadors

Since the staff at AIR Studios became familiar with the island during their "rotations," bands often relied on them to be ambassadors for the island. Montserrat's unique culture and its limited entertainment options presented the staff with the opportunity to act as local guides as the artists learned their way around the island. Since the studio sessions tended to be high stress affairs for the staffers, they often would want to get away from the studio complex at the end of the day. Ken Blair said, "If you were busy with a session, you could end up at the studio for quite long periods of time. Starting to feel like you really wanted to get out and have a trip at least into the middle of town so you could have a break from studio life. This culture developed where Friday night was the night for going out. We always made sure that we impressed this on the band that Friday night was our night for going out in Montserrat so hopefully they would give us some down time on Friday night." He said that the bands would tag along. "We'd often take the bands with us so they come out and see the delights of a Montserrat night life," he said. Artists would find their favorite spots for food, dancing, and partying and would often become regulars. Places like Andy's Village Place, The Agouti club, and La Cave disco were frequented by the musicians, engineers, and producers. The intense working environment combined with the friendly island culture and small town atmosphere led to a bonding between the artists and the AIR staffers that persisted beyond the studio's confines. Everyone worked hard and partied hard as well. Ken said, "I remember having some really good times [there]...In fact, I don't really remember the good times there because usually there was too much beer involved."

The staff at AIR Studios Montserrat integrated with the island, partaking in the culture, and becoming part of it for the brief time they were on the island. Parties were attended, friendships and romances bloomed, and vices were partaken in. New experiences were had, there were high levels of stress during sessions, and soul-crushing boredom came with the territory. They worked hard, played hard, and often had long bouts of mind-numbing down time. Regardless of what happened, no one that I interviewed regretted going to Montserrat. For most of the staff of the studio, it was a special time in their lives that is looked on with great reverence, broad smiles on their faces as they regaled me with their stories of AIR Montserrat.

THE CYCLE OF A SESSION

While every recording session varied depending on the artists and their various requirements, there was a general cycle of how the sessions were carried out.

AIR Managing Director John Burgess was responsible for seeking out potential clients to book sessions at the studio. In many cases, the studio sold itself through word of mouth and reputation, but a great deal of the work was through the salesmanship of John. Relying on his extensive personal relationships in the recording industry that he had fostered over the years, John's reputation allowed him access to those who held the power over where and when artists could record and mix their albums. The artists could easily be sold on the idea of recording on a beautiful Caribbean island but those who controlled the purse strings at the record companies often needed to be courted in order to get a solid commitment to book as session at AIR Montserrat. If the artists or their management wanted information about the studio or to book a session, they could call the studio itself or AIR London but these requests were routed to John.

Once they had a commitment from an artist and their record company, John and his secretary Carol Weston would work out the logistics of getting the artists, their entourages, and their gear to the island. The packing of the musical gear prior to the journey was handled by the artist, sometimes by their touring companies. AIR took it from there. Getting everything to the island was expensive and could become very complex logistically depending on where the people and equipment were coming from. Carol said, "[John] would do the selling bit and then we had to work out how we were going to get them all out there, where to put them up in different [villas]...and get all of the equipment out there. We had a very good bloke at British Airways that we use to liaise with...he was wonderful. He would work out how to get them out there and give them the best possible journey. Without people like that, it would have been very difficult." Regardless of the help that the airline provided, Carol found arranging the logistics quite frustrating. She said, "We'd had to get the people out there and I used to nearly cry. I thought, 'Why has George picked such [a] remote island of all places...' It's all very good having these ideas but in the normal run of things, it was quite hard work."

AIR staff would work with the artists' management to find out any unique requirements that their client needed for the session. This included special gear, dietary requirements, and preferences for food, drink, cigarettes, etc. Because of the isolated nature of the island and the difficulties obtaining specialty items, this had to be worked out well in advance so that arrangements could be made for importation of these items prior to the artists' arrival. With the isolation of the island, some specialty goods may have taken days or weeks for them to arrive so preproduction was a requirement. Artists' accommodations would also need to be worked out since they varied greatly from session to session depending on the size of the party, their preferences, as well as their budget.

At the studio, everyone would go into what Yvonne called "work mode." Since most of the Montserratian staff did not work at the studio when it was empty, they needed to be called back to work, often leaving part time gigs or side hustles that they were doing during the down times. Staff members would check on the stock of consumables that would be needed for the session, everything from food, to blank tapes, to toilet paper. Low stock items were brought up to acceptable levels by buying from local businesses or from other islands.

The artists and their personnel would fly from their source location to Antigua since there were no direct flights to Montserrat from anywhere in the world. Usually, the studio manager from AIR Montserrat would be waiting for them to arrive and to help facilitate the next part of the journey. Special arrangements were made to whisk the artists through Antiguan immigration and to get their gear through customs. The artists would then board a small passenger aircraft seating less than 10 people and were flown to Montserrat. If there were more people than could fit on the plane, multiple flights were booked. Small amounts of gear could come over on the planes, but those artists with a large amount of heavy equipment would have their gear sent over via boat where it would arrive at the port and then be processed through customs.

In interviews, many people commented that the flight into Montserrat was a harrowing experience. The pilots were often nonchalant about the flights, having made the trip hundreds of times, sometimes leaving windows open with their arms hanging out, or flying at low altitudes. Then there was the approach to the island's Blackburne Airport runway. The runway ran north to south on the east side of the island. It was on the coast almost at sea level with the sharp crags of the mountains rising sharply behind it. The flight path had the planes approach the island directly from the east with the airport located to the left of the aircraft. Artist Anna Dam's description of the flight to Montserrat echoed the sentiments of many people I interviewed: "They used to fly straight at what looked like you were flying straight at the side of a mountain. [The pilots] would suddenly bank. The wing would go very abruptly, the right wind would go up in the air... make the hard left turn, level it out, and then just drop onto the runway. It was a horrifying landing in Montserrat every time. And you had come in with speed or you'd end up crashing short of the runway because of the downdrafts off the mountains. You could see the planes in the water that didn't make it because they never hauled them out [of the water]." Many of the passengers were unaware of the bovine borne dangers that could be lurking on the runway. Frank Oglethorpe told me that whenever a plane came into land, someone at the airport had to drive up and down the runway to make sure that none of the island farmers' cows had wandered onto the runway.

The Entirety Of The Check-In Area At The Airport
Photo: Frank Oglethorpe

Once arriving at the Montserrat airport, they would then have to go through island immigration again to enter the country. AIR Montserrat's manager would be onsite to help facilitate a quick trip through immigration. The studio manager would also be working with island customs agents to get the artists' gear cleared for importation. At some point, the studio was designated as a bonded customs warehouse so that the artists' gear could be transported directly to the studio with customs agents completing their duties there rather than at the airport or docks. The artists and their entourages would be whisked off to wherever they wanted to go such as to see the studio, but much of the time they were taken to their villas to receive their hired cars and to settle in and relax after the long trip. Regardless of destination, they were treated to a ride across the island in the studio vehicles or in local taxis. Yvonne said that, "If they'd never been there before, then they'd probably pile into my car [or] pile into the studio Hilux [truck]. And if there were more people, a taxi. We would always make sure a particular taxi. Someone that could tell them all of the history as they went through." The drive from the airport on the east coast to the island's west coast where the studio and villas were located allowed the artists to take in the lush jungle views, hilly vistas, and local villages and traffic. For many, this was their first trip to a Caribbean island and for almost all of them, their first trip to Montserrat. Coming from cities such as London, New York, or Los Angeles, that first drive across the island was a new experience for a lot of artists with the island's unique sights, sounds, and smells. The drive would set the stage for what they would experience in Montserrat over the coming weeks. Yvonne said that the artists were presented with their rental cars once at their villas. She said that she would ask them if they felt comfortable driving themselves

149

to the studio when they were ready to head up to see the facilities. I suppose the drive from the airport with its windy steep roads and unfamiliar terrain put some fear into them because Yvonne said that the answer was "Invariably, NO!"

While the artists got acquainted with their new surroundings, their gear was brought up to the studio from the port in Plymouth or the airport. Anything brought into Montserrat was noted on its way into the country and when the artist left the island, it was again noted on its egress. There was no importation duty levied on the equipment so long as it only stayed on the island for the session.

As far as accommodation went, most big-name stars, producers, and their families stayed in large, luxurious (by Montserrat standards) villas located in close proximity to the studio property. Arrangements for the villas were booked through a local rental agent. Often, session musicians, engineers, and other artists' staff stayed at Olveston House which was owned by George Martin and John Burgess. Although not as private as the rented villas, Olveston House had high quality rooms with beautiful grounds, a great sound system, a swimming pool, and tennis courts.

After they had settled in, the artists would often come to the studio villa for their first dinner with Chef George Morgan. This meal set the stage for the incredible feasts that they would experience during their stay on the island.

Once the artists were settled into their accommodations and setup in the studio, the pressure on the studio managers would ease while it would often increase for others working at the studio. Steve Jackson said that one the bands were "up and running, there was little for us to do." Denny Bridges echoed the sentiment by saying that "people would arrive and disappear into the studio and you wouldn't see them much of them at all...other than dinner." The studio and its staff were available 24 hours a day to accommodate any schedule that the artists decided to keep. Bartenders, drivers, technical staff, tape operators, and engineers were expected to be available to the artists around the clock. This could mean a very disjointed schedule for them since every artist had their own routine for recording.

Breakfast was usually served at the artists' villas prior to travelling to the studio in the mornings. Lunch was served midday at the studio villa or in the studio itself, catered by the daytime culinary staff which was usually Franklyn Allen. Dinner was served in the early evening in the dining room or patio of the studio villa. A multicourse meal was served. It was up to the artists how long they wanted to hang out and socialize after dinner. Some chose to go back into the studio for more work while others would relax on the studio patio well into the night.

Entertainment during their stay was at the whim of the artists. Like I explained earlier, Montserrat was not a tourist destination so there was not an industry built around this. There were a few activities that artists tended to experience in Montserrat: hiking to the Soufriere volcano, visiting the large island waterfall, windsurfing, renting a boat for a cruise around the island, swimming, beach BBQs, shopping in Plymouth, and hanging out at local bars and restaurants, often jamming with the local musicians playing there. Otherwise, artists were usually working.

Sessions could last from as short as a few days to many months such as with Dire Straits, although that was the exception. Mixing sessions tended to be shorter than tracking sessions due to the minimal setup required as compared to recording a live band. The average session length tended to range from two to six weeks.

Once the session had completed, all tapes were given to the artists, even the outtakes. AIR wanted the artists to have possession of all the material that was recorded in the studio so that they would not be held liable for the leaking of any unauthorized recordings. No tapes were reused from previous sessions. New tapes would be ordered for the next session. Depending on the studio manager's personal preference, bills for the car rentals, equipment rentals, liquor (which was not included in the studio cost,) and other ancillary expenses were presented to the artists' manager at the end of the session, or these expenses were tallied later and sent to the artist after the fact. Yvonne Kelly preferred the former because she felt that presenting the bill when the expenses were fresh in the artists' minds led to "more clarity" and less cases of expenses being challenged later when the bill came due.

Leaving the island was the reverse of the arrival. Artists left via the island's airport and caught a flight home via Antigua. Their equipment was accounted for by local customs agents and left on a boat or airplane heading for Antigua. The staff would clean up, fix any faults in the studio, and prepare the property for the next artist. Whether the next artists was arriving immediately or there was a long gap between sessions, the studio and facilities were prepared to be used within a short timeframe. As the saying goes..."Lather, rinse, and repeat."

TIDBITS

I had some great stories and interesting information about the island that did not fit directly into any chapters but that I thought readers might enjoy. Here are a few tidbits about Montserrat and the studio.

Studio Vehicles

The studio itself had several vehicles over the decade. The manager had their own vehicle which was originally a Ford Cortina Estate. This was replaced with a Honda accord in later years. There was also a Mini Moke that was retired sometime in the earlier years. They also had a Toyota Hilux 4x4 truck, a "people mover" van, and a Volkswagen Beetle.

Artists would hire cars from locals who had vehicles to rent to tourists and part-time residents of the island. The studio would make the arrangements for the rentals for the artists but the artists would pay the locals directly for the rentals although it was not clear if this was always the case.

Dangerous Driving

A common theme that I heard in many interviews was how dangerous the driving was on the island. I can attest that the roads in Montserrat are very narrow and are littered with tight blind turns. This is common on many small volcanic islands where roads must conform to the terrain which is often steep. Couple that with rapidly changing weather conditions that can occur over the island, and this was a recipe for many an automobile mishap. For the AIR staffers that came from off island and many of the artists, driving in these conditions was completely foreign. Couple this with the amount of drunk driving that frequently occurred on the island and it was a recipe for frequent automobile accidents. Dave Harries said, "We crashed so many cars. Everybody crashed cars. Geoff and [AIR Engineer] Colin Fairley, on the first day they arrived, their car went off the road and down into a ditch in the mud and the rain." Frank Oglethorpe says that while he was working at the studio, his experience was that there "were more drunk drivers on the road than sober ones on any given night." Dave Harries was concerned about the amount of drunk driving on the island and spoke to the island's chief of police. He recalled, ""I remember saying to the chief of police about U.K. law. '[In Montserrat] There's no seat belt law and there's no 'drink and drive' prosecutions.' He said, 'Man, if you stupid enough to drink a load and then drive round these roads, then you'll get your own punishment. We don't need to punish you.' And I suppose he's right really."

Ron Eve After His Encounter With Montserrat's Roads
Photo: Frank Oglethorpe

Many an artist had an automobile mishap while driving on the island. Ron Eve remembers that "We wrecked a few cars there." He himself ran off the road while Dire Straits was recording there but swears he was completely sober when it happened. He said that, "I just went off the road. On the island, you would get little microclimates and by this point, it was after Christmas so I was staying in a different house. [He had been staying at Olveston House.] It was up...big winding hill. And as I came up the hill, there'd been a little bit of shower, of rain. As I came around, it just went 'whoop' down the side. I nearly went down the cliff. I was stopped by a small tree. I was unbelievably lucky. They said, 'Your drunk.' I said 'I wasn't actually.'" AIR studio driver Carlton took the studio truck out to the crash site and pulled the car back to safety.

AIR Staffer Frank Oglethorpe remembered that OMD "put a Mini Moke through the roof of a house." It may be this story that Yvonne told me, although she did not mention the artist's name. She remembered, "We had a situation when one of our clients drove his car into somebody's front room. And Judy [Martin] and I had gone to the house and sit with the car 'just there' while we apologized and sorted it out. It's that awful feeling where it looks so surreal and it looks like if you just pulled it out of everything would stay, but you know it won't." Of course, the artist was responsible for the damages, but studio staff management had to be the interface between the artist and the poor Montserratian who had a car sitting in their living room.

Another artist drove a car into the pool at Olveston House. Matt Butler remembered the story vividly because he was in the car at the time. He remembered, "I was in it. We didn't get very far in the pool. I think 2 wheels were in the water and we got told off, not for driving the car into the pool, but because [he] had flattened a few flowers on our way. It was a rock star thing to do."

Car rental costs were a large expense for the artists, especially when the entourages were large and the vehicles were damaged. As was said, the hired cars for the artists were rented from local Montserratians as there were no professional car rental agencies on the island. Franklyn Allen, daytime chef at the studio, remembered that he rented his new car to an artist before he even had a chance to drive it himself. Yvonne remembers the shock of one local lady, who had purchased a few Jeeps to rent to tourists, when she saw the condition of the cars then they were returned to her: "When it was Dire Straits, there weren't enough cars because they were there for such a long time. You have to remember that a lot of 'snow birds' came [retirees who would stay through the winter] and they wanted cars as well. There was one lady called 'Pauline' and we used to rent her Jeeps. And just remember when she got four brand new Jeeps and she almost cried when we gave her them back. I mean, we paid for everything [the damages] but they were not in pristine condition anymore. And she's like, 'I can't believe it' because she'd been used to little old ladies renting her cars...Eventually, she was quite alright about it but honestly, they expected the old-style rentals where you give it back with a full tank."

To drive in Montserrat, you need to have a driver's license from your home country. Most countries' licenses are accepted and to drive on the island, you simply need to pay a fee to the local police to obtain a temporary Montserrat driver's license but some artists and staff members were from large cities such as New York or London where they used public transport exclusively for getting around and thus never had obtained a driver's license at home. An example was producer Chris Thomas who arrived in Montserrat in 1983 to record an album with Elton John. He recalled: "I said to Yvonne, 'I need a car.' She said, 'Do you have a license?' because she knew I didn't drive. I said, 'No.' So she said, 'So you won't have any insurance?' But I said, 'But I need a car." So she said [hesitating], 'Alright...'" Chris laughed profusely when delivering this line knowing how illegal it had been. Sometime the rules were bent to keep the client happy.

Here is another example of what drivers had [and still have to] contend with in Montserrat. Steve and Jan Jackson were driving home from the studio in her Mini Moke as the sun set. She said, "There were cows all over the place [on the island]. This one was tethered on one side [of the road] but he'd walked to the other side of the road but you couldn't see the chain. I hit that frickin' chain and pulled the head of the cow, who had huge horns, right into the [side of] the car. Scared the crap out of me!" Wandering livestock and wild animals were quite a danger for drivers on the island.

For many years, the AIR staffers who were assigned to Montserrat had a Volkswagen Beetle at their disposal for traveling around the island. The poor car was used and abused by the staff. Paul Rushbrooke remembers: "It was a really great Beetle. It was a semi automatic, white. We used to drive everywhere...It was like a hired car. Nobody respected it whatsoever. Our deal was that one of us was trying to wreck it from the outside and the other was trying to wreck it from the inside." AIR engineer Stuart Breed remembers having an incident in the Beetle: "Frank taught me to drive. I went down there and I had a learner's permit and they went, 'Well, you're going to have to drive.' Well, I've never driven a car before in my life. I was driving this old...beat up Volkswagon...Some gears worked and some didn't. [Finally] I've got a driving license. I'm driving this thing most nights drunk around an island [where the] roads were like the side of a volcano and I'm still here to tell the tale. There was 'Breed's Bend' which was the bend coming out of Plymouth and you turned right. There was a sharp right-hand bend to go back up towards the road that led up to the studio. I came round in third gear and went straight into the church wall there. I pulled the [fender] and drove it up to the studio...we looked at the car and front fender...was caved in. I was like 'Hi Yve! I put a little bit of a dent in the car last night.' So yeah, she was used to it." At one point, Yvonne had the Beetle painted white which Frank Oglethorpe said, "It looked a lot nicer...Yvonne was selling it. And she's sold it and Paul Rushbrooke went out up to Andy's [Village Place] one evening...Impaired judgment on the way back, he kind of misses a turn and puts it into a telegraph pole. He's fine fortunately. The car, not. Poor Yvonne. It was being sold the next day. Somebody'd already agreed to buy it. No. It was a write off, I think." Paul said. "I was quite lucky actually. I hit a telegraph pole coming down. I was near the Belham golf club. [I was lucky] to have hit the pole. If it hadn't done that, I would have probably gone down the bank into the golf club and that would have been bad."

An Awkward Introduction

A band was in the studio and Dave Harries was in Montserrat at the time and was helping get some of their equipment through customs and up to the studio. There were some really nice chaps working down at the docks that Dave liked so he told them, "If you ever fancy looking around the studio, come on up." Later, Dave was up at the studio when one of the guys from the dock showed up and brought a mate with him. They wanted to see the studio, so Dave told them to wait while he checked to see if the band was recording at that time. Dave went into the control room and asked the producer and engineer if they were busy. They said that it was ok. They were taking a break at that moment and had no issues with Dave bringing in the locals to see the studio. Dave brought the visitors into the main recording room and the band's drummer was still in the room, "smoking a massive spliff," as Dave describes it. "The smell was horrendous!" Dave recalls, "I just ignored it, I didn't say anything. I just carried on, showed them around the studio very nicely." When they finished the studio tour and were outside of the facility, the customs dock worker decided to introduce his friend to Dave. He said, "Mr. Harries, I'd like you to meet...Constable so-and-so from the Montserrat Police." Dave thought, "Oh no! [Montserrat] is a British protectorate so that sort of thing is against the law." The Montserrat officer turned to Dave and said, "Man, we used to come up here a lot because people used to grow marijuana up here and we would collect it up and burn it." Dave slyly says to the policeman, "Oh, we don't have any of that sort of thing up here anymore!" Dave said to me, "I never heard a word. Nothing from the police. Nothing." The tacit agreement between the police and the studio regarding marijuana use at the studio was exemplified that day.

PRODUCERS

So why would artists and producers choose to come to Montserrat considering the logistical challenges and elevated costs of doing so? The obvious answer is "Who wouldn't want to work in a Caribbean paradise?" Well, that was a big part of why AIR Montserrat proved popular with artists. Other reasons were not so apparent.

One reason, early in the studio's history, was for tax purposes. For U.K.-based artists in the 1970s and early 80s, there was a tax advantage to recording away from England. An example of this was Sheena Easton recording her first album in Montserrat in 1981. Producer Chris Neil said he was advised by her accountants and manager to find a studio outside of England to record. He recalled them saying to him, "Record where you like but if you record overseas, i.e., not in the UK, you have 20% tax relief off the top of all your royalties because you didn't perform in the UK, you performed the services [overseas]." Beyond the tax relief on a particular recording, the extremely high income taxes of the time had led many U.K. artists to choose to become "tax exiles." They would setup financial entities for themselves in countries like France and the Netherlands where the tax rates were significantly lower than in the U.K. These artists could only reside in England for about two months per year. This disincentivized spending their few precious days in their home country in a recording studio rather than spending that time with family or friends. Having a session in a far-flung location like Montserrat appealed to those who became tax exiles. The Police were tax exiles when they recorded their album "Ghost In The Machine" at AIR Montserrat. Unfortunately for these tax-savvy artists, the takeover of the British Government by the conservative Tories in the early 1980s quashed many of these tax loopholes. Margaret Thatcher's ascendence to Prime Minister was certainly not welcomed by those artists wishing to save on their tax liabilities.

Another reason to come to Montserrat was to help artists escape the trappings of their fame. Boy George was going through a tough time in his personal life when he came to Montserrat. Dealing with addiction and the death of several friends due to drug overdoses, the U.K. press and paparazzi coverage had led to a very intense and public scrutiny of his private life. He came to Montserrat to not only record, but to decompress away from the pressures of the press that was constantly hounding him about his personal issues. Ken Blair said that Boy George arrived on the island a week prior to the start of his session. He said, "He was just on holiday with us for a week...It really was a sanctuary [for him.]" Similarly, The Rolling Stones came to the island to record "Steel Wheels" in 1989 just as the press was attacking bassist

Bill Wyman for the 52-year old's marriage to Mandy Smith, who was only 18 years old at the time. The physical isolation of the island and limited ways to travel there allowed the Stones to record without the intense scrutiny that they would have had if they had booked the session anywhere else. In fact, the Stones sent Bill on a solo trip back to Antigua during the session to deal with the press away from Montserrat..and the rest of the band.

Opinions Of the Studio and the Island

So what did the producers and engineers think of recording at AIR Montserrat? The following is how they felt about the studio in their own words.

Ray Bardani

Producer Ray Bardani And His Then-Wife At The Studio
Photo: Frank Oglethorpe

Engineer and producer Ray Bardani worked with Luther Vandross on two records at AIR Montserrat. He had this to say about the vibe of the studio: "The atmosphere was so beautiful. The way they had it was when it was sunny, there was a control room window...so you would see the ocean. The sun would be coming through...As the day shifted, it would get darker and the light would change so your body would be adjusting with that. But I remember some of the songs that we did were done like at noon while it was bright and sunny and it was exciting and stuff. And then there were some of the most beautiful songs that we did were done late at night and then the stars and sprinkling and its dark and the vibe was like, 'Where are we?' We were in our own world and the concentration level was high because there was no distraction. There were no cell phones. There were no computers going on. You didn't even know what was going on outside of that place. You had no idea. So what you did was you focused on whatever it took to get the sound."

Ray continued, speaking of how much AIR Montserrat differed from other studios: "The beauty of it also was once we were setup, it was always there. Everything was ready all of the time. I had the piano. I had the electric piano. I had the two guitar amps. The bass. The drums. Luther's vocal setup was always setup. Basically, all we had to do was load the tape up, put the console on input. Headphones were routed. Everybody's ready to go. Whereas in New York. You'd have to book the hours. You'd get in. You'd do a couple hours of setup and then record. Then you'd have to get out. It was just different. It was really beautiful in the sense that there was no time limit to anything...However long it took, it didn't matter."

When I asked him if he thought there was a general misconception about how Montserrat and the studio were viewed as a playground for artists, he said, "When you were in the [studio] complex, it was like paradise but on the way home, you would see the people with the tin huts living by the side of the road. There were goats walking down the road and cows. The island wasn't not a very rich neighborhood or whatever you want to call it. So basically, you live in this paradise, and you are there and you feel safe, and you're surrounded by beauty and technically it's amazing because, coming from AIR London...You were covered. So it does look like a paradise to people when they see The Police jumping on the console and they see the trees outside and people doing stuff. It's a misconception of what that island really was."

When I asked him why AIR Montserrat was chosen for Luther's sessions, he said, "How we found about Montserrat. I was really always inspired by English records and recordings and stuff, so I knew about AIR Studios and Abbey Road in London and all that. And I had seen that The Police had recorded there and Paul [McCartney] at that point. [Luther] comes in one day and he goes, 'Ray, I want to get out of here' because at the time [in] New York City, we were doing sessions and all the musicians in the band were great musicians but everybody was doing record sessions, jingles, [other] sessions. People were coming and going. [Luther said] 'I heard about this place called Montserrat. What do you think about that?' And I'm thinking to myself, 'I know exactly what that is.' He said, 'I think it would be fun if we took everybody there so then nobody can leave. No distractions. I think it would be really fun. Why don't you find out about it.' Of course, I knew about everything. I said, 'Alright. I'll check it out. It sounds like it could be fun...I think that would be really great. They've got everything. Wonderful. They've got a custom Neve. Beautiful room, beautiful island. Accommodations.' So he said, 'Why don't we just get everybody and I will fly out you and your wife...and the band and their wives and girlfriends and we'll go for a couple of weeks. What do you think?' I said, 'That sounds good to me!' So it was like a dream for me because being a young guy and being inspired by getting to work at such as luxurious kind of place was an exciting experience."

Chris Neil

Chris Neil produced two records for Sheena Easton in the early 1980s, including her debut album, as well as Mike + The Mechanics later in the decade. When I asked him about his opinion of the studio, he said, "To answer your question...it was a great studio. It was very much of its time. i.e. late 70s, early 80s. Everything worked. It was in good condition. They had to keep everything air conditioned permanently. But in terms of studio design, it was very dry and very dead as were most studios at the time. It wasn't until the mid-80s that you started to get 'hard rooms'...It being George Martin's [studio], there was a great selection of microphones. It was all there for you to make a record. Everything was there. You just needed to bring the talent there." He continued: "Because it was George Martin, everything was self-contained, everything you could you want. The desk was fabulous. 24-hour maintenance engineer. The whole thing. It was a London studio stuck in paradise or stuck in the middle of nowhere."

Regarding George Martin's choice of Montserrat for his destination studio: "I used to go to AIR. I worked at AIR Studios in London. I had heard...very bravely, George had opened this studio in the middle of nowhere on a tropical island. I thought it was a brave decision."

Chris was enamored with the island: "I remember one of the trips saying I really don't want to go home. It was probably in the winter months. It might have been March...I settled straight into Montserrat. I got it. I mean, I just got it." In her interview, Yvonne said that Chris Neil won "'The person who most did not want to leave' award."

Chris Neil and Sheena Easton Working At The Neve Console
Photo: Chris Neil

Chris Kimsey

Chris Kimsey came to Montserrat twice, first to record Anderson, Bruford, Wakeman, and Howe in 1988, and then again in 1989 to record the last album before the studio shut its doors forever, The Rolling Stones' "Steel Wheels."

When I asked Chris about his opinion about the studio, he had strong feelings about the studio's main room: "It was boxy sounding. You had to work hard to get a sound in there. Apart from having the great desk, you need great musicians obviously. I remember when I set Charlie's [Watts] drum kit up in there it was like 'Oh shit. This is not translating very well. I mean Charlie doesn't hit the drums hard anyway but that doesn't really matter if you've got a good room. It should help the sound rather than reverse it. So I remember I had to build [something]...the bass drum went 'Pfft', there was no depth to it at all. So I built like a tunnel to get any resonance out of the bass drum. Also, there was no kind of, how can I explain, there was no nice 'crack mid sparkle in the room.'...When I was going somewhere that I'd never worked in before, my main thing with drums was that sound, that mid-range bite so I always travel with this very cheap Sony stereo microphone that was really, it would come with a Walkman back then, [it did a] good job. I had it because it was quite a bit of Charlie's drum sound there. That helped. The guitar sounds were not really a problem they were just in the room but boothed off and that was easy and Mick was in the [vocal] booth so that's normal. The actual room as a room sound, not my favorite place at all...Bit of a difficult room to work. It was ok for ABWH because we were doing

161

everything at once and I think that Bill Bruford had an electronic drum kit as well so the room wasn't necessary for that. Keyboards and piano, that's simple and the organ and whatever Rick was playing."

He continued: "I was surprised by the smallness actually. The actual recording room. The performance room was quite small considering that they could have made it as big as they wanted in building it. That was interesting that it was relatively small. I thought it was going to be bigger but it wasn't a problem. It's the same at Compass Point. [Recording studio in the Bahamas] Actually, Compass Point was a small room as well. [But] the control room was great."

Regardless of the shortcomings of the studio, he loved the studio and island vibe: "All of the staff were terrific. You kind of became instant family with everybody. Everybody was very well accommodated and looked after and fed."

Neil Dorfsman

Neil Dorfsman Relaxes By The Studio Pool
Photo: Frank Oglethorpe

Neil produced both Dire Straits' "Brothers In Arms" and Sting's "...Nothing Like The Sun." He absolutely loved Montserrat and the vibe of the island: "It was kind of paradise, man. Even though there was nothing to do. There was a disco in town. There were a couple of bars which got frequented pretty heavily but there was nothing else to do except to swim and windsurf and work. So, it was like a dream. It really was like a dream...It's so special in my heart, you know...It's like you couldn't make it up. It really was like a fantasy place in certain ways."

The Neve console, which was used on Dire Straits' session, was key for Neil: "The main thing about Montserrat, and I loved it...was the Neve console. That was worth the price of admission right there."

With that said, he echoed many of the same sentiments of other producers who pointed out the shortcomings of the studio: "I was coming from the Power Station in New York which is a big live ambient space with multiple isolation booths so you can get a live sound and still keep the isolation...So I was kind of stunned when I go there. It's like you have this whole island and you've got this pretty tiny recording space and it kind of bummed me out. It was like 'Ugh! What are we going to do here?' I really did not expect that and I did not know what to do." He thought about moving the drums outside of the studio similar to what Hugh Padgham did with The Police: "I actually thought of putting the drums up in the dining area...[but] it wasn't glassed in so I was like 'Well, the sound is just going to go out. We're not going to get a room sound but it will be 'liver' but there's staff cooking and cleaning and doing stuff there [and] I can't see the guy. There was no video hookup that we had. So I [thought] 'That's way too much trouble.'...I just dove in. I kind of built booths in the studio. It was really, really hard and [even] harder on Sting's record because he had a saxophone and leakage into the saxophone...It was really hard... It was just like 'I'm not sure I can get what I'm hearing.' But it all worked out somehow."

Not having the ability to quickly rent gear he needed was the main differentiator for AIR Montserrat compared to studios Neil was used to working in: "The biggest difference was the ability to get what you needed gear wise...The studio down there, as I recall, did not have a lot of outboard gear at all. Thank God I had the Neve because I could get a good sound on things without doing my usual things. I like to EQ while I record. I like to make records sound as close as I want it to be while I'm tracking. So I looked around [at the control room] and was like 'There's no outboard gear here.'... this studio really had very minimal...couple of tube equalizers, a couple of compressors. Not a lot of stuff. That was the main difference for me technically."

Chris Thomas

Chris Thomas produced three of Elton John's early 1980s releases that were recorded at AIR Montserrat: "Jump Up," "Too Low For Zero," and "Breaking Hearts." His familiarity with the standardized studio setup that AIR had carried from Oxford Circus to Montserrat helped him get up and recording post haste.

"I loved it because it was everything that I knew...I knew what a Neve desk sounded like intimately...When I got to Montserrat, I picked up and carried on. It was the same deal [as Oxford Circus]. It was a Neve desk and it was fabulous. [All of the outboard gear] was there. And the speakers were great. It was a breeze. To the point where when we did "Too Low For Zero," we were doing a song almost every day. We did the whole thing in 18 days, bar a few overdubs...So within that very short space of time, Elton had written those songs and we recorded them.

While producers like Hugh Padgham and Neil Dorfsman thought that the studio design made it difficult to record drums, Chris thought that the studio room and gear made it versatile for recording. He told me: "There's pretty much a different drum sound on virtually every song and the drums never moved [in the studio.] They just stayed in that same little place the whole time...That's how malleable everything was there and how good it was to use... Back in the old days, it was always a joke. The first day was spent getting a drum sound. It was always overcoming this, that, and the other. It is such a yawn. When we did Too Low, it was just "Come up with an idea and manipulate it." And there are pretty much different drum sounds on every song. And it was the same basic starting point. Same mics. Same this and that. Same drummer."

After recording "Jump Up" in 1982, he found that coming back to record "Too Low For Zero" was easier the second time around. "The whole process of doing 'Too Low For Zero', for a number of different reasons was a lot easier, a lot more efficient that the first time we went down there...I was more familiar with the place...We understood more...Was it me getting used to it or was the studio starting to run a bit better because everything had been worked in properly? I don't know...To be able to knock off a record that quickly of that quality...The facility to be able to do that really says, 'This is really top notch now. It's really running like the old bullet train. You don't actually feel it moving too much. It's just all working.'" He felt that he never had to worry about the AIR technicians in Montserrat, which was not always the case at AIR London. He said, "If there was a new tape op, if you went there on a new visit...if you haven't worked with him before, you can see he was on the ball straight away. Because obviously sometimes back at AIR London, when you guys came in [referring to Dave Harries and Malcolm Atkin] came in, there would be a bit of holding hands...going sort of softly with these [new] guys because they don't know the job particularly well. But by the time they got down to Montserrat, [they knew what they were doing.]"

Producer Hugh Padgham probably said it best: "I could probably sum it up as it's probably the only studio I've ever been to in shorts every day, you know?"

TUG OF WAR

In late 1980, Paul McCartney was recording his latest album in AIR's Oxford Circus studio in London. At the time, there were a swirl of rumors that the Beatles were going to get together and record for the first time in over a decade. Any hopes of this happening were dashed when John Lennon was murdered in December 1980. Was there really going to be a Beatles reunion? Both Steve Jackson and Malcolm Atkin say that there was. Malcolm said that he had spoken to engineer Geoff Emerick about it: "Geoff told me it was due to happen before Christmas, but they all wanted to wait...[Paul] said 'I wanted to finish my album first.'" To quote Steve, "That's what it was. It was a Beatles reunion. We had everyone's tickets and then that guy shot John." Paul, distraught the death of his friend, promptly put his current session on hold, not wanting to continue with the project.

But Paul was not idle for long. Arrangements were made for him to start a new recording project in Montserrat and three weeks after the death of John, on January 4, 1981, the Tug of War session in Montserrat was started. Malcolm thinks that the quick pivot to Montserrat and the invitation of a procession of famous stars to come record with Paul was intended to help him cope with the loss of John. He said, "Why are all of these living legends being invited down to Montserrat to play with Paul? The more I think about it, the more he's trying to soften the blow so that it's not a Beatles reunion, it's a bunch of people, superstars all having some fun together." Musical heavyweights from around the industry came to help Paul with the album such as Stevie Wonder, Carl Perkins, drummer Steve Gadd, bassist Stanley Clark, and Paul's Beatles bandmate, Ringo Starr.

Although he was the lead technical manager for AIR who normally worked out of London, Malcolm wanted to be at the Montserrat McCartney session to have the chance to work with one of his musical heroes. He asked Geoff Irons, Montserrat technician at the time, if it would be ok if he relieved him of his duties. Geoff, a team player whose supervisor happened to be Malcolm, gladly relinquished his role and Malcolm slid into the position for the session.

The logistics of getting Paul, his family, guest stars, and his plethora of musical gear to the island was difficult. It was on a much larger scale than a normal client. To help facilitate the entry into Montserrat, Steve flew over to Antigua to meet everyone and to usher them onto a plane bound for Montserrat with Jan waiting at the island airport to greet them on arrival. Steve stayed behind to deal with the "hard bit": air lifting four tons of equipment from Antigua over to Montserrat. It took multiple flights back and forth to Montserrat and full lorries between the airport and the studio to get all of Paul's gear to the island, not to mention the reams of customs paperwork involved.

Steve described how he met Paul for the first time: "So I walked in several hours after Paul was there and they were all in the lounge having some drinks. And I walked in and George [Martin] went 'Ahh. Here's Steve now.' Paul gets up and comes over and says, 'Hello Steve. I'm Paul McCartney. I'm really pleased to meet you.' And I laughed, "Well, yeah. I know you're Paul McCartney. [Steve laughed as he delivered the line.] I mean, that's how he was. 'I'm Paul' like I didn't know. That's the way he was."

Maureen Hodd told me the legend of Paul's reaction to taking a view of the island for the first time. She said that he and his family had rented a large villa on the island called Providence Estate and arrived at the property in the evening after a long day's travel. It was after dark and after a bite to eat, he went to bed. When he woke the next morning and opened the doors, he was greeted with a spectacular view of the tropical hills below the villa that ran down to the blue Caribbean waters. He said, "Oh my God! I've died and gone to heaven."

With the death of John still in the news, a heightened level of security was called for. A UPI news article reporting on the session said that the island police increased security on the island, fearing that there might be an attempt on the life of one of the remaining Beatles who might arrive on the island. In the article, a police spokesman was quoted as saying, "The possibility that some deranged foreigner may attempt to repeat the Lennon tragedy cannot be ruled out." Another news article said that local security was beefed up with eight private security guards arriving from New York and Ringo showed up on the island with his own security force, but it was all for naught. This was Montserrat and it was quickly apparent to Paul that the high level of security was not needed. Soon, he would be traveling around the island on his own without a security guard in sight.

Speaking of Ringo's arrival, Steve says that Paul insisted that they go to the airport to greet Ringo when he landed. You must remember that Montserrat's air terminal consisted of a single small building next to a short landing strip. Greeting someone on arrival is as easy as pulling up at the airport and standing next to the landing strip with no security or barriers. Jan set the scene: "We all went to the airport. [Paul] insisted that all of the families, our family, their family, all went to the airport to meet Ringo and we had to act like screaming fans. We all had to scream when Ringo came off [the plane.]" While waiting for the plane, everyone is facing east, looking east towards Antigua in anticipation of the plane on the horizon. Paul turned to Steve and said, "So where is Antigua?" The island was clearly visible from the where they were standing at the airport. With a deep level of sarcasm, Steve said to Paul, "'Well, it's there between the sky and the sea.'" Steve continued, "And he just goes Whack! around the back of my head. You could talk to him like that. He was cool."

Paul became integrated with the island culture quickly. Before long, he could be seen driving himself around the island in one of the open-aired Minimoke cars. If he came across someone needing a ride, he would gladly lend a hand. Local Rose Willock told me the story of her encounter with Paul:

"One time I was walking down somewhere and this chap stops next to me and says 'Want a ride?' [I said] 'Sure!' When I sat in [the car], I looked at him and said 'Oh wait. You're Paul McCartney, aren't you?' And he says, 'Uh huh.' And I just left it like that because I recognized him. He was driving somewhere and just offered me a ride. And that was it! [I wasn't like], 'Oh my God!' We're not like that in Montserrat." Paul and his wife Linda could be seen strolling through Plymouth, shopping, and taking in the local flavor. This was one of the major advantages for famous artists such as Paul. Here was Paul McCartney, one of the most famous musicians in the world, only weeks from John Lennon's death, able to move around in public without being hounded by the press and fans. Steve told me that the proprietor of the local t-shirt shop came to him and asked when Steve was going to bring Paul by the shop so the owner could meet him. Steve replied, "Actually, he was here yesterday. [He] went down and bought a whole load of t-shirts...him and Linda." The shop owner was shocked: "That was Paul McCartney? No shit!"

Wonder-ful

Paul invited fellow superstar musician Stevie Wonder to come to Montserrat and collaborate on some songs for the new album. He recorded two songs with Paul including the international smash hit, "Ebony and Ivory." The impact that Stevie Wonder had on the island cannot be understated. He was universally loved by Montserratians because he was extremely talented, a warm person, and black like most of the islanders. Malcolm Atkin said, "Stevie Wonder going down to that island was just magic" and Steve Culnane, who came back to the studio in 1983, said, "The biggest thing that happened as far as AIR Studios was concerned [for] the Montserratian people was when Stevie Wonder came over with Paul McCartney. They were still talking about it 2 years later...Such a major thing to happen to the island." I was told many stories about Stevie's trip to Montserrat. Here are a few of them.

When Stevie arrived on the island, he brought a large entourage of managers, lawyers, and handlers. Steve Jackson said that Stevie and his group were in the studio control room "blathering about" while Paul was in the main performance room, tinkling about on the Bosendorfer piano. Realizing that the entire reason that Stevie is here is to work with Paul and not to hang out in a control room with lawyers, Steve took Stevie by the arm and said, "C'mon. Let's get out of here", leading him into the studio performance room with Paul. He led Stevie to the piano bench where Paul was waiting and introduced the two, "Stevie. This is Paul. Paul, this is Stevie. Listen. You do what you do. I'm going to go into [the control room] and sort that out." Paul saw the commotion through the control room window and said, "Yeah. I think you better." Steve came into the control room and said to the suits, "Gentleman. Those two guys in there are going to make your salaries for the next five years. Let's take this somewhere else", leading them back to the villa and leaving the talented twosome to work their art. Steve said, "That's what we had to do."

There was a washroom on the main floor of the studio villa that everyone would use regularly. It was located behind the manager's offices. Each morning, Jan would be working in the office and Stevie would go into the bathroom and warm up his voice before recording. She said, "It was like I had died and gone to heaven."

Malcolm remembered being serenaded by Stevie one evening. "We're all having dinner together up there [at the studio.] And [Stevie] says, 'Can you bring my piano up on the balcony? I'll play a couple of songs after dinner.' And blow me, he sat there for two and a half hours as the Caribbean sun's going down. Stevie Wonder on a Fender Rhodes. Played the lot to an audience of ten of us...McCartney was in the corner, just playing the bongos. It was brilliant."

Another evening, everyone is gathered around the villa dining room table, having an after-meal coffee. Steve Jackson said that Stevie was quite the raconteur, weaving tales and leaving everyone in stitches. In the middle of the story, Stevie, who is blind, got up from the table and excused himself to use the restroom. He started heading toward the washroom without a handler to assist him. Steve Jackson, realizing that there is a flight of steps between the dining room patio and the washroom, started to panic and jumped up to help him. As Stevie reached the top of the stairs, he surprised everyone by deftly leaping over them, landing on the floor below. He turned to the dinner guests and said, "You all don't think I can see, do you?" and continued on his way. Everyone at the table was in shock. Although Stevie was blind, his ability to memorize the space around him and navigate using his other senses was amazing.

Both engineer Mike Stavrou and Malcolm Atkin recalled a story from the Tug of War session that could have had a shocking end: Stevie had brought a Linn drum machine to Montserrat with him. This was one of the first great sounding commercial drum machines available. He used it to create a rhythm pattern to use as a guide for one of the songs they were working on. Suddenly, halfway through the song, the Linn stopped working. Stevie came into the control room and asked one of his helpers to open the drum machine for him. They hand Stevie the opened drum machine with all its wiring and circuits exposed...and it powered on! Stevie tells everyone, "I got it. I got it" and starts pressing on various components inside the Linn. The AIR staffers in the room, including Malcolm, George Martin, and Mike were looking at each other in astonishment, imagining the newspaper headline, "Stevie Wonder gets electrocuted at AIR Montserrat," but they cannot say anything. "It's Stevie Wonder." Mike said. "The level of respect that everyone had for each other would have made it inappropriate to slap his hand and stop him." Malcolm had to intervene to save Stevie from electrical shock: "We took the lid off and he started tapping things inside. I did actually push him off at one point as he was getting very close to the high voltage wiring. I retreated to the workshop with it and eventually got it working again. No one had ever seen such a thing before and it was a big novelty."

Stevie cemented his place in the legends of Montserrat with an impromptu concert at a local club. Malcolm tells the tale: On a Monday night, around midnight, Stevie says, "Guys, I want to go downtown. Is there a nightclub?" They tell Stevie about The Agouti nightclub in Plymouth. Knowing it was close to closing time, Steve Jackson made a call to the club and asked them if they could stay open so Stevie could come down and play. The club was glad to indulge Stevie's need to perform live. The house band, The Agouti Brothers (local Errol Eid on drums), was on stage at the time and Stevie went up to them asking if they would be open to have him sing a few numbers with them. Of course, they welcomed the opportunity to perform with a living legend like Stevie Wonder. A number of the band members were American and they knew how to play many of his songs. Malcolm said, "It went from about a handful of people in The Agouti at midnight...Word went around the medical school and within about 45 minutes, there must have been 400 people in there. Stevie Wonder, live on stage and it's going crackers." Stevie improvised a song about Montserrat while playing on stage about what a wonderful time he was having: "The people here are so friendly. The staff at the studio are wonderful. You are going to see my black face around here again." Malcolm continues: "And then he starts singing this Montserrat chant and the whole lot's going. The whole place is stomping...He became an absolute overnight legend. Here we are 40 years later still talking about it." Malcolm says that he still has a cassette recording of the concert. Others had made recordings of that night as well and I was told that this impromptu concert was replayed on the local island radio station for years.

One more Stevie Wonder story from Montserrat that personifies his immense musical talents. The studio coordinated a barbeque for Paul, Stevie, and the studio musicians. At the barbeque, a local steel band (also known as a pan band) was setup to play for everyone. Jan told me that "before we knew it, all the guys were playing with the band." Paul was playing drums and Stevie, who had never played a pan before in his life, was up on stage, wanting to play one. Barman Desmond Riley remembers Stevie saying, "I've got to have a go at this." Desmond called the leader of the pan band over and told him that Stevie wanted to try the steel drums. The band leader said to bring him over. Desmond again: "So his [helper] took him over. They put him behind the drums. It's unbelievable what I saw. He picked the notes and started playing. Just like that. It was unbelievable...People went mad!"

When reflecting on McCartney's session, Jan and Steve described it as "the worst session...and the best." The pressure was immense, so immense that Steve remembers one moment where he was especially upset and Malcolm grabbed him by the arms and told him, "You're thinking about committing murder. Steve, you WILL be a murderer." On the other hand, Steve got to meet one of his musical heroes and have both of their families have some great times together on the island.

Tug of War went on to top the charts around the world and sell millions of copies, reaching platinum and gold sales milestones in many countries. This was the first blockbuster release from AIR Montserrat but far from the last.

SYNCHRONIZING GHOSTS

The Police headed to Montserrat in June of 1981 to record their fourth record, "Ghost In The Machine." According to various sources, including the autobiographies of drummer Stewart Copeland and guitarist Andy Summers, the band were entering a very tumultuous time in their history. The intense pressure of their fame was taking its toll. Andy's marriage was about to end. Sting, as the main song writer for the band, started exerting more and more control over the arrangements of the music which did not sit well with the other two members of the band, especially Stewart. This would come to a head when they came back to record their final album, "Synchronicity" less than two years later.

Drumming In The Living Room

One of the unique aspects of The Police's sessions at AIR Montserrat was that Stewart recorded his drums, not in the studio, but in the living room of the studio villa, immediately behind the studio manager's quarters. Producer Hugh Padgham said, "The biggest problem for me was getting there and discovering really that I didn't think I was going to get the sort of drum sound that I wanted to get in the actual studio room. It was kind of a bit too dead really and so that's when we did this whole thing of moving the drums out to the dining [and living] room area which was semi-open and it had a nice bright acoustic [resonance] which made it much easier and better to get a drum sound there." The studio design of having a "dead sound" that had been so fashionable in the 1970s was falling out of favor by the early 1980s. Hugh was part of the production team that developed the big, booming "gated drum" sound that is featured on many Peter Gabriel, Phil Collins, and Genesis records of the time. Phil's "In The Air Tonight" is the quintessential example of this drum sound. The gated drum sound needed the reflective properties of hard surfaces and although this particular technique was not used on The Police's records, the lesson Hugh learned of using a live sounding room had come into fashion. So, when Hugh found that the Montserrat studio had a very acoustically dead room, he moved the drums to where the acoustics fit his musical sensibilities, the villa living room. The stone fireplace and hard walls of the room gave the drums the "presence" that Hugh was looking for. While providing a great space for recording drums, this set up had its own challenges. A mass of long cables had to be run from the studio to the villa in order to connect the large number of microphones needed for recording a drum kit. While the studio was acoustically sealed to keep the loud sounds of a band recording from disturbing the surrounding neighbors, the living room had none of this. In fact, it had many windows that where open for ventilation. The sound of Stewart's drums would echo across the valley. I was told that when Stewart's drum technician was setting up the kit, people on The Belham Valley golf course could hear the drums, which were over a mile away. Also, the villa did not have air conditioning so recording in the early summer in the Caribbean was a very hot endeavor. Stewart had issues with slippery drum sticks and hot headphones while recording, with Hugh trying to help the situation by taping the headphones to Stewart's head with gaffer's tape. An obvious answer to this problem would be to avoid the heat by recording at night but the island would not allow it. Hugh said, ""Because [the room] was semi-open, we couldn't record at night because at night, all of the tree frogs came out, woke up, and they sound...LOUD! We literally couldn't record the drums at night at all." Another major issue was communication between Stewart, who was in the villa, and Hugh with the other band members in the studio control room. Hugh explained: "The biggest problem was, in those days, that there wasn't nearly such a good sort of audio/visual vibe in terms of equipment. So we put up a camera so that we could see Stewart but he couldn't see us. We didn't have enough stuff to do that. Of course, this problem only arose after we got there so it was really difficult. We repeated the whole thing two years later. I mean, it was quite fun to start with. When I say 'Fun,' Stewart was very game for it, he wasn't sort of complaining in any way. But the frustration, which got harder for him, was the fact that the only way he could hear us was us opening the talkback and speaking through the headphones. So if it got to the end of the take and somebody didn't turn the headphone switch down straight away, he didn't know what was going on. And I must say, I really take my hat off to him because it was very frustrating."

Having Stewart in the living room also presented a challenge for the staff who had to work around his recording schedule. Since the living room was adjacent to both the kitchen and manager's offices, problems arose from staff going about their daily duties of prepping meals and cleaning the facility. Lloyd Francis said, "What [Stewart] don't realize, people there never understand how recording works. The workers there would not understand. But he felt that they should understand. So they come in and...pull the door or people talking. Then they would try to tell [that] the artists are recording...but the people don't know that if you talk, it will pick it up." Their interruptions led to more than one outburst from Stewart who was not in a great headspace due to the band's ongoing internal strife.

Scaring The Children

Jan Jackson told me a story about a scary moment during the session: "When The Police played, Stewart had his drum kit setup in the living room...my son was obsessed with this drum kit. He was two. Totally obsessed with it. Dylan was in the office and as Dylan walked out of the office, Stewart hit his drum kit really hard. Bear in mind, Stewart's got a pair of headphones [on] so you don't hear [the playback] and then he gets to the bit where he's got to come in and 'BANG!' Scared Dylan so bad, he peed his pants. And after that, he wouldn't go anywhere near Stewart and Stewart felt really, really bad. So eventually, Stewart grabbed him and said, 'C'mon, I don't want you to be afraid' and sat with him behind the drum kit and they played the drums [together.] He gave [Dylan] some sticks, which I've still got!"

Bouncing To the Beat

With Stewart setup in the living area of the villa and Sting recording his bass in the control room, Andy was the lone person in the main recording room. The floating floor of the control room was a problem due to Sting's enthusiastic performances. Hugh explained: "He had this like a mini trampoline. It's called a jogging mat. And he used to have that in the control room and he'd be bouncing up and down on it while he was playing the bass with the band going on. And the whole floor, everything was shaking because it was a floating floor. It was sprung. Literally, everything, the machines were almost bouncing around as well and you'd say, 'Look, Sting. Without being a killjoy. It's a bit of a problem.' 'Oh fuck off,' he'd say. 'I'll do what I want to do.'"

Bumpy Flight

After they finished the session for "Ghost In The Machine," the band was leaving the island to go directly Caracas to play a concert. They needed a plane large enough to carry the band, crew, and their gear to Venezuela but small enough to fly out of the island's airport. An old DC-3 was contracted by their manager to deliver the band to Caracas. Everyone and everything was loaded into the cabin of the plane since it had no cargo hold. The plane looked worse for wear but the band climbed aboard anyway. As they flew towards South America, they hit a bit of bad weather and the plane was battered with turbulence. Suddenly, the emergency exit door was torn from the plane! The cabin was swirling with the rush of wind and a loss of pressure but there was nothing that could be done but continue the flight. Luckily, no one was injured but it was quite a harrowing experience.

Not In Sync

When The Police returned to Montserrat to record their follow up record, 'Synchronicity,' the personal problems between the band members were peaking. The magic was waning. Hugh explained: "On the...Synchronicity session, we were there working every day, pretty well every day, for two weeks when we got there and we did not have one, kind of what I would call, piece of music to play. It was that bad. There was a meeting called and [Police manager] Miles [Copeland] flew in...and the meeting cumulated in 'Are we going to stay together and make an album now or shall we call it quits now?' Literally break the band up now. It was that bad and everybody said 'Nope. We're going to make it.' And therefore, we then went back in and dogmatically struggled to make the album. In a way, the bliss of being in this wonderful exotic and romantic or whatever place wasn't kind of there the same way as it was on the first album. Especially from my point of view. I remember going into the office because you didn't have mobile phones or anything in those days. I remember going into the office and ringing up my manager going, 'I'm not sure if I can handle this anymore." It was that bad."

Regardless of the difficulty of the recording process, Synchronicity was a blockbuster release for the band. The band broke up after the ensuing worldwide tour, but Sting's love for Montserrat would continue. He returned to vacation on the island, one of which holidays resulted in him being asked to sing backup on Dire Straits' huge hit song "Money for Nothing." I was told that some of the demos for Sting's for first solo album were recorded at AIR Montserrat and that he used local island vocalists as backup singers. Sting also mixed his live album, "Bring on the Night" at the studio in 1986 and returned once again to record "...Nothing Like The Sun" in 1987. AIR engineer Ken Blair told me a story from the "...Nothing Like The Sun" sessions: "When all of the flight cases and equipment arrived, it wasn't just musical instruments. We opened these flight cases and there was a kind of Aladdin's Cave of really amazing early valve microphones which all looked like they'd just came out of the packing and yet they were mics from the 50s, 60s, [and] 70s...We [Ken and producer Neil Dorfsman] hung this metal bar which I think we had taken off a mic stand...and we hung it from some rope from the ceiling of the studio. Then from that bar, we hung about 4 or 5 valve microphones. Sting could stand in front of those and he could have all 5 routed to the tapes and we'd record them all and compare one from the other and then choose the one that sounded best. There were always interesting things like that going on."

ELTON

Elton John was enamored with Montserrat, so much so that he returned to record three albums in three years at the studio: Jump Up in 1982, Too Low for Zero in 1983, and Breaking Hearts in 1984. Barman Franklyn Allen said that the thought that, out of all the artists he served at AIR Montserrat, Elton "enjoyed himself to the fullest, more than anybody else." Not only did Elton love the island and its people but the staff at the studio and Montserratians loved Elton back. When I asked Desmond Riley about Elton, he said, "Elton John. Oh my God...I can't even put words to describe this man. This man is so...how to put it? I love him. Put it that way. He's genuine. He's not like putting on or showing off. He's just genuine." Steve Jackson said, "He was a lot of fun. He kept on going up to Janet saying, 'How's my baby?' (Jan was pregnant at the time.)...He was cool. Very, very kind person...Couldn't be nicer."

Delivered From Temptation

The decision for Elton to record in Montserrat was initially made to help him through some personal issues that were causing problems during a recording session. In 1982, he was working on a new album with producer Chris Thomas in Paris, France. Chris said that the session was "not going very well at all. It was very, very slow...Elton was going through various sort of problems then, addiction problems." Elton bravely talks about his addictions and depression in his excellent autobiography entitled "Me" which I highly recommend if you want a deeper insight into what he was going through during this period of his life. Chris was very frustrated with how the session was progressing so one particular Monday, Chris rang up Elton's manager John Reid in the U.K. and told him that, "This is a nightmare. I'm going home. I'm going back to England. There's just no point." John told him to hold tight, that he was going to fly out to Paris and get things sorted. A meeting was convened the next day, Tuesday, and everyone went home, albeit only briefly. During that week, a decision had been made that the session was moving to AIR Montserrat and by Friday, the planes landed on the island with Elton, Chris, and the band. Chris told me that the choice of Montserrat was made because of its isolation from normal life. He said, "The whole idea was to get away somewhere that was away from, sort of, temptation."

Montserrat was the perfect place for Elton to mellow out and concentrate on his music. The lack of readily available vices and the laid-back vibe of the island helped Elton decompress and concentrate on his creative process. Lloyd "X" Francis had been hired to build a pond at the studio. Frogs lived in the pond and X said that Elton and John Reid would spend time at the pond, relaxing and reflecting while watching the frogs hop and listening to their croaking. Chris said that Elton and his personal assistant Bob would drive around together on the island in open air Minimoke vehicles looking like "a couple of old dears going shopping." Regarding the island's effect on recording, Chris said that the calm of the island "just concentrated everything because there was nothing else to do but work." A strong work ethic and regular routine fell into place. The lack of nightly distractions was welcome according to Chris: "Instead of all the...side attractions [you would have] if you were someplace like Paris, there were no distractions. Where in other places, there are distractions, left, right, and center. That was the main thing. More than anything else." Chris described the routine: "We would start working early. The band would arrive 10 o'clock in the morning and Elton would be there earlier than that because he would be writing. And I would get there earlier as well, so we were setup to record at 10 o'clock and we would go through to about 8 o'clock at night." They would stop for lunch midday and call it a night after dinner at the studio villa. "Everyone is pretty much onsite the whole time...It kept everything together so you were there for a very short time, but you worked very efficiently."

Security Detail

With the heightened level of exposure and security of Paul McCartney's Tug of War session fresh in everyone's minds, Elton's personal manager was approached for additional security, according to AIR manager Steve Jackson. There had been some history of using the local police for additional help with studio operations occasionally but not for Elton's session. One day, Elton's personal assistant, Bob Halley came to Steve quite agitated. He said, "Where is this all going to end? We are coughing out all this money!" Steve was confused since he knew what costs were being billed for the session. Steve asked Bob what this money was being spent for. Bill said it was for security services from the local police. Steve said to him, "You don't need security. You're fine." Bill asked, "But what if we go somewhere?" Steve replied, "No one is going to bother you...Don't worry about it." "But we've just paid all of this money and they're now asking for more," Bill complained. Steve was not happy with the situation because not only was a client being harangued for security services they did not need, but also because it was being done without his knowledge or consent. Steve went down to see the police commissioner exclaiming, "You are not taking money off of my clients!" The police commissioner was confused. He had no idea what Steve was talking about. He had not offered Bob any security detail. Steve said to him, "Well, somebody is because they are complaining to me." After some investigation, it was determined that the assistant police commissioner was running this scam unbeknownst to the head of police. The police commissioner called the assistant commissioner into his office, demanding that the assistant commissioner return the money he had collected from Elton for the unwarranted "security services." With the money returned, Steve made sure that he would be immediately notified if anyone else approached Bill looking for payment for services that did not come through the studio.

Food Fight

One night during the Jump Up sessions, there was a massive food fight in the studio villa dining room. Steve said that, "Food was everywhere!...It was ridiculous." Chris Thomas and Elton took a trash can full of vegetable clippings, which Steve referred to as "pig swill", and dumped it over Steve's head. Rum punch was spilled all over the dining room floor. When it was all over, Elton went to leave to head back to his private villa. Steve said to him, "Where the fuck do you think you're going?...You caused this. You're going to help me clean it up!" And Elton, being the genuine person he is, did indeed help Steve and the staff clean up the mess. He grabbed a broom and started sweeping the floor. Desmond Riley said that Elton made amends to one of the cleaning staff for the mess. He said, "Irene [housecleaning staff] got some pie all over her. [Elton] gave her his coat. That jacket cost about £5000. He gave it to her as an apology." After the mess was cleaned up and the musicians had left, it became apparent that the floor finish had been ruined. The rum punch had eaten off much of the floor wax in the dining room. When he saw the remaining wax, Steve joked to Franklyn, who was tending bar, that he might want to make some more rum punch so that they could remove all the floor wax since it was so effective. Steve said that post food fight, they varnished the floors so that the finish would be impervious to any subsequent alcoholic assaults.

Dropping Like Flies

Elton's hit song, "I'm Still Standing", had an interesting genesis story as told to me by Chris. This was the first session that the original Elton John band had been together since the mid-1970s. During the "Too Low For Zero" sessions, the band was having health issues. "Poor old Dee Murray [bassist] had cancer. He had good days and bad days." One day, Dee was not feeling well and could not come into the studio for a day or two. Guitarist Davey Johnstone had flown into Montserrat sick with the flu and had "a temperature of 100 and God knows what." Elton and Chris had arrived early to the studio and were hoping to do something productive that day. The phone rang and they were told that Nigel Olsson, the drummer, was ill and was not going to come in that day. All the key members of Elton's band were down for the count. Chris recalled that Elton said to him in the control room, "For fuck's sake, what's happening to everybody? They are all dropping like flies!" Suddenly, they see a huge plume of smoke rise from between the Neve console and the glass of the main recording room. An anonymous voice came through the smoke saying, "Well, I'm still standing." Elton and Chris hit the deck, howling with laughter. It was Adrian Collie, Elton's logistics and studio coordinator, rising through the smoke and declaring that he was "still standing." Chris said that Elton "dragged himself off the floor a few minutes later and phoned up Bernie [Taupin, Elton's lyricist] and said, 'I've got the title for a song I want you to write the lyrics for.'" The rest is history. The song became a massive worldwide hit in early 1983.

Village Place

Andy's Village Place was a small bar and restaurant located in Salem, less than a mile from the studio. Also known as "The Chicken Shack," it was quite popular with the locals on the island and was described as "The life of Salem" by X. Elton loved Andy's and it became a mainstay for Elton to let off steam and "let his hair down." He would dance to the Soca music played over the bar's sound system and would open the bar and give everyone free drinks. X remembers him giving away his sunglasses and jackets to locals who were having a great time with Elton.

Chris Thomas told me on the story of Elton's introduction to "The Chicken Shack": Early one morning during the "Breaking Hearts" sessions, Chris had just woken up and was feeling quite groggy from the partying of the previous evening when Elton showed up at the door of Chris' villa. Elton asked where Chris had been to the night before to which he answered, "The Chicken Shack." Elton was intrigued. Chris took a detour on the way to the studio to show Elton the bar. Chris continues the story: "We went by and it is nothing but a little tin shack with a bit of corrugated on top of it." Elton exclaimed, 'I love places like that. Nobody ever invites me to places like that.' Later in the afternoon, Elton declared that that, 'We are all going to the Chicken Shack tonight!'" Chris and Elton spent the evening together in the bar when Chris suddenly realized that it was getting quite late. He wanted to get some sleep before the next day's session, so he grabbed a ride home with a local who promptly drove Chris' rental into a ditch. The next morning, Chris met Elton at the studio. Elton, quite bubbly from the evening prior, said to Chris, "Oh. That was fantastic. That was the best night of my life. I had the best time ever!" Chris was surprised and asked when Elton had gone home. "About 4 or 5 o'clock," he replied. But that was not the only surprise. Elton proceeded to tell Chris, "I asked Renate to marry me." [Renate Blauel was an AIR recording engineer, the only female engineer at the time.] Chris was flabbergasted and did not believe Elton. This was completely out of the blue and even more odd since Chris knew Elton was gay. Only hours later, after Elton kept insisting that he was serious, did the news finally sink in for Chris. Until the engagement was officially announced in Australia later, only Elton, Renate, Chris, and an AIR tape operator were privy to this important step in Elton's life.

Elton's love for Andy's started a long-term trend of Andy's Village Place becoming a mainstay hang out for the artists who came to AIR Montserrat as well as the AIR staff members who came to work at the studio.

Other than Sting, Elton is the only artist to return to Montserrat more than twice. He clearly loved the vibe of the island and its people. AIR Montserrat gave him the perfect place for creativity as he was seeking to revitalize his career in the early 1980s.

BROTHERS IN ARMS

In 1984, Dire Straits was planning on recording their new album in Montserrat. That album, Brothers In Arms, would spawn multiple hits worldwide such as "Money for Nothing," "Walk of Life," and "So Far Away." Released in May 1985, it would go on to sell over 30 million copies and would have the distinction to be the first album to sell one million copies on the new-at-the-time compact disc media format.

When Mark Knopfler, Dire Straits' guitarist, lead vocalist, and principal songwriter, approached producer Neil Dorfsman about recording overseas, Neil was excited. Neil told me, "When I got into the business, I sort of [had a] mental list of places I always wanted to work and one of them was Power Station in New York, and then one of them was AIR London. And I had heard about Montserrat, but I thought there was no way. I'm never going to get to work there. So when Mark said, 'What do you think about recording in the Caribbean?' I was like 'Yeah!' I had no idea what the studio was like. All I knew was that it had a vintage Neve console and that was enough for me...So when he suggested that, I was like 'Yeah! Please, man! That sounds amazing.' Turned out to be quite a challenge but I'm happy we got to do it." Arriving in November, they had no idea that it was going to take three months to complete their blockbuster album.

Dire Straits' technician, Ron Eve, remembered arriving on the island and finding out how isolated they were from a technical standpoint. He said, "We quickly realized that we were stuck with what we had [on hand], which in hindsight was absolutely fine." Because speakers and full-sized organs were quite heavy, "we were told to keep the weight down because it was vastly expensive. And we were told there were speakers there...We took out the expensive keyboards [but] they had a Hammond [organ] there and a Leslie which I fixed. I had it in pieces at one point to get it working properly. That was fine. They thanked me for that. AIR Studios...Back then, you just did what you had to do. Make it work."

Band Technician Ron Eve Repairs The Studio Leslie Organ
Photo: Frank Oglethorpe

As the band arrived on the island, studio manager Yvonne Kelly was leaving. She was heading back to England to give birth to her first child. Her husband Malcolm stayed behind to manage the studio in her absence. Coincidentally, it turned out that Malcolm had grown up only three miles from where Straits' keyboardist Alan Clark lived as a child. Alan said, "In fact, from my bedroom window, I think I could see his house across the valley."

New Fangled Tech

One of the unique aspects of the Brothers In Arms sessions was the arrival of a Sony DASH 3324 24-track digital tape recorder to the studio. At the time, AIR Montserrat only had 24-track analog tape machines available for artists. Mark liked the lossless, high-quality sound of Sony's digital tape machine so he brought one of the 440 pound, $150,000 recorders to the island with him. The problem for the technicians on site was that no one had ever used or serviced one of these units before and replacement parts were days and thousands of miles away. Frank Oglethorpe, AIR technical manager at the time, was quite nervous when he saw the Sony 3324 roll into the studio for the first time. If something went wrong, he would be responsible for getting it up and running again. He was hoping Ron Eve might be familiar with the unit. Ron said, "Frank was just fantastic. I used to play jokes on him mercilessly because when I arrived, he obviously had no information about the Sony 3324 at all. So when I arrived and we were setting it up, and he said...I didn't know Frank until this point. He said 'Do you know about the machine? You know how it works?'" Frank distinctly remembers Ron's reply to him. Ron said, "You're fine. What I don't know about this tape machine would fit on a postage stamp." Frank said that this significantly lowered his anxiety about having to care for this critical and unknown piece of gear. Little did Frank know, "It was a complete lie," Ron laughed as he told me this. Ron had tinkered with the DASH machine during rehearsals but knew little of its technical operations. "I let him believe it for a while. He's never forgiven me for that one, actually. But from then on, we were best of mates."

Football Finger

Before tape started rolling on the session, Frank almost unintentionally ended it. The band headed down to the beach to have some fun and decided to play some American flag football. To those unfamiliar with the game, it is like standard American football but with the exception that tackling is not allowed. Flags are placed on either side of the waist and instead of tackling an opponent with the ball, you simply pull one of the flags from the ball carrier's hips to stop the action. Frank, who had only had experience playing rugby, did not understand the rules and promptly tackled Mark when he got the ball, bringing him down to the sand hard, injuring the finger of the esteemed guitarist. Luckily for Frank (and Dire Straits fans), it only turned out to be a temporary sprain rather than a break and Mark was able to start playing again soon afterward.

To NYC And Back Again

The session was originally scheduled for six weeks with the intention of wrapping up recording by late December and then moving the session to New York for mixing at the Power Station. As the session entered into December, it was apparent that things were not going well. Ron said, "They thought they would have the album on the bag at that point...But we got to the end of the time in November and there was virtually nothing in the can." For one thing, the Sony DASH tape machine was having issues. Ron again: "We started to get dropouts on the Sony. Stuff disappearing...We couldn't figure it out. Searching for problems. Calling out Sony. Everything. And it transpired that it's the effect of the error correction in the Sony. If it didn't see the [error correction] bit quite properly, it would drop it out. And the way to cure it...get this. This is the weirdest bit which we found out after a little while was to copy the tape to another Sony and by copying it to another tape, it cured it. Against all reason, that's the cure...copy the tape to another machine and then you're fine. And of course, it's digital so there is no quality loss." So the solution was to copy the tape from one Sony DASH machine to another. I asked Ron if they had a second Sony DASH in Montserrat to copy the tapes to. Ron said, "No. [laughing] We had to ship the tapes to New York. Could you imagine how we felt about that? So these were the masters and someone had to go up to New York and copy them and bring them back. Pray nothing happens in the meantime." If they had been recording in New York or London, they would have simply had to rent a Sony DASH machine for a day to perform the copy but because they were in Montserrat, the critical original master tapes had to make a full round trip to New York and back to fix the problem with the error correction. Additionally, Ron said that there could be customs issues shuttling the tapes back and forth to New York. He told me, "If you told them they were master tapes, they would charge you tax. If you said they were backup copies, that was fine."

Band Tech Pete Brewis With John, Alan, and Ron In The Game Room
Photo: Frank Oglethorpe

The Rhythm Wasn't Right

Not only was the tape machine giving the band issues, but Mark and Neil were not getting the "feel" that they were looking for from the band's drummer, Terry Williams. Neil told me, "The way Mark was hearing the music at that point in his writing, it didn't seem like Terry was the right guy, even though he's a member of the band. So, from the very beginning I was sort of worrying, as I do, and also saying to Mark, 'This is not really holding together. It doesn't have the right feel, the right energy, the right orchestral aspect'...he's like 'No. No. It's fine. It's fine' and we kept going." But it was not fine. Ron remembers the situation: "The way Mark works in the studio is very different [than what Terry was used to.] [Terry] worked with people like Dave Edmunds, Rockpile, and so on where they would go into the studio and all play together and knock out the tunes. Mark doesn't work that way particularly. He builds tracks. He needs to start off with a drum track which I think Terry found very hard to get in his head with songs that he's not familiar with and they're not just rock and roll songs. Very different. And he struggled. I remember watching him in the studio. I was feeling really sorry for him." The band went on holiday at Christmas and while away, Mark made the decision that they had to bring in another drummer to get the feel right on the album. Neil continued, "I think Mark realized that this is not right. So

182

we had a little pow wow and we debated about what to do about it. We'd already cut the tracks with Terry with no click I might add. No click track! So we're screwed. We have to do all this over again." A click track is a rhythm click sound that is included on the recording so that the musicians have a rhythmic reference point to sync to when playing along with the track. The problem was that the plan was to re-record the drums which, without a click track in place, are the only rhythmic reference point in the recording. The drummer would have to base their playing on non-percussive references such as the guitars, vocals, and keyboards, which is a very difficult task. Neil knew he needed an extraordinary drummer to retrack the songs and he had an idea of who might be able to pull off this miracle. "I had the idea of getting Omar Hakim down who was, to me, the premier drummer of the time," Neil said. With the decision to bring in Omar made, Mark did not want to tell Terry that he was being replaced so he asked Neil to do it. Neil explained his feelings at the time: "The crazy thing...it was like diving into the deep end of being a producer for me...Mark wanted me to tell Terry it wasn't happening and he was going to be replaced. I had no bedside manner at that point. I didn't have enough experience to really know how to do that except to just straight up tell him. That was really painful for me and him. It was hard. Super hard... Made me hate being a producer." With only one flight a day coming in and out of the island and the tiny size of the airport, there was bound to be an awkward moment when Terry left Montserrat. Ron Eve remembers: "Terry was flying back to England and as he walked out onto the tarmac to the plane, Omar is coming in and they passed and it was like...excruciating. It must have been so bad for Terry."

With the new session drummer in the studio, the band was able to move forward, albeit way behind schedule. Neil said, "We got Omar in and [he] redid the drums to existing tracks without a click track. Now, we're [recording] over the original drums so if it wasn't right, we were triply screwed. And Omar came down and in two and a half days, redid all the drum parts to the existing band takes. Played without a click except for the intro to Money for Nothing which was Terry's tom tom tracks. So he basically, like my joke is, 'He saved the project.'...Effortlessly too. He did 'So Far Away From Me' in I think it was one take...I was like 'Oh my God! Thank you! There is a benevolent and loving God in the universe.' It was that kind of feeling."

I Want My MTV

During the session, Sting, from The Police, had come to Montserrat on a family vacation. He had made a connection to the island and its people far beyond the confines of AIR Montserrat while recording two albums with The Police. (He went on to record a solo album and mix a live album at AIR Montserrat a few years later.) While on the island, he went to AIR Studios to have dinner with the band. After hearing a rough mix of the song "Money For Nothing," Mark invited him to add some vocals to the track. He can be heard singing harmonies with Mark throughout the song and he also contributed the classic line "I want my MTV" sung to the melody of The Police's hit, "Don't

Stand So Close To Me." The addition of that single improvised line earned Sting a rare co-writing credit with Mark...and a share of the song's profits.

Roundtrip To Redonda

The guys in the band did the normal things that artists do on the island for entertainment: BBQs on the beach in Little Bay, nights hanging out at Andy's Village Place, and hiking to the waterfall and the Soufriere. But what really caught on with keyboardists Alan Clark and Guy Fletcher was windsurfing. Guy and Alan were sharing a villa on the island and had a spectacular view of the Caribbean Ocean west of Montserrat where they could see the boats and windsurfers riding along the horizon and the tiny uninhabited island of Redonda out in the far distance. Local islander Danny Sweeney ran a boat and windsurfing rental shop on the beach below the studio, and he gave lessons for sailing and windsurfing to those needing training with these activities. Alan remembers that the weather was awful the first few weeks they were on the island, so he jumped at the chance to get on the water once the weather cleared. He had experience with sailing, so he rented a dinghy from Danny. While out sailing, Danny came out on the water on a windsurfing board. Alan thought, "'OK. I'll give that a try.' That's how the windsurfing started." Alan and Guy went to Danny for lessons, and both proved to be rather adept at windsurfing which can be quite a difficult sport to master. It quickly became a cornerstone daily activity on the island for the keyboardists, whether day or night with the latter aided by headlights of cars parked on the jetty, lighting up the bay at midnight. Seeing the small island out in the distance, Alan used Redonda as a reference point for his daily windsurfing trips. He told me, "So every day, I would be sailing out in a direct line towards Redonda which is 18 miles away. And every day, I'd get more and more confident, and I'd go out about two miles or so...I'd sail towards Redonda for a half an hour or so and turn around and head back." Intrigued by the small island jutting above the horizon and knowing that the upcoming Sunday was a day off for the band, he came up with an insane idea. "I said to Danny, 'On Sunday, we're going to sail to Redonda' and he said, 'You're crazy, mon.' [I said again] 'You and I are going to sail to Redonda.' And that's what we did!" What you must keep in mind is how dangerous this trip can be. There are many dangers in the sea such as sharks, barracudas, and whales, not to mention the large waves and high winds. On a trip as long as this, weather can change quickly with terrible consequences not to mention the long exposure under the hot Caribbean sun while under heavy physical exertion. This would never be allowed by a record company handler if they had caught wind of this. (Pun intended.) Losing both of the band's keyboardists to an ocean-bound mishap during recording an album would present too much risk, but since Montserrat was so far from the prying eyes of Warner Brothers representatives, no one was there to stop them. Guy was concerned about his bandmates finding out, as he said on his website: "We set a day for this epic adventure and were careful not to let too many people know about it. I doubt if the rest of the band would have agreed to our endangering our lives in such a way, with a world tour approaching and a very expensive album in the making."

Guy And Alan Prepare For Their Adventure
Photo: Frank Oglethorpe

For the trip, Danny enlisted the help of his brother, a fisherman, who went by the moniker 'Englishman.' He would follow the group at a distance in his boat, available in case there was an emergency. Danny, Alan, Guy, and Danny's brother set sail from Little Bay on the north west side of the island. The trip to the island took several hours. As they were approaching the island, they took a break to rest and were sitting on their boards. Suddenly, there was a loud ear-splitting noise that startled everyone. A 30-foot whale was breaching the surface very close to the group! Alan recalls: "It just leapt out of the water right in front of me, between me and Danny. That was amazing...It kept coming right up to my board and rolling over and I could see its eye. At one point I could have jumped on its back, you know? It was that close. I got the distinct impression that it was very happy to see us." Being a seasoned sailor of the local seas, Danny had a different reaction to the whale encounter. He told me that he was thinking to himself, "Oh my god. I have brought these men down to be killed by a whale!" Danny's brother leapt into action, bringing the boat close to the whale, revving the motor to make a loud noise which drove the whale off. Crisis averted, they continued on, meeting up with some people on a catamaran on the far side of Redonda where they were invited onto the boat for lunch. Returning to the windsurfing boards, they headed back towards Montserrat.

Because the direction and speed of the wind is variable, luck had a hand in avoiding another crisis. Sunset was imminent as people on the shore saw the returning windsurfers on the horizon. Ron Eve: "We were all seriously worried because when we first spotted them. They were still quite a way out and we knew when the sunset was coming obviously." They made a bonfire on the beach at Fox's Bay to help guide them into the shore as dusk approached. Had the wind not cooperated, the trip could have taken hours longer and the group could have been lost at sea in the dark, but fate was with them that day and they returned to a beach BBQ unscathed. Ron said that "I hit the beach and it was like 'Jesus, guys! In the middle of recording an album? Crazy stuff!'" Guy said that their tour manager was waiting for them and gave them "an earful" for taking such a dangerous trip during the recording session. Regardless of the dressing down they received that day, it became a truly legendary tale for all involved. Ron said, "That was truly memorable. Really speaking, it was mad...People talked about it for years afterwards."

Heading Out With "Englishman" In Tow, Redonda Is On The Right
Photo: Frank Oglethorpe

Frogs

The song "Ride Across The River" had a distinct "island vibe" and Neil Dorfsman wanted to capture some of the local night sounds of Montserrat to include on the track. So late one evening, he and AIR assistant engineer Steve Jackson, along with Frank Oglethorpe hiked up to the waterfall below the volcano to record the unique evening chorus of the local tree frogs. With recording gear in tow, they trudged into the jungle in the middle of the night. I asked Neil what possessed him to go so far out into the wilderness in the dark to record these night sounds. The same frogs would be singing all around the studio and could have been recorded on the property. He said, "[It was] my obsessive nature. People had talked about the volcano and going up the volcano. I always wanted to do it. Not many people did. I wanted to experience the more raw jungly aspect of Montserrat. And just the challenge. It's funny because...we recorded it and when we got back, of course, our flashlights died on the way down which was treacherous." Frank said that he thought, "It was a badly prepared trip." Neil remembers, "Getting back down the mountain probably two in the morning...and calling up Andy [from Andy's Village Place.] 'Andy. Can you please open up and give us some beers and make some chicken for us and he got out of bed and did that. That was the vibe in the island. Like 'It's All Good.'" The next day, Neil presented the recording to Mark. The reaction was not what Neil was hoping for. Mark did not want to use it. He said that "It's corny." Neil told him, "Oh no. we're using this, dude. I don't care... People almost died for this." Neil said that, "You can tell in 'Ride Across The River' there's only like a 6 second break where you actually hear the tree frogs and just because I insisted."

Cover Shot

The iconic cover photo of Mark's 1937 Resonator guitar was shot by famous celebrity photographer Deborah Feingold. Frank remembers that the picture was captured over by the studio's generator shed, shot against the blue and pink Caribbean sky, the metal of the guitar reflecting the colors of the sunset and capturing the vibe of the session. Ironically, Deborah told me that the picture was not shot as a cover for the album. She had been contracted by Warner Brothers to shoot some publicity photos for the upcoming album so she flew down to Montserrat with her assistant. The band were working hard in the studio at the time and she recalled that she was having a difficult time getting Mark to stop recording long enough to take the publicity shots for the record company. She said, "I was just worried that days were going by. My ticket home was booked and I didn't have anything." One late afternoon, she headed up to the studio hoping to get some shots of the band but they were working so Deborah had some free time while she waited. Deborah said, "It was just a beautiful pink sunset and I went inside the studio where they were recording and I asked if I could photograph the guitar up against the sky...A roadie or someone held it up while I shot two frames and then they went back into the studio." The guitar shots helped ease the anxiety she was feeling "for about two seconds," she said. "Shooting that picture was a creative relief for me." She spent a few days on the island, taking photos of the band when they were available. When she returned home to New York, the film was developed. "I forgot that I had shot that and when the film came back...I saw the two frames [of the guitar] and I thought 'Oh, this is cool' so I kept one for myself and sent [the other] along with the publicity photos of the band." The next thing she knew, her impromptu "creative relief" photo was on millions of album covers around the world. She told me, "I never knew it was a cover until it was made the cover."

Money For Nothing

Although this is not a Montserrat specific bit of trivia, it is a session-specific bit of trivia to help clear up a bit of misinformation about the guitar sound on the track 'Money for Nothing." Stories about the iconic and unique guitar sound have been floating around the Internet for years so I wanted to find out what the real story was. People have speculated that it was a Laney amp or perhaps a Fender and that the sound was created by a lucky happenstance of microphone placement. Ron Eve set the record straight.

"It was a Marshall JTM45. Because it was mine. I took it out there because...we were short on gear," Neil told me. "We didn't take any speaker cabinets out there because we had Marshall 4x12 cabinets but they were fitted with EV speakers which made them really heavy. And I thought surely they were going to take at least one but they said 'No. Apparently there's speakers out there.' And I think it was a Laney cabinet...I'm sure that what it was. This is the confusion. But I'm absolutely certain there was no Laney amp and certainly not one used for that track because it was my JTM45 on that track because I set it up." Ron was assisting Mark get setup for the track. Ron continues, "So I said 'Any idea what sort of sound?' And Mark said 'Well, it's a sort of ZZ Top sound.' So 'Oh, OK' So I got the amp. Plugged it all in and the amp would have been on the floor so you would only see the cabinet. Probably another reason why [people have said] it was a Laney amp. And putting the mics up. They were just put there, just ready without any real placement. And of course, the wahwah pedal...As we kind of switched it on and Mark was playing and suddenly they shouted from the control room 'Stop, stop, stop! Don't touch anything! That's the sound.' So that was it. And so mics were not in the best position with the way Neil works. He always used several mics in different ways, in different angles, and different distances. And Neil, as I know, he always went in with a tape measure and measured stuff and drew diagrams of where everything was. He was an absolute persnickety. But then when they tried to reproduce it in New York, they couldn't. That's the story. It was a JTM45 which I eventually sold to Mark...The sound was a complete chance...this was just standard amp, guitar, speaker cabinet. Put some mics in front of it...I guess this is why I went on to be his tech but from what he said, he said 'That ZZ Top sound.' And I thought 'Oh. That's like when you are using a wahwah pedal in a stopped position.' So I did that and it all just came together in seconds. It was a complete accident."

So the real story of the Money for Nothing sound was Mark's guitar playing with a stopped wahwah pedal (for frequency filtering), through Ron's Marshall JTM45 amplifier into the studios' Laney speaker cabinet. Mics were not placed with any precision. They just happened to be sitting in the perfect place in the studios' main room during setup to get "that sound." A sound that was not reproducible when they tried it again in New York. Montserrat magic, you might call it.

Moving Out

After three months of recording, Dire Straits were ready to leave in February 1985. Alan Clark told me a story that summed up how long they were in Montserrat. He said, "There was a 45-foot yacht that broke its moorings and got washed up on the rocks. And we were there so long that...the insurance paid out and [the owners] turned up with a new one."

Ron told me a funny story about leaving the island that made him think he would never be able to. Ron: "I've got one last little story for you which is leaving the island. So my man Pete Brewis (Mark's guitar tech)...we were very good friends...When it came time to leave in the beginning of February, we packed everything up and it all went off. So we go down to the airport and we say goodbye to the staff at AIR and we get on the plane and fly to Antigua. We get to Antigua. We go up to get the plane back to London. The tickets were invalid. 'What?' 'This ticket back to England it is invalid.' It had expired. The tickets we had were for before Christmas...We hadn't really checked especially Pete and I coming off, we just assumed it's all organized. So this is about 8 o'clock at night on Antigua. So the plane goes. There's no plane 'til the following day. 'What am I going to do?' We phoned up Ed Bicknell the manager of Straits. Woke him up and said 'Um Ed. It's Ron' He said 'What is it Ron?' I said 'We're stranded' He said 'What do mean?' I said 'We're on Antigua. We tried to board the plane for London but they said our tickets are no good.' He said 'Just get a hotel. I'll sort it out.' So I went back to Pete. I said 'Hotel for the night.' We just picked a hotel and the next day, we had all day on the beach before [the flight.] So we basically had an extra day. But while we were on the beach that day, we ran into this very friendly chap that had a little smoke. And then we went back to the hotel to get ready and fell asleep. We woke up with like a half an hour to spare and we still had sand on our shoes. We were in swim costumes. We just grabbed our bags and ran to the airport with minutes to spare. It would have been very unpopular to have missed it for a second night. So Pete and I were laughing...we were laughing so loud. He said 'We're not destined to leave Montserrat.'"

With all of the fond memories of Montserrat and AIR Studios fresh on his mind, I asked Alan Clark if he had ever gone back to Montserrat after the Brothers In Arms session. He said that he had not. He conveyed a sentiment that was echoed by many of the people that I interviewed: "I've been back to the Caribbean quite a lot of times but I've never gone back to Montserrat. I think maybe I don't want to break that spell. It was just a magic time...I would rather remember it the way it was which was absolutely fantastic."

ARTISTS

S peaking with various artists and performers, I had many anecdotes and personal impressions of AIR Montserrat that did not fit perfectly into any particular chapter. These stories range from funny to sentimental and all captured the vibe of what it was like to work on the island. Rather than omitting these stories, here is a smattering of random vignettes into the lives of the artists who came to Montserrat to ply their craft.

A Beautiful Distraction

While the lack of a tourist economy limited the number of entertainment options for artists, some found the beauty of the island distracting in itself. Derek Holt from The Climax Blues Band said, "We were in, no word of a lie, it was paradise. What a beautiful island! The emerald island of the Caribbean they call it. To be sort of allowed to be at a place like that it's such wonderful surroundings, the jungle, the sea, state of the art facility, thousands of miles from anywhere. It was quite strange. I wouldn't say it was good from the point of view from the work ethic because it was just too beautiful. We used to say, 'Let's take a couple hours off. Let's go have a game of golf or something.'" Alan Clark from Dire Straits echoed Derek's sentiment when he recalled being in the studio, looking out the studio window across the Belham Valley: "I'd be looking at the bay and looking at the wind whipping up and watching the white caps on the water and thinking, 'I could be out there windsurfing!'" He also said this of Montserrat: "It's an island, so you have to get to it, but once you were there, you were stuck on it, pretty much, which is a nice thing."

Entertainment

The breezeway that connected the studio villa to the studio itself ran parallel to the pool. Its height and close proximity to the pool proved to be a great temptation to artists (and AIR staffers as well.) Many would climb to the roof of the breezeway from the patio above the pool and leap off into the pool.

Taking A Leap During A Luther Vandross Session
Photo: Frank Oglethorpe

Crab racing was another way to pass the time. Mo Foster, bassist for Sheena Easton and Gerry Rafferty, said they would capture crabs from the beach, place them under a container, and then lift the pot, allowing the crabs to race to freedom. He did not mention whether money was won or lost on wagers of whose crabs were victorious.

The TV and VCR in the living room was a hub for entertainment for the artists. Yvonne Kelly said that they bought "the biggest TV they could get." They had a massive library of videos available for viewing with new additions regularly sent from England. This allowed the artists to catch up on shows, movies, and music videos that they might have missed while on the road. Eventually, the studio got satellite TV but that was later in its history.

Prior to the studio getting its own satellite dish, the only way to receive overseas video feed was via rebroadcast. A local expatriate owned a satellite dish and had the equipment to rebroadcast the signal to those on the island who happened to have television, which was rare, especially in the early days

191

of the studio. The issue was that he could only rebroadcast what he was currently watching so locals were at his mercy as to his tastes in television programming. Also, if he decided to stop watching TV and go to bed, everyone else had to stop watching as well when he shut off his equipment.

Rush was on the island to record their album, Power Windows, in 1985. Hailing from Canada, the members of the band were rabid hockey fans. AIR staffer Matt Butler said, "They wanted to watch the hockey, of course. The ice hockey was a big thing and they were desperate, so actually they got in touch with him and paid him to keep the transmission going and they gave him a credit on the album." If you check the liner notes of Power Windows, he is credited as "The King of Antilles Television."

Foreign Food

Montserrat, culturally closer to a small colonial village in the 1800s than a modern city, had a very direct line from "farm-to-table." Much of the food served at the studio was harvested locally and that led to an eye-opening experience for one of the artists. Franklyn Allen said that a band told the studio manager that they wanted to have a big party. Studio chef Tappy Morgan told the band that if they want to have a real party, they need to have the locally famous dish, Goat Water, and a suckling pig for the event. This being Montserrat, instead of heading to the local market to pick up meat for the dishes, Franklyn headed to Spanish Point on the east side of the island to buy the ingredients for the meal: a live pig and goats, which would be slaughtered at the studio by Tappy in preparation for the party. Franklyn returned to the studio and tied them up on the grounds since the meal would not be prepared until later. When Tappy came to get the animals, he found that they were gone. The band members had found out that the "cute" animals were going to be their meal and were upset. Tappy said, "I was mad! [Franklyn] bought a pig and the guys [in the band] just says 'This is what we're going to eat?' They cut the pig loose. They cut the rope. We didn't even find the pig again...So I had to go do the menu over. Some of the guys wanted to have roast pig but it is a good thing for them not to see it." Culture shock gave the pig a new lease on life.

Two Grown Men

The island had its share of native life that found its way into the lives of the artists. An example of this was a story told to me by producer Chris Neil: "With Mike and the Mechanics, Mike [Rutherford] and I stayed in another house and we used to go [home] every night. We both have a thing about cockroaches, and on those islands, that's where they live. It has nothing to do with dirt. Beautiful house but we were both terrified. We'd have our shoes in hand and I'd go into his bedroom and look around for cockroaches. 'I can't see one. Ok. Come and check [my room]. We would check each other's bedrooms...Two grown men."

Eddie Jobson

Eddie Jobson is a keyboardist and violinist known for his virtuosic playing for groups such as Roxy Music, Frank Zappa, and the prog supergroup U.K. In 1987, he moved to Montserrat to compose and record the album "Theme of Mystery" which was a follow up to his 1985 all-Synclavier electronic music release "Theme of Secrets." Once again, this album was going to be recorded using the Synclavier synthesizer exclusively. The gigantic (by today's standards) Syclavier synthesizer system, which was over six feet tall and cost $200,000 USD, was shipped to the island and setup in a villa. Once Eddie had composed the music and programmed the Synclavier, the synthesizer was shipped up to AIR Montserrat and setup in the control room to record. Producer John Punter, who Eddie had worked with on albums with Bryan Ferry and Roxy Music, was flown in to assist Eddie in mixing the album. All this expense and work was for not. Eddie said, "For an assortment of reasons after the album was completed, I decided not to release it, get out of the record industry altogether, and focus instead on scoring soundtracks. I stayed on the island for three-and-a-half years composing music for movies, TV, and commercials." He told me of the toll that the island environment had on his equipment: "One technical issue that both the studio techs and I had to deal with was that the sulphur particles in the air from the Soufriere Hills volcano corroded the gold contacts in the electronic circuitry. I had to remove the circuit boards from the Synclavier computer tower regularly and clean the contacts with an eraser." When I asked him about how the island affected his creative process, he said, "Living in Montserrat was the most relaxing and tranquil period of my life—it provided a peacefulness that I found most conducive to creating some of my most rewarding work."

Old Man Cricket

Anderson, Bruford, Wakeman, and Howe came to Montserrat in 1988 to record their eponymous record with producer Chris Kimsey. Well, it was more like Anderson, Bruford, Wakeman, and Tony Levin (bass player) as guitarist Steve Howe was not a fan of the Caribbean and was concerned as to what the climate might do to his precious guitars. He elected to stay back in London and record his guitar parts later after the main tracks were completed at AIR Montserrat.

While the guys were working at the studio, Jon Anderson struck up a friendship with one of the locals. Knowing that the band and their producer hailed from Mother England, Jon's new friend asked if they might want to have a friendly game of cricket against some of "the local boys." Chris Kimsey remembered: "So at dinner one night, Jon says 'We're going to play cricket tomorrow.' I was like 'Who's playing cricket? What do you mean?' [Jon says] 'We're going to play the local [team]." Well, it turns out that the local team consisted of 15 to 18 year old lads Chris described as "all young, so fit and great cricket players. And we struggled on, the old boys." At the time, Jon, Chris, and the crew were all in their late 30s to 40s. Jon said that they showed up at the pitch in t-shirts and jeans drinking beer only to find that the local boys' families and others had gathered to watch the match. John said, "These kids come up hill onto the pitch all dressed in white in classic cricket gear with pads and gloves and everything. A real team. And obviously, they beat the hell out of us." Chris told me, "The pitch wasn't green grass. It was grass about 10 years ago. It was like hard baked earth to if you took a fall you'd know about it. I think I was bowled out twice. I didn't get out straight away...but it was terrifying. They were throwing balls at 100 miles per hour plus."

Although the band had been annihilated by the local cricket team, they took it in stride. Being good sports, they had a trophy made at a local shop and asked for a rematch. Needless to say, they did not leave the island with the cricket cup but instead with some fun memories of the local cricketers.

Summing It Up

For many artists, the lack of things to do on the island became tedious as the sessions wore on. Studio manager Denny Bridges told me this story: Roger Daltrey was recording the McVicar soundtrack at AIR Montserrat. Denny, Roger, and drummer Kenney Jones are sitting on the studio villa veranda when Kenney starts counting palm trees, "1...2...3...4..." like there was nothing else to do but acknowledge the number of palm trees on the horizon. Kenney sighs and says, "Another boring day in paradise." Denny said, "Sometimes, that was all that there was to do on the island." What gave this statement, "Another boring day in paradise," even more credence was that, less than a week later, I was in Mo Foster's house in London, watching some very rare footage that he filmed of his session in Montserrat with Sheena Easton. As the footage played, one of his fellow musicians says from off-camera, "Another boring day in paradise." Coincidence?

A PARADIGM SHIFT

A IR Montserrat's Neve recording console is regarded as one of the best sounding desks ever built. Revered for its legendary rich sound, it seems almost counterintuitive that AIR decided to sell such an important asset of its remote studio in 1986. Some have theorized that AIR needed the cash due to the studio's financial situation while others think that the Neve had fallen out of fashion with artists and producers. The answer falls somewhere in between.

In the 1980s, computer automation was making its way into many industries. From the auto industry with its assembly line robotics to the financial sector with computer-based trading, computer automation was streamlining workflows and processes that were once human-controlled affairs. The recording industry was no exception.

A Deeper Discussion of The Recording Process

Before we move on, I must give a brief explanation of what a recording desk is and its place in the workflow of recording so that you understand how critical it is to a studio and why the following story is important to the history of the studio. The terms console, desk, and board are all used to describe this integral part of a studio and are used interchangeably throughout this chapter. In audio recording, a control desk is the central piece of gear in a recording studio. It performs most of the functions in the path the audio takes from performance to what you hear as a listener. Some of the functions of a recording desk are:

· It receives the audio signals from musicians and their instruments as they perform and controls the filtering of these sounds using equalizers, volume controls, panning between speakers, etc.
· It sends sound signals through different effects such as echoes, reverbs, gates, etc.,
· It sends and receives the sound signal to and from the tape deck for recording and playback.

Prior to the early 1980s, all the various knobs, sliders, and buttons that control these functions needed human intervention of some sort. If the volume needed to be raised on a track, a person's finger needed to push the volume slider up. If the track needed to be panned further to the left speaker, someone had to turn the panning knob left. When recording a band's performance, the engineer would need to take the time prior to the recording to setup the sound parameters on every track being used to capture the performance. For the most part, these settings remained static while the artists' performance was occurring. The true difficulty of using manual adjustments came during the mixing process. After the songs have been recorded to tape, these recorded sounds need to be blended together into a "mix." When you hear a song (or the sound in a movie, TV show, etc.), this is the result of the mixing process. The performance that was initially captured through the recording desk likely sounds quite different than the final mix that you hear when you press play on your home audio system. In the mixing process, a myriad of parameters can be adjusted or applied to the recorded tracks' audio signal: Volume can be adjusted, effects could be turned on and off, equalization changed, etc. Depending on the number of tracks, this could quickly become a problem if there were many tracks simultaneously needing adjustment during the mixing process, since the changes needed to be made in real time as the track played through the recording console. A punk band with four tracks of audio with limited effects was an easy task for a single recording engineer but as the number of tracks and the complexity of the arrangements increased, so did the difficulty of mixing. A band may have needed many people working in unison to get the final mix that the artist and producer were looking for. You needed human intervention for every sound parameter needing adjustment and when you have dozens of tracks needing adjustment at the same time, it could be a difficult task. For example, at AIR Montserrat, an artist might have had over 40 individual tracks of recorded sound for a particular song, with every track having its own volume, panning, EQ, effects, etc. With the song playing through the recording desk in real time, every parameter that they wanted changed in the final mix needed a person to adjust that knob, slider, or button at the exact moment that it needed to happen and for it to be done with high precision. With 40+ tracks playing in real time, there may have been a half dozen people or more working in concert to make every adjustment required for the mix to sound as the artist intended. Mixing on non-automated desks was and still is a performance within itself.

When AIR Monserrat was conceived and Rupert Neve was tasked with building the recording desk for the studio, computer automation for recording desks was in its infancy. The standard workflow of how recordings were made had remained rather static since sound recording was developed in the early 1900s. At the time AIR Montserrat was built in the late 1970s, engineers and producers were comfortable with the manual recording and mixing techniques that they had been using for decades. When George Martin, Geoff Emerick and others at AIR made the decision to buy a recording desk for Montserrat in the late 1970s, it was going to be a traditional, manually controlled recording desk...albeit, one of the best sounding consoles in history.

SSL and Automation

Enter Solid State Logic (SSL). In 1977, they introduced the SSL 4000B, one of the first commercial automated recording desks. By the early 1980s, SSL and their computer automated desks began to change the recording industry in a major way. With SSL desks, adjustments made to any parameter during the mixing process were encoded onto the master tapes along with the audio. This automation feature was called Total Recall and soon became a boon for the industry. Once adjustments were recorded by the SSL's computer and committed to tape, the desk would automatically adjust the sliders, knobs, and buttons in real time for the engineer. If a producer raised the vocals in one section of the song and then lowered them later in the track, from that point forward, the desk could automatically move the physical volume slider just as the producer had but without the need for human intervention. This allowed an engineer or producer to mix as many tracks they needed with only a single desk operator since the SSL desk would perform the physical parameter adjustments for them as the audio playback was occurring. This made mixing exponentially easier and cost effective as it now required less time and staff to perform a mix. Additionally, it allowed studio operators to rent out their studios more frequently. With a manual desk like the Neve, if an artist was in the middle of a mix and decided to call it quits for the day, there were two options: the desk would have to be left as it was with all of the settings in place so it would be ready for the next day, which prohibited a studio owner from renting the studio to another artist, or if another artist was coming into the studio for a session, every parameter would have to be noted by the outgoing engineer who would then have to reset every parameter on the desk to where it had been the previous day when returning to the studio. This was very time consuming and could introduce errors. SSL's Total Recall allowed multiple artists to use a studio because all sound settings would be instantaneously recalled as they were already saved to tape.

SSL's computer automation had even more benefits logistically. A producer could take master tapes to any studio with an SSL desk and all the desk parameters would be recalled and set automatically. They could start mixing in one studio and then move to another and it would be as if they had not moved at all. From the record companies' standpoint, Total Recall benefitted them as well. It allowed them greater control over the final product. For example, with a non-automated desk, if the record company thought that the vocals were too loud on a final mix submitted by an artist, it was often too difficult to ask the artists to remix the song because there was no way to replicate the settings on the mixing desk again without spending a significant amount of money and time to do so. With Total Recall, all individual track settings were intact, encoded on the master tapes, so changing the volume would be as simple as replaying the song and making the single change to the vocals. The impact of automation on the recording industry cannot be overstated. It was a game changer, a paradigm shift, and by the mid-1980s, a studio was almost required to have an SSL recording desk to be competitive in the market.

With all the benefits of SSL's automation apparent, many people in the recording industry did not like the sound of the SSL desks. They thought that the sound was thin, tinny, or harsh compared to the older Neve, MCI, and Trident desks, especially for tracking (another name for capturing the live performance of artists.) So, with the older desks having a better sound profile and the SSL desks having an advantage with mixing, many studios that had the available space would have both onsite.

AIR Becomes Automated

With the recording industry enamored with automation, AIR was feeling pressure to have SSL desks in their studios. They had purchased an SSL desk for their London studios in the early 1980s where they had the space to have both the older Neve desks and an SSL coexisting together, but they were not sure what to do with AIR Montserrat. Considering that the studio only had the space for a single recording desk, it was thought that having the Neve as the only option in Montserrat was costing the studio session bookings. Since most studios were adopting SSL desks, not having one in Montserrat was seen as detrimental, regardless of the superior audio quality of the Neve. Without an SSL in Montserrat, artists were going to take their business elsewhere, especially mixing work. AIR's Managing Director John Burgess said to Malcolm Atkin, "We've got to keep getting the work out there." So, the decision was made to replace the Neve console with an SSL. Dave Harries said that although "[the Neve] was a fantastic desk and it still is, we had to sell it because of marketing pressures." So in late 1985, AIR started planning the switch to an automated recording desk in Montserrat.

The Master Negotiator

John Burgess went into action to secure an SSL console for AIR Montserrat but as was John's modus operandi, he was aiming to buy an SSL as cheaply as possible. John was known as a master negotiator and approached SSL directly about purchasing a 6000 series desk for Montserrat. Carol Weston, John's secretary said of him: "John was very charming. [Laughing] He would charm the bird off the trees...That was the side of him that was so good for AIR that he was the money man. He'd do his best to get something for nothing, I'm sure. [He'd] charm his way around it." And in this case, he did. Malcolm Atkin was at the meeting where John met with a sales director at SSL. He said that the female director was "known in the industry for demolishing people [in negotiations]" and thought that she could "walk over these men and do deals." Malcolm said that he simply sat back in the meeting with a glass of wine in hand and watched John handle the negotiations. John worked his magic: sweet talking, chatting her up, and flirting with her. "The poor woman was demolished by John." Malcolm remembers that at the end of the meeting, she said, "I can't believe I've agreed to a price like this. I've never done this for anybody." He continued, "It was a master class on how to negotiate...Hats off to John Burgess. He was great at that. He could be bloody annoying in other ways but he was great at doing that stuff."

With the SSL purchase finalized, the question remained: Who was going to buy the old Neve desk since it represented the non-automated paradigm of desk design which had gone out of fashion? Enter Shelly Yakus and Jimmy Iovine at A&M Studios.

Ken Blair At The Helm Of The Montserrat SSL
Photo: Ken Blair

The Neve Finds A New Home

A&M Studios in Los Angeles, California was owned by Herb Alpert and Jerry Moss and had been operating there for almost twenty years by the mid-1980s. (The "A&M" stood for Alpert and Moss.) The studios were showing their age and Jerry and Herb were looking to refurbish the studios to make them modern and reliable by industry standards. Not having any experts in-house to handle a project of this magnitude, they began searching for someone to head up the task. Rather than seeking out someone who had extensive expertise in studio design, the heads of A&M took an unorthodox approach by looking for someone who had produced records that they thought sounded great. Their search led them to the production/engineering team of Jimmy Iovine and Shelly Yakus. The pair had recently had success in producing several popular albums together for artists such as Tom Petty and the Heartbreakers (Damn the Torpedoes), Stevie Nicks (Bella Donna), and U2 (Under A Blood Red Sky). Shelly said that A&M called them and asked, "Can you build us studios where we could make records that sound like yours?" Shelly replied that although they were not in the construction business, if A&M allowed them to bring in people that they wanted to assist with the project and to finance the purchase of the equipment they selected, they would be able to update the facilities and meet their goal of having studios that could record great sounding albums such as theirs. They were promptly hired by A&M in September of 1985.

Shelly knew that they would need some SSL desks as they had become an industry standard at the time. The A&M Studios complex had five individual studios on the A&M lot in L.A., so they purchased three SSL desks. Knowing how the SSL desks were prized for mixing, they were installed in the studios most suitable for that task. Studio A, which was the biggest recording room at A&M, was designated a tracking room where the priority was focused on the quality of sound for live performances. Shelly knew that the recording desk in that room would have to be a superior sounding desk so they knew that an SSL was not going to be installed there. Shelly and Jimmy discussed several options and decided on a vintage Neve console for Studio A. In an effort to find a used Neve, Shelly reached out to Paul Sloman at Atlantic Records Studios in New York. Paul had purchased a vintage Neve desk from AIR London recently so Shelly was hoping that Paul might be able to help. Paul told him that the one they had purchased from AIR London was the same design as the one in Montserrat. Paul provided Shelly with the contact information of the broker he used to negotiate the deal with AIR, Malcolm Jackson, who was in the U.K. Shelly reached out to Malcolm to see if he had any leads on vintage Neves that were on the market, especially the one in Montserrat since Paul had talked so positively about the quality of its sound. Malcolm knew of a few Neves that might be available and said that he would look into the option of the Montserrat Neve although it was not officially for sale at the time.

In the meantime, Shelly wanted to get some other opinions of the quality of the Montserrat Neve, especially from those who had used it. He rang up producer Neil Dorfsman who had recently recorded Dire Straits platinum-selling "Brothers In Arms" album there. Shelly had to be coy in the conversation, not letting on that he was looking to purchase the Neve. With the vintage gear market, if the word got out that the Montserrat Neve was for sale and A&M was looking to buy, others might start bidding on it as well, driving up the price. Neil told me that, "Shelly...called me under the pretense of 'I'm thinking of going to Montserrat. What do you think of the board down there?' I was like 'It's the greatest board in the world. You've got to go!' Little did I know, he was planning on buying it for A&M." After his conversation with Neil, Shelly was convinced and was ready to move forward with the purchase if AIR was willing to sell it to A&M. What Shelly did not know was that when Dire Straits was in Montserrat, George Martin had visited the island and Mark Knopfler and Neil had said to him, "If you ever sell this board, please give us first right of refusal on it because we'd like to buy it together." What Neil did not realize at the time of Shelly's call was that George did in fact come to Mark with an offer to sell him the Montserrat Neve prior to any other deal. Mark was not sure he wanted to spend the money on the board at that point in time and turned him down. Neil said that "[Mark] never called me to say 'Should we do this?' I would have said 'Yes! Yes! It's going to be worth its weight in gold.' And the next thing I know, Shelly Yakus had bought the board."

At Shelly's behest, Malcolm Jackson approached AIR management about the possible sale of the Montserrat board. Fortunately for A&M, the SSL console swap was being planned at that time. With Shelly satisfied that the

Neve was the board he wanted to install into A&M Studio A, both parties moved forward with the deal. The logistical plans of moving the board from Montserrat to Los Angeles were initiated.

Mr. Emerick Is Upset

It cannot be understated about how much AIR engineer Geoff Emerick loved the Montserrat Neve desk. It has been said by those who knew him that he thought it was the best recording console that he had ever worked on. He had even purchased a home on the island so that he would be in close proximity to his beloved desk. The problem was that no one at AIR had told him that the Neve was being sold and replaced with an SSL desk. Shelly said that Geoff called him out of the blue, sometime after the sale was put into motion but before the Neve had been shipped to A&M. Shelly recalls the call:

"He called me personally. I didn't know that he lived on the island. I didn't know that he was still connected to the board and he was really upset. He said, 'I can't believe that you're buying this board. I moved to the island to live here and to be able to work on that board in that studio and do my work here.'…I said, 'Jeff, I'm really sorry. I had no idea you were living there and depending on the board.' I felt awful but I explained to him, 'AIR London was putting this board up for sale so if we didn't buy it, someone else was going to buy it. I'm really sorry.' I mean, I was squirming. The guy was really upset about it and I said, 'Look, if they weren't selling it, we wouldn't be buying it. We would [have] just looked elsewhere.' I explained to him how it all happened and he understood but he wasn't happy because it really affected him professionally."

Unfortunately, according to the album archive website Discogs, Geoff would never have another production credit at AIR Montserrat post-SSL desk installation. Whether it was because the Neve was sold or for some other reason, we will never know. Only Geoff could have answered that question.

A Compromise

Chris Thomas, blockbuster producer known for The Beatles' White Album, The Pretenders, The Sex Pistols, and many, many others had recorded at AIR Montserrat three times with Elton John. He had strong feelings about the superior sound quality of the Neve desk and about the perceived lower fidelity of SSL consoles. He had used an SSL on a Pete Townshend solo album a few years prior and did not like the sound at all. He told me the tale of how he heard about the swap in Montserrat and how he offered some advice to AIR management. (As a funny aside: When I was interviewing Dave Harries and Chris Thomas, Dave knew Chris' strong feelings about the SSL swap and brought up the subject by saying to Chris, "Tell Brian what you thought of us taking the Neve out and putting in the SSL." Chris promptly rolled his eyes and exclaimed, "Oh!!!" with Dave saying to me. "I knew that would set him off!" with everyone laughing.) By this time, Chris had completed what was to be his last album with Elton John in Montserrat. One day, he was in AIR London and John Burgess said to Chris, "Chris, we're going to pop an SSL into

Montserrat." Chris exclaimed, "WHAT?!?" John said, "Everyone wants us to put an SSL in there." Chris promptly replied that "Well, I'm never going back there again then." When John asked why, Chris told him flatly: "Because they sound terrible." (Another side note: Dave interrupted Chris at this point during the interview to interject his opinion into the story and perhaps defend AIR's decision. Referring to the sound quality of SSL desks, he said, "No, they didn't [sound awful]. Not by then.") Chris said that the SSL that he used on Pete's record "sounded like a tin can...really horrible." To help make the audio sound better while tracking, Pete had brought in some Neve channel modules to run the live performances through rather than the SSL modules. This had helped the sound situation. Chris suggested to John Burgess that they install some Neve channels into the SSL desk to give producers the option of getting the "Neve sound." John asked how many channels Chris would want if this turned out to be a viable option and left the conversation at that. Later that year, Chris found himself in AIR London again and bumped into George Martin. Chris said that George told him, "I've had this fantastic idea. I thought of having some [Neve] modules installed in the desk." Chris thought to himself "What do you mean YOU'VE had this frickin' idea?" since he was the one who had made this suggestion to John Burgess previously. What AIR had done was to contact Rupert Neve about the possibility of making some tracking modules based on his designs. By this time, Rupert no longer worked for the Neve Company and had started a new company, Focusrite. Rupert had agreed to create some modules that could appease those producers like Chris who wanted that classic "Neve" sound. Paul Rushbrooke and Malcolm Atkin helped design a sidecar for the modules that would be installed directly into the new desk, which SSL gave them permission to do since it altered their product. While this might be seen as a hack, it would allow those artists and producers wishing to use Rupert Neve-designed electronics for tracking to be able to do so.

A Logistical Nightmare

With the sale of the Neve in place and the SSL desk scheduled for delivery, the Neve had to be moved...safely. This was no easy feat considering the weight of the Neve, the sensitivity of the electronics, and the distance it was going to have to travel. Malcolm Jackson's brokering firm was responsible for the transportation of the Neve desk from Montserrat to Los Angeles. AIR staff was on-hand to assist in decommissioning the desk in Montserrat. Electronic modules were removed from the desk and studio wiring was disconnected. The studio game room, located directly off the pool deck, was rearranged so that it could be used as a staging area while the desk was prepped for shipment. The famous control room window overlooking the Belham Valley had to be removed so that the desks could be swapped as they were too large to make it through the narrow studio vestibule. Dave Harries said that he was temporarily made deaf on one ear when removing the glass of the window. The panes were wobbling in the frame but would not budge. Dave held the window in place as a precaution while Malcolm Atkin tried to free it. Malcolm came up next to Dave with a wrecking bar and a "lump hammer" (a single hand sledgehammer) and placed the bar inches from Dave's ear when he struck it, metal on metal. Dave said his ear "went completely stone deaf." Fortunately for Dave, whose career relied heavily on his hearing, the deafness only lasted twenty-four hours. With a sly smile, he joked, "It's my best ear now."

Even with all the modules removed, the desk was still incredibly heavy so when it came time to move the Neve from the control room, Malcolm Jackson contracted a local rugby team to lift and carry the desk from the control room. It took the strength of seventeen men to carry the desk around the backside of the pool deck and around to the game room. Once set in place, a local furniture craftsman built a mahogany shipping crate around the desk for protection. Now it had to get to Los Angeles.

Moving The Heavy Neve Was A Group Effort
Photo: Stephen Barncard

According to Montserrat studio manager Yvonne Kelly, John Burgess wanted to use air transport to get the Neve off the island. Working with artists' logistical needs regularly, she knew the cargo capacities of various local aircraft available. John had selected a plane which could theoretically carry the Neve but the layout of the doors of the aircraft would not allow it to be loaded. Yvonne warned him of this but her advice was not heeded. The plane landed and then promptly left Montserrat as it was clear that the Neve would not fit through the door. AIR technician Paul Rushbrooke, who worked on the console swap, said that another option for transport that was explored was via helicopter. "We were racking our brains trying to work out how we could get the desk[s] [to and from] ...Montserrat...We went to see the French army in Guadaloupe to see if we could borrow a helicopter because we thought we maybe could get it on a helicopter. We thought it would be easier.

203

But we didn't get really far with that because they said, 'If we have a problem...the first thing we are going to do is drop the payload into the sea, so you are never going to get any insurance,' so we thought maybe that wasn't a great idea." With other possible shipping options not coming to fruition, transport was still needed. Finally, Malcolm Jackson made arrangements to have the Neve transported to Antigua on the personal steamer boat of the Chief Minister of Montserrat. Insurance requirements for the Neve required that someone from AIR had to accompany the board as it made its way to its destination. Again, Dave Harries was drafted into accompanying the Neve as it made its way across the sea. He showed up at the dock in shorts and flip flops to check everything before heading home to pack for the trip. When Dave turned to head home, the captain of the ship promptly told him, "No. We are leaving now." So Dave had to leave Montserrat with only the clothes on his back and had to sleep on the floor of the captain's office where he said that he caught conjunctivitis. "That's what it was like there," he said when he told me this story. Once it safely arrived in Antigua, the Neve was then transported via plane to Miami and then on to Los Angeles to its new owners, A&M Studios.

Shelly, Herb, Alan And Others Inspect The New Arrival
Photo: Stephen Barncard

Shelly says that his recollection is that A&M purchased the Neve for $200,000 U.S. dollars. He estimated that with the cost of the rugby team, Governor's boat, customs, insurance, and plane flights, that they had paid an additional $25,000 U.S. to transport the Neve to Los Angeles. Total cost would be over half a million dollars U.S. in 2020.

Once the Neve arrived in Antigua, the SSL desk, which had arrived from London, was loaded on the Chief Minister's boat and it arrived in Montserrat the next day. A funny anecdote about shipping the SSL from the U.K. came from AIR technician Paul Rushbrooke. Knowing how expensive shipping goods to Montserrat was, AIR staff in London packed the outgoing SSL crates with everything they could whether they were related to the SSL install or not. "One of the guys in London said to Yvonne 'Do you want anything else?' She said to bring some nappies because she just had a daughter at the time. 'So put as many nappies as you can inside.'" The SSL crates arrived bearing not only a state-of-the-art recording console, but baby diapers as well.

Malcolm, Dave, and Paul set about installing the new SSL console, a 6000 series desk that had the capacity to do film work, although that was not the intended function in Montserrat since the studio's small performance room could not house a large group of musicians such as an orchestra. (That was the purpose of Studio 1 at AIR London.) It took several weeks for the team to get the swap completed but Paul said that the installation did not pose a problem since they had an SSL engineer onsite to assist them and the AIR technical team had already had the experience of a previous SSL installation at Oxford Circus. AIR intern Ken Blair remembers that he and AIR Technician Frank Oglethorpe finished up the desk swap by installing the Focusrite modules at the tail end of the project. A technological new era had started for AIR Montserrat.

Fast forward months later to when the Neve is installed and operational in Studio A at A&M Studios. Malcolm Atkin and Dave Harries went to L.A. to see the console in its new home. Chris Thomas and engineer Steve Churchyard were at the studio for a project, possibly INXS' Kick album which was recorded at A&M around that time. Malcolm said that everyone was standing in front of the Neve and Steve turns to Malcolm and Dave and says, "Why did you flog a Rolls Royce and buy a Datsun?" Chris was about on the floor with laughter, but Malcolm said that he and Dave were feeling a bit uncomfortable...because they knew he was right. Trends in the recording industry and space limitations of the small studio in Montserrat forced their hand into selling what was arguably one of the best recording consoles ever made. AIR engineer Matt Butler put it this way: "Nobody for one minute said that 'This is a better sounding console than the Neve. Let's get this old thing out.' Nobody thought that. But people did look at it from a business point of view...' Without a doubt, we can have more sessions coming in with a Solid State Logic.'" As an aside, Dave and Malcolm went beyond just helping with the physical move of the Neve to A&M. Dave said, "When it arrived in A&M, Malcolm actually installed it there. I was engaged to redesign the acoustics in their studio at the same time. The room sounded terrible and Shelly wanted it to sound like a cross between Air No 1 and Power Station in New York. I knew how these two were constructed and the project went well I'm glad to say."

Surprise, Surprise

Some of those booking sessions at AIR Montserrat had no idea that the Neve was no longer there. Ray Bardani had worked at AIR Montserrat in 1985, engineering Luther Vandross' "The Night I Fell In Love." When Luther had decided to return to Montserrat to record his next album in 1986, "Give Me The Reason," Ray was in for a surprise. He told me: "I remember walking in. Yvonne took us down [to the studio] and she said, 'We've had a couple of changes'...So I walk in and I see an SSL. Right? And I'm freaking out because I'd never worked on an SSL...I remember saying to her when we got back to the villa, 'What am I going to do? I don't know how to work that thing. I don't know what to do!' I didn't know what it sounded like...The Neve was...great sounding. But the SSL was new and it was different and it had a lot of bells and whistles...So I was like freaking out and she goes, 'Don't worry. You'll figure out something. Maybe the assistant can help.' So luckily, I had a great assistant and I got there a couple of hours early. I said, 'Listen, I've never worked on one of these and we have to setup the whole band and I don't know...' He said, 'We'll get it together.' And we got it together."

Walt Whitman, who produced The Fixx's "Calm Animals" album at the studio said, "I was a little disappointed that not long before we went in there, they had removed the really wonderful custom Neve desk and replaced it with an SSL which I hated. I had worked on those AIR custom Neves at AIR in London many times and loved them and that's why it would have been much more attractive if it had been still there in Montserrat." Walt said the addition of the Focusrite modules was a saving grace for the session, "We basically avoided the SSL entirely and used outboard racks of Focusrite...modules to record through...I recorded almost nothing except some synthesizers through the SSL."

Upgrading The Past

What would be ironic is that the Neve's main limitation would not exist for long as A&M's hand was forced as well by the need for automation...a fact made even more ironic because it was put into motion by a band whose previous studio album was recorded using the SSL at AIR Montserrat. In 1993, the Rolling Stones were looking for a studio to mix their latest album, 'Voodoo Lounge.' Shelly's good friend, Don Smith, was working on the project and called to tell Shelly that the Stones were looking to mix the album in Hollywood. He asked the dreaded question, "Shelly, do you have automation on the [Neve] board?" Shelly was not about to lose a Rolling Stones gig so he told Don, "No, but if it means getting the Rolling Stones in here, it will. We've been talking about putting automation on it." Up until that point, there was not enough mix work for the Neve to warrant the high cost of grafting automation into the old console but Shelly had a discussion with Herb, Jimmy, and Jerry and they decided that if the Stones would commit to mixing on the Neve at A&M, they would install automation on the board. So the Neve, which was sold by AIR because of its lack of automation, became an automated console seven years after it left Montserrat.

The near-mythical stature of the Montserrat Neve was exemplified in a personal anecdote from my research for this book. Producer Chris Kimsey had produced two records at AIR Montserrat: one for Anderson, Buford, Wakeman, and Howe and another for The Rolling Stones. These albums were recorded in 1988 and 1989 respectively, well after the SSL was installed into AIR Montserrat in 1986. When I interviewed Chris in London, he swore to me that he used the Neve on those albums. When I tried to correct him (gently, of course), he did not believe me. He was so convinced that the Neve was there that he jumped on his smartphone and texted Keith Richard's guitar technician who was at the studio during the Steel Wheels session with the Rolling Stones. Keith's tech also believed that the Neve was at the studio for that session. I tried laying out the timeline for the Neve swap for Chris (again, gently), not wanting to push the issue too hard with someone being so generous with their time and information. We decided that the only way to get the real answer was for Chris to go directly to an authority on the subject matter, Malcolm Atkin. Chris texted Malcolm and within minutes, we had our answer. Malcolm confirmed that there was no way that he could have recorded those albums on the Neve as it was at A&M in L.A. by then. Chris was taken back a bit since his memory was of him using the Montserrat Neve. The almost mythological reputation of the Montserrat Neve had trumped his own personal memories. You can see how important this particular console was to so many of the people in the recording industry at the time.

The legacy of Neve lives on to this day. After a long tenure of service at A&M, it was sold to Allaire Studios in upstate New York where it was completely refurbished to bring it back to Rupert's original specifications. After several years of service there, it is now located at Subterranean Studios in Toronto where it is still in use today. What cannot be denied is the Neve's long history of great recordings on its travels around the globe, from Britain to Montserrat to Los Angeles, New York, and Toronto, still recording music over four decades since Geoff Emerick, Malcolm Atkin, George Martin, and Rupert Neve put their knowledge and expertise together to build one of the best sounding recording consoles ever made.

NATURAL DISASTER

On September 10, 1989, 2500 miles east of Montserrat, a tropical depression formed off the west coast of Africa. The storm started tracking west along the 12th parallel north, following the path of trade winds that flow from Africa towards the Caribbean. The next day, it became a tropical storm and was upgraded to a hurricane the following day, September 13th. Within three days, it had travelled more than half of the distance from Africa to Montserrat and was 1100 miles east of the island. By September 15th, it had become a dangerous Category 5 hurricane with sustained winds of 160 miles per hour (260 km/h). The storm had been named Hurricane Hugo and it had Montserrat in its crosshairs.

No One Was Prepared

In Montserrat, people were not taking the dire weather warnings quite as seriously as they should have. The island had not seen a hurricane make landfall for over sixty years so there were few islanders old enough to remember how destructive they could be. For decades, there had been predictions of hurricanes that might make landfall in Montserrat, only to have the storms veer off to the north or south. Many residents of the island had grown immune to hurricane warnings over the years and besides, the days preceding this storm were absolutely gorgeous. The beautiful weather completely contradicted the storm track warnings coming from Britain and the United States.

As the hurricane made its way towards Montserrat, Minetta Francis said that she had a vivid dream telling her that "something big is coming" so on Friday, September 16th, she started barring up her house and trimming the trees around her home in preparation for the storm. Her neighbors said she was crazy, laughing and asking her, "What are you doing?" She told them that they had better do the same because "something big is coming." Pleas from the local government coming over local radio and television grew more frequent in an effort to get Montserratians to prepare for a likely storm strike.

The Fury of Hugo

By early in the day of Saturday, September 17th, the storm was bearing down on the island. Winds were picking up and the storm's angry clouds were casting an ominous shadow over the West Indies. Montserratians clamored for any supplies that they could find to secure their homes. Once they had finished whatever hasty preparations that could be completed quickly, there was nothing to do but wait. As evening fell, Hugo's intensity steadily increased, unleashing its worst in the early hours of Sunday, September 18th. Sustained winds were estimated to be 140-150 mph (225-240 kmh) with gusts over 200 mph (320 kmh.) Hugo relentlessly pummeled the island for hours upon hours until 7:30am when the storm's eye passed over the island. This only provided a brief respite for the islanders as hurricane force winds quickly returned and the storm's assault on Montserrat continued until around noon. By the time Hugo had moved on to wreak havoc on islands further to the north and east of Montserrat, the island had endured over eight hours of Category 5 force winds and rain.

The island was devastated in every imaginable way. The Emerald Island was no longer green. The rolling hills previously covered with trees and jungle had been stripped of all leaves and vegetation and were now naked and brown. Property damage was extensive. 90% of the buildings on the island had sustained some sort of damage with 50% being severely damaged and 20% completely destroyed. Many of the houses on the island used galvanized sheeting for their roofs which had been ripped off during the storm and had become large, fast-moving projectiles causing further damage. 2500 people were homeless and 1200 were forced into communal shelters. Those whose homes were still standing opened their doors to fellow Montserratians who had no shelter. The water supply had been damaged across the island with many water towers blown away and water mains compromised. Water had to be collected at springs in the hills and manually treated before being used to avoid water-borne illness. The main hospital building lost its roof and all patients had to be relocated. The air traffic control tower at the airport was destroyed and the runway was clogged with debris. It could not be used for the first few days after the hurricane which led to a delay of deliveries of essential supplies needed in the storm's aftermath. The main jetty at the port was destroyed by the storm surge, limiting ship docking at the main port. Telecommunications systems across the island were unusable. Radio transmission and microwave towers were ripped from their perch atop Chance Peak. It would take several days to get basic telephone service working with the outside world. Long queues would form to use the single working telephone on the island to call frantic loved ones desperate for some assurance that their family members were ok. Carol Weston, John Burgess' secretary at AIR, told me that Yvonne Kelly used Carol to relay information about her wellbeing to friends and family in the UK since the very limited access to phone services would not allow her to do it herself. The main power plant also sustained damage and could not supply electricity to the island but even if it had been functional, power distribution systems had been demolished by the wind. Power wires were down everywhere and poles around the island were snapped or torn from the ground. 90% of the power poles in Plymouth were destroyed. Roads were washed out and covered in dense debris. Fuel was severely rationed to residents so that the government would be able to use any available gasoline and diesel for repair and recovery services. All this material destruction paled in comparison to the ten Montserratians who lost their lives to Hugo's rage.

Typical of the nature of Montserratian culture, the people of the island took the destruction of their home in stride and immediately looked to the future. Then-Governor of Montserrat, Christopher John Turner, described the attitude on the island after the storm by writing: "I had never seen such destruction. Yet there was an astonishing cheerfulness. Everyone met in the streets grinned ruefully but with enormous relief. Rightly, the very first reaction of everybody was not so much over what had been lost but gratitude for what had been saved-their lives. Time and again one met people who said: "My house and everything is gone but thank God we are all alive and all right."

Unlike other islands that were hit by the hurricane such as St. Croix where there was looting and violence in the wake of the storm, Montserratians banded together and immediately started the process of getting the most basic of services up and running and people's needs met. The British government sent a ship of seamen to help with the recovery process. Countries around the world sent supplies, equipment, and experts to the island.

Even Midge Ure, who was in Los Angeles at the time, jumped into action. He had just finished up a tour with Howard Jones and was taking a few weeks to relax in L.A. He had been following the news as Hugo was bearing down on Montserrat. When he turned on the television on Sunday morning on September 18th, he saw that the hurricane had hit Montserrat directly. He told me an epic story of heading to the island to help and what he encountered when he arrived:

"I packed my stuff and went out and bought sterilization tablets and batteries and a tent, hurricane lamps and anything I could get my hands on. I got myself on a flight to Miami. I made my way from Miami to Antigua. I managed to get on the first flight on Monday morning over to the island and when I landed on the island, I'd never seen anything like it. I think the British Navy had followed the hurricane in its tail. So the moment it hit Montserrat and moved on, they got in as quickly as they possibly could with some of their...machinery and cleared some of the roads. So when I arrived at the airport, taxis could get through so I managed to get a taxi straight to the studio. I didn't even go to my house to check on that first. I went straight to the studio and expected to jump out like Indiana Jones with my batteries and my water sterilization tablets and all of that and Malcolm met me at the door to the studio and said, 'Oh great your back! Come in. We're having Duck L'Orange today.' And I said, 'What?!?' He said, 'Well the freezers are off. Everything is off. All of the electricity is gone but The [Rolling] Stones have just left so, for weeks afterwards, we were all brushing our teeth in Evian and Perrier... So we had to eat up what was left in the freezer.' So when I got to my place, the roofs had been ripped off. I set up a tent in the middle of the sitting room because the windows were all hanging off and the roof shingles were all gone. There were holes in the roof and the holes came from coconut husks because they were flying through the air at 180 miles per hour. They were like cannonballs...I was seeing what was this green lush jungle-like island reduced to nothing green at all. No leaves. Just bits of broken wood sticking up out the ground which were the palm trees. Everything had snapped off and blown away. It was bizarre. Within weeks, all of the vegetation all kind of came back again. So I was there on the island for quite a while after the thing. Trying to get electricity up...The power cables were all overhead, so they all came down... for a while, it was kind of like the wild west...There were no lights. No street lights. Just headlights of cars...Word would go out that there was a cooler running off of a generator somewhere where you could get a semi-cold beer and people would drive to the other side of the island just to find them. They could not get them in one end of the cooler fast enough to get them out the other end cold. So it was an interesting, weird, and wonderful time. The big drawback, I suppose, was that, being a tiny island, there's only so many builders on the island. [Only so many] building materials. So everyone was a builder all of a sudden. Everybody and his brother were builders...I had this Mercedes jeep that I'd shipped out a few months beforehand and everyone thought it was crazy to have this old Mercedes jeep...And of course that was the jeep that saved the island. Malcolm and I used it to carry these massive tarpaulins around that [had been] sent to the people of Montserrat. We could climb up on the back of the Jeep and throw these tarpaulins over the damaged roofs. So [it] just turned into everyone just helping each other which was an amazing experience."

Up at AIR Montserrat, Yvonne and Malcolm gave out frozen meat and fish from the studio's kitchen freezer to help the community during its time of need. Their thought was that if the studio food stores were going to spoil, better it go to the people who could use it during this crisis. Minetta Francis told me that she took meat from the studio, salted it, and then fire dried it in her backyard so that it would last without the need for refrigeration. She said it was like "in the old times when there were no fridges...to survive." She would give it out to neighbors who needed something to eat in the aftermath of the storm.

What was clear was there was going to be a long-term recovery period for the island. With most aspects of infrastructure either severely damaged or completely destroyed, Montserrat would not be returning to normal anytime soon. There were huge lines at the local bank to get cash since most businesses on the islands did not accept credit after the storm. For the chance to buy gasoline, Montserratians had to wait in queues lasting ten to twelve hours long. It would be weeks before Plymouth would see electricity return. The Hodd family did not have power at their home until two days before Christmas. Some areas on the island would not have power until May the following year. The tourism industry, as limited as it was, was devastated. 80% of the hotel rooms on the island were unusable. Rental vehicles were destroyed. Basic transportation, communication, and utilities would take months before they would be functional. With the help of governments and people around the world, Montserrat began the slow process of returning to its former glory.

For Yvonne, the storm was not the only source of sadness. Two days before Hugo hit the island, AIR Montserrat family member and studio dog Bosun died. He had been a constant companion and source of joy for many staff members and artists over the years since his arrival in the initial months of the studio's opening. His passing represented the loss of what many considered one of the best "staff members" at the studio. Yvonne said that she was heartbroken at his loss.

But what of AIR Montserrat itself? What effect did the storm have on the studio? The studio never hosted another recording session post-Hugo. Why? There is no clear-cut definitive answer but here is what I know...

THE END OF AN ERA

On September 22, 1989, The New York Times published a news story about the devastation of Hurricane Hugo and Montserrat's start on the road to recovery. The journalist wrote that the studio had survived the hurricane's assault saying, "Miraculously, one of the few places that was spared was the island's best-kept modest secret, the state-of-the-art Air Studios recording operation."[1] In the same article, Yvonne Kelly was quoted as saying "Down here it was brilliant and the studio built like a bunker...This was paradise. It still is when you hear on the radio about them shooting in St. Croix...The next band that's got the guts to come out to record, we're ready for them." If this had been the case, that the studio had sustained no serious damage and was ready for artist sessions, why did the studio close its doors forever immediately following Hugo? The answer is a bit complicated and after interviewing many AIR staff members and others who lived on the island at the time, I believe that there was a confluence of factors involved in the studio's closure beyond damage to the property itself.

What is clear is that in the aftermath of Hurricane Hugo, a decision was made by AIR management to cease operations in Montserrat. Statements about the closure made by George Martin during interviews in the years after the studio closed can be summed up as follows: He came to Montserrat six weeks after the hurricane to take a survey of the studio. As he entered the studio, he went to the Bosendorfer piano and opened the keyboard cover only to find it covered in green mold. He thought that if the piano had this much damage, the electronics installed in the control room must be as bad as the piano or worse. With damage this extensive, there was no way to salvage the studio and he made the sad decision to close its doors forever. I'm certain that George's explanation has some truth to it, but it is a very simple answer to a decision-making process that held much more nuance and depth than "there was mold on the piano."

It Weathered The Storm

AIR Technical Manager Chris Mason had weathered the storm in the studio itself with local Danny Sweeney and Danny's girlfriend. It was one of the best places to ride out the hurricane on the island since the studio had been designated as an official hurricane shelter. It was truly "built like a bunker." He told me that the studio held up very well. Initially, they had setup in the studio itself, safely surrounded by the thick concrete walls of the inner studio building. He said that they were "suffering terrible pressure changes" in the studio but could hear very little of what was going on outside, so he and his guests climbed atop the inner concrete studio building. One panel of plywood had torn off the roof and they watched the storm pummel the Belham Valley through the hole. Other than this small hole in the outer roof of the studio building and the pool's sliding board being blown away, the studio and villa had suffered minimal damage. This is likely the reason why Yvonne was quoted as being ready for operations so shortly after the storm had hit.

One theory that was repeated to me many times regarding the studio closure was that the studio complex's generator was not operational at the time Hugo hit the island. Without consistent power, there was no way to run the air conditioning system in the studio which would quickly lead to the ruination of sensitive equipment due to the humid, salty Caribbean air. This would correspond with George's story of the studio's closure. Chris Mason, who was responsible for maintaining the generator, said that the generator's alternator windings "blew up" three days before the hurricane hit. He said that the entire winding would have had to be sent to Antigua for repair and that it weighed 400 lbs. which complicated the repair. Malcolm Atkin confirms that the generator was not working at the time. He told me that "I remember screaming, trying to persuade anybody I could find to take a small part [for the generator] onto an airplane so that I can get that generator to work." He tried convincing an international rescue team, who were one of the first groups to respond to the crisis, to take the part to the island with them, but in the confusion of hastily throwing together a support team, the part never arrived. Others who were on the island at the time, such as Desmond Riley and Lloyd Francis confirmed that the generator was not operational in the aftermath of the hurricane. What is strange is that when I asked Yvonne about the state of the generator, she said that she remembers the studio complex had power from the generator after the storm. This contradicts what I heard from many others so the truth may be one way or the other, or perhaps somewhere in between...but does the state of the generator really play into the real decision to close the studio?

The Millstone

Another factor that cannot be ignored is the near complete destruction of the island's infrastructure. Villas and hotels needed to house potential studio guests needed major repairs or to be completely rebuilt. Cars for rental were nonexistent. Electricity was going to take 6 months or more to come back online and to be made reliable once again. Basic needs such as clean water and fresh food were scarce in the near term. Both Malcolm and Yvonne estimated that they thought it may have taken up to a year before an artist could have come to the island to record and have the experience that the studio was known for. With the possibility of having no artists working at the studio for a year, there would be no money flowing into the AIR Montserrat's coffers for the foreseeable future.

An extended period with no incoming revenue represented a huge problem for AIR. Contrary to the public image of a prolific history of huge albums and famous artists recording at the studio, what is not widely known is that AIR Montserrat was never profitable, even in the early to mid-80s when

215

the studio had a large book of business. Carol Weston, who was privy to the company's financial books, put it this way: "[The public] thinks everything is roses around the door [but] there's a lot of hard grind at the back of it and you don't always get the reward money wise." She continued: "When I think back, they must have been crazy to do such a thing really because it never made any money...It was just almost like a whim of George's that they'd gone along with. It was crazy really...They probably would have made more money if they'd hadn't done it at all. As I said, it wasn't a money-making machine. It was definitely a loss account...It was an indulgence, I think, really more than anything." When I asked Dave Harries about the studio's profitability, he said to me that "You know it wasn't there to make money. Never did make a penny...It was more a benefit to George and AIR and prestige for Chrysalis [and their artists] ...It was extra work for everybody [at AIR]....hard work." Financially, the overhead costs of the studio were extraordinarily high, from the importation of goods and transportation/logistics to facilities maintenance and staffing overhead with electricity being one of the highest cost centers for the studio. Power on the island was generated using diesel-powered generators and this led to very high prices compared to most developed countries. The predominant wisdom at the time was that all the studio equipment needed to remain powered on 24 hours, 7 days a week, regardless of whether an artist was booked in the studio or not. The thought was that power cycling the gear could introduce failures which would be especially dire at a studio that was days away from any replacement gear. So, if there were no sessions booked for two months, the studio remained powered up 24-7, profusely bleeding money the entire time. As bookings began to happen less frequently and for shorter periods as the 1980s wore on, the high operational overhead became more and more of a problem for AIR. Malcolm Atkin, who was Managing Director of AIR Studios at the time, said that after the studio had been open for six or seven years, they needed approximately 38 weeks a year of booked sessions to break even. He said that "In [one of the later years], I think we got about 18 weeks...It was becoming more and more of a millstone." John Burgess, who handled the finances for AIR, was constantly pressuring Malcolm to find ways to cut costs of the studio. He asked Malcolm if the studio could run exclusively on its generator since it would be cheaper than paying for island power from Monelec. (This was not allowed on the island, by law) One unfortunate casualty of the cost cutting was Minetta Francis, head housekeeper for the studio and long-term loyal employee of the studio. She was "made redundant" in 1988 with her position being eliminated to save on staffing costs.

The Free-Wheeling 70s Were Over

As alluded to previously, the number and length of bookings at AIR Montserrat were tapering as the decade wore on. This was not just a problem for the Montserrat studio but for any recording studio in the late 1980s. There had been multiple paradigm shifts within the music industry that affected studio usage.

Firstly, record companies started restricting budgets for recording projects. In the "freewheeling 70s", when George conceived the idea of a destination studio, artists had seemingly unlimited budgets and the freedom to take as much time as they wanted to make an album. It was not uncommon for a big-name artist to take upwards of six months to a year to record a new album. That meant long term studio bookings and with that came extended periods of continuous revenue for studio owners. In the early 1980s, record companies started controlling costs by strictly managing recording projects and tightening their purse strings. While the daily price for recording at AIR Montserrat was not extraordinarily high by industry standards, the costs of logistics to bring a band and their entourage to the island made using the studio a tough proposition. Malcolm Atkin pointed out that, "In a London studio, they would not have to pay hotel bills, a stupid amount of airfares, or deal with hangers-on." Additionally, being so far from any record company representatives made record companies hesitant to send bands to a far-flung Caribbean island where the artists could not be monitored so easily. Records could be made in more convenient places like large cities. The main draw for Montserrat was the island location which was for the benefit of the artists' comfort and creativity. Budgets shifted the priority from artists' choice of environment to controlling costs and session management.

Secondly, the benefits of an artist having exclusive "ownership" of the Montserrat studio for their session was a double-edged sword for AIR Montserrat. Creatively, this was a great proposition for the artist who could use the island studio as if it were their own at all hours but this restricted the profitability of the studio. At a studio complex such as AIR London, a studio could theoretically be booked and in use 24 hours a day by different artists who only needed a studio for a specific amount of time, renting out the remainder of the time to other performers. Having multiple studios in one location allowed staff to be utilized for many different sessions rather than be tied to a single artist like at AIR Montserrat. In Montserrat, you had to have an engineer, tape operator, and maintenance engineer available to a single artist 24 hours a day whether the artist was recording or not. In AIR London, the staff could move from session to session as needed. If an artist only used a studio for four hours, the same AIR staff could then move to another session thus generating additional revenue with a set staff cost for AIR. That could never happen at AIR Montserrat with only one artist in the studio at a time.

Lastly, music was becoming more and more electronic-based, rather than acoustic. Synthesizers and drum machines were replacing pianos and drum kits. With these new technologies, the need for a great sounding recording space became less and less important. For electronic-based artists, rappers, and sampled music, the location where the music was recorded was not important since the space did not dictate the sound as much as the gear did. Additionally, setup and recording time was often less with this type of music than a traditional band. This made the logistics and investment of time to travel to a distant destination studio such as AIR Montserrat less attractive to these artists.

Another issue that came to light after the fact was that there was a problem with the insurance coverage for the studio. AIR had contracted with an insurance broker who, as it was revealed later in court, defrauded AIR and many other Caribbean policy holders by taking payments for policies that he did not secure for them. It would take years for the defrauded companies and individuals to recover any funds related to losses due to Hurricane Hugo.

A Financial Decision

While the hurricane's physical destruction might have seemed as if it was the cause of the studio's demise, it was ultimately a financial decision. As Malcolm told me when I asked him about AIR Montserrat's profitability: "[It was] not good. That's actually why it closed." The confluence of extremely high operating costs, the studio's exclusivity, and many various changes in the recording industry made the studio perpetually unprofitable. The destruction of Montserrat at the hands of Hurricane Hugo was simply a logical place to pull the plug on George's pet project. All hopes of reopening the studio were dashed with the insurance debacle that ensued later. While it was clear that George loved the island and its people, returning often before and after the studio's closure, by 1989, he himself had not used the studio that he spent so much time, effort, and money building for many years. The last production credit he had at AIR Montserrat was Ultravox's "Quartet" album, recorded seven years prior in 1982. Did he fall out of love with the studio or was he winding down his career in production? His hearing started to seriously degrade in the 1970s making production much more difficult for him. Any guesses are pure speculation at this point since these questions could have only been answered by George himself who unfortunately passed away in 2016 at the age of 90.

Although the studio closed its doors as a recording studio in September of 1989, the property did not cease having some utility on the island and the legacy of AIR Studios continued on.

[1]Kifner, John. "Devastated by Hurricane, Montserrat Starts to Rebuild." The New York Times, 22 Sept. 1989, pp. A22

AFTER THE HURRICANE

With the studio closed after Hurricane Hugo in 1989, Malcolm Atkin was sent to the island to remove all the technical equipment from the studio. Malcolm said that John Burgess had done "one of his dodgy deals" to sell the SSL desk and the echo plate to Funhouse Sapporo Studio in Japan. The remaining gear was to be sent back to the U.K. When Malcolm saw the condition of the studio's piano, he said, "This piano is absolutely fucked." The heat and humidity of the Caribbean had wreaked havoc on the Bosendorfer. Believing that the piano was not worth trying to salvage, he left it behind when he returned to England with the rest of the salvaged gear, but the piano had sentimental value to George Martin, as he considered it his personal piano. George wanted it to return to England so a few months later, Dave Harries went out to Montserrat to prep the piano for transport. He had brought a special sealed bagging system that allowed the piano to be wrapped and sealed completely air-tight to protect it from any additional liquid damages that might happen during the trip back to the U.K. Dave described the piano's state: "The piano was in a terrible state. The cellulous paint had come away all over the surfaces. It had descended down the legs in rolls leaving the bare wood showing." Dave locked down the mechanical parts of the instrument and vacuum sealed the package. He had some local carpenters make him "a beautiful packing case out of mahogany-faced plywood" and then had it wrapped in steel bands for additional security. With the shipping container looking quite good (as opposed to its contents), the piano made its way home.

By the time the piano arrived in the U.K., AIR was transitioning from its Oxford Circus location to the new studio facility in Lyndhurst. The new studio was consuming a huge amount of time and resources for AIR and thus, anything having to do with Montserrat was considered, as Malcolm said, "last decade's problem." When the piano arrived, it was not a priority for the staff and its fate was passed off to others. Les Pierce was AIR's piano technician, and he was asked to rebuild the Bosendorfer by George but he had no available space for it in his workshop. With his incredibly busy schedule dealing with the new studio, Malcolm needed to quickly find a place to store the large piano. Pioneer, a Japanese electronics conglomerate, had a stake in AIR Studios at the time so Malcolm asked them if they had any room in the warehouse that they were providing to AIR to house old gear from Oxford Circus. They did, so the Bosendorfer was stored in their Greenford warehouse. A few months later, out of the blue, Pioneer informed AIR that they were closing the warehouse and that AIR needed to promptly remove all their gear from the property, including the piano. Knowing that the piano was

George's personal property, Malcolm again asked Les if he could store the piano at his workshop until he could start restoring the instrument. Les agreed and sent a van to pick up the Bosendorfer.

About a month later, George asked Malcolm to check on the piano restoration project. When Malcom rang him up, Les said, "Oh fuck! Hasn't anyone told you what had happened?...Are you sitting down? The piano is in Japan!" Malcolm was flabbergasted. He said, "I only wanted it moved from Greenford to your workshop. That's about eight miles. Why is it in Japan?!?" Les explained that when he went to have the piano picked up, he still did not have room in his workshop, so he asked Piano Transport Services, who performed local transportation of Steinway pianos, to store it at their warehouse for a few days until he had made some room in his shop. In the intervening days, the transport company declared bankruptcy. Steinway had a piano stored in their warehouse that was supposed to be shipped to Japan so they asked the receiver who was handling the bankruptcy to collect the piano and send it to their buyer, The Tokyo Opera House. The receiver went to the warehouse, saw a piano in a beautiful custom-built mahogany shipping container, assumed it was the Steinway, and promptly shipped it to Japan. The piano arrived at the opera house and when the box was opened, inside was not a new shiny Steinway piano, but the weather-ravaged Bosendorfer. Steinway wanted nothing to do with the destroyed piano and sent it back to Haneda airport in Tokyo without anyone having a plan of what to do with it. By this time, real ivory was illegal for import in Japan and with the Bosendorfer being built decades before, its ivory keys were considered contraband, so it was impounded by customs officials. AIR received a call from Japan informing them that it was going to cost $4,000 U.S. per week for the piano to remain in Japan's customs warehouse. The piano was only worth about $20,000 at that time.

Malcolm had to tell George the bad news. The original bankrupt piano company had been purchased by another in the interim and the new company had offered to ship the piano back to England albeit via sea freight since the cost of shipping via air for such a large and heavy item would be extraordinarily expensive. With the waterproof seal breached when the piano was opened at the opera house, it would not survive the trip back to England on a ship. George was livid. He threatened the new owners of the piano shipment company with a promise that if they ever wanted to work in London again, they would get his piano back using air freight. George's clout within the music industry could not be underestimated, so the company relented and the Bosendorfer returned to England on a plane.

It took several months for Les to repair the piano and return it to its former glory. Once complete, it was delivered to George's estate where it remains today. As an aside, Malcolm told me that the poor Bonsendorfer's bad luck with water continued. Several years ago, a pipe burst in the bathroom above the piano and once again, the Bosendorfer was drenched, not with hurricane rains but with water from the loo.

In Limbo

Yvonne Kelly left the studio property in 1990 and other than a brief stint as temporary housing for the Governor after Hurricane Hugo, the studio and villa laid dormant. The electronics were removed from the studio itself but everything else remained, from the furniture to the kitchen appliances to the studio bar. Lloyd "X" Francis was hired to manage Olveston House by the Martins and as part of those duties, he helped care for the studio property as well. I was also informed that a technician from the Climax Blues Band moved to the island and helped with the maintenance as well. Over the next few years, the property was unused but could have been ready for visitors with only a thorough cleaning. There was hope that AIR Studios would once again open its doors in some capacity, but catastrophe struck only a few years later.

She Awakens From Her Slumber

The Soufriere Hills volcano had been active on the island for centuries but without any disastrous effects to the island's communities. There always had been sulfur vents around the island, occasional mild earthquakes, and plumes of ash venting at the volcano's dome. These are common occurrences for islands in the Caribbean as most lie on fault lines that run along the ocean floor. The oceanic tectonic plates grind into each other causing earthquakes and allowing hot magma to escape from below the earth's crust. The venting magma cools and creates volcanic islands such as Montserrat. Unseen pressure had been forming under Soufriere Hills for many decades but without much fanfare so there was no expectation of any danger from Montserrat's volcano. With the volcano lying dormant for 350 years, the local islanders looked to the volcano with reverence because of its beauty and its positive effect on the quality of the island's soil, so they were caught by surprise when the volcano decided to come alive in July of 1995.

Earthquake activity had been increasing in the days leading up to the first eruption. On July 18th, the volcano started venting an unusual amount of ash and the situation only worsened over the next few weeks. Lava domes formed and collapsed many times, causing huge clouds of ash to form, often blackening out the sky and covering the island with thick, heavy blankets of ash. Residents had to repeatedly shovel ash from roads, walkways, and most importantly roofs which were subject to collapse due to the weight of the ash. The most dangerous element of the eruptions were the pyroclastic flows that followed many of the eruptions. Unlike other volcanoes that release slow moving lava, the pyroclastic flows from the Soufriere consisted of hot gas, mud, boulders, and debris that moved at more than 70 miles per hour down the sides of the volcano. The materials in the pyroclastic flows are extremely hot, up to 250 Celsius (480F). Anything in their way is quickly destroyed by the heat, weight, and energy of the pyroclastic material. As the flows became more frequent, the capital of Plymouth was evacuated as it was directly in the path of the volcano's wrath. Over the next few years, the frequent ash clouds and pyroclastic flows covered much of Plymouth and devoured the island's airport. With Plymouth and the areas surrounding it uninhabitable, much of the population moved northward on the island, often living with family members or in temporary housing what was built for them by the government. Since Montserrat was a British territory, the U.K. government offered Montserratians a chance to move to England and settle there, which many decided to do. Others moved to the U.S., Canada, or other islands around the Caribbean. Over the next decade, the population of the island decreased from around 12,000 inhabitants to less than 5,000. The bottom third of the island, which was where most of the population had lived and where the majority of businesses were located, was designated an exclusion zone. Today, no one is allowed to live there, and travel is severely curtailed in the area due the present danger posed by the volcano. Many of the Montserratian staff members of AIR Studios had left the island by the year 2000, including Minetta Francis and her daughter Stephanie, Desmond Riley, X, and Blues (a driver). Midge Ure had been planning to sell his home on the island in the months leading up to the eruptions but his procrastination cost him. Without insurance, his home, which was in the exclusion zone, quickly fell into disrepair and has long been destroyed.

AIR Studios Montserrat is located on the northern edge of the exclusion zone. Although it was not directly in the path of a pyroclastic flow, it was only 450 meters (.25 miles) from large flows that ran down the Belham Valley River which subsequently destroyed the island's golf course. During the first few years of the volcanic eruptions, the ash was cleared from the studio buildings and the pool emptied as needed, but with no interest in using the property again, the Martin family allowed maintenance of the property to lapse throughout the 2000s. In 2003, Malcolm Atkin and his wife Debbie returned to Montserrat. He told me, "I said to Deb, 'I've got a key. I think it opens AIR Studios.'...We went to the studio, put the key in the door, bang, I opened it. We walked into a room that nobody had been in for about 15 years. That was spooky. Because it was all intact at that point...A lot of the spares were still sitting in the workshop. [I thought] 'This is weird.'"

After the volcano started devastating the island, George Martin continued his dedication to Montserrat buy pulling together a huge concert with many of the artists who recorded at the studio with the proceeds going to help the islanders cope with the volcano's destruction. Called "Music For Montserrat," it was held at the Royal Albert Hall in the U.K. on September 15, 1997, and featured artists who had recorded at the studio such as Sting, Elton John, Eric Clapton, Paul McCartney, Midge Ure, Arrow, and Mark Knopfler. Jimmy Buffet, whose song "Volcano" was written about the Soufriere Hills volcano, performed the song but changed the lyrics to have a more positive message for the islanders. It raised about 1.5 million English Pounds and a DVD of the concert was released with all proceeds going to support the island.

Completed in 2006, the Martin family also built a cultural center for the islanders in the northern part of Montserrat, to be used as a performance place, community center, and event space. Dave Harries was sent to the island to setup the sound system for the cultural center. The shuttered studio helped him with an issue he encountered while working on the project. Yamaha had provided a huge amount of audio gear to George at cost. Dave said, "I didn't anticipate all that number of power amps...so we had to rack them up. I had to...get police permission and go up to the studio and take the control room racks out. Take all of the rack bolts out of them and clean all of the rust off of them, give them a spray of paint. And then we put the power amps that are in the cultural center, those two racks for the power amps were from the studio, from the control room."

The Montserrat Cultural Center
Photo: Brian Sallerson

Everything Has A Period

There has always been speculation of a revival of the property for another use, but nothing has ever come to fruition. After Hurricane Hugo, artist Eddie Jobson, who lived on the island at the time, approached George Martin and John Burgess about purchasing the studio but to no avail. There had been rumors of investors wanting to buy the property to make it into a museum and performance space. X told me that in the early 2010s, the then-current premier of Montserrat was working on plans to make the studio into a heritage museum of sorts but a change in administration quashed those plans before they could be implemented. Even John Silcott, AIR's Montserratian success story, wanted to buy the studio from the Martins because it had such a huge positive impact in his life and he wanted to preserve it. None of these plans have ever had a chance of becoming a reality because the Martins have refused to sell the property. When I asked Malcolm his opinion of why nothing was done to preserve the studio, he had this to say: "The volcano blew up. It was in the exclusion zone. So although it wasn't physically damaged by the volcano, the pyroclastic flow went straight past it...right across the Belham Valley. Who on earth is going to buy a studio or a building where...you can't physically go in there? There's roadblocks up so you physically can't get there...even with the volcano calming down, it's still in a semi-exclusion zone so there's no building permits...To do anything with the studio now, you wouldn't get any insurance...It's an absolutely blighted situation...Yes, it's been handed down to the children. I think the children would love to wash their hands of it because the problem will be, the moment it is moved out of the exclusion zone, somebody will be demanding rates [taxes] off of them." Yvonne and her daughter went back to the studio and seeing the terrible state of the property, she was moved to ask Giles Martin, George's son, why nothing was done with the studio. She said that Giles replied that "There was no sense doing anything with it." Perhaps George said it best when interviewed for a BBC documentary: "It's like everything in life, isn't it? Everything has a period. You bring something out of nothing and it always goes back to nothing again."

Over the years, the property has been pillaged by tourists and locals, sometimes with permission from the Martins, but often without. In 2011, George had all the furniture, fixtures, and appliances removed to make the property safer for those who insisted on trespassing within the studio ruins. In 2010, the Martins allowed a team of archeologists from Brown University to take a survey of the property as part of a Caribbean archeology project. Although the studio was quite young compared to other sites where you might expect to find archeological studies, the degradation of the island's structures due to the volcano's eruptions gave the team a sense of urgency to document the studio's state before it was too late to do so. They surveyed the site and created a cache of data about the state of the property and the artifacts in and around it. They returned two years later in 2012 to document the decay of the property since their last visit and had this to say in a published article: "The degree to which the property and its structures have changed since our initial survey is astonishing. In contrast to 2010, when the fairly well-preserved residential area and studio spaces still held potential for renovation and reoccupation, the present state of the property is one of rapidly accelerating and irreversible decay...Gaping holes now exist in the wooden roofs, termites are causing irreparable damage to walls, floorboards are rotting as rain enters through the roofs, windows and doors are missing, and the courtyard is completely choked with vegetation. Over the next few years, this complex will inexorably be reduced to the shell of a structural ruin, indistinguishable from other abandoned, decaying buildings in Montserrat's exclusion zone. Nature is reclaiming the studio space, delivering an emphatic final verdict on the viability of AIR Studio's long-term physical preservation."[1] The early 2010s seemed to mark a turning point in the viability of the studio ever returning to its previous glory. When I visited the site in 2019, seven years after the archeology team's final assessment, the property was in a derelict and dangerous state. The roof of the villa had collapsed, and the patio roof had begun to succumb to the elements. Termites have ravaged the flooring, walls, and fixtures. Trees and grass grow on almost every surface and out of holes in the roofs of the structures. Wasp nests are everywhere. The once-beautiful lawn below the pool has been completely reclaimed by the jungle. The courtyard is impassable, and the front of the villa is completely overgrown to the point that it is almost impossible to see it from the driveway. I can only imagine what condition it is in, almost three years later, as I write this. I will reiterate the policy that the Martins have regarding visiting the studio property: Please do not enter the property. To do so is trespassing and the property is extremely dangerous at this point. Floors and roofs can collapse at any time. There are many sharp and rusty surfaces protruding everywhere and the pool is septic. There is a fence built around the front of the property with warning signs discouraging anyone from entering with good reason. Even the island's taxi drivers are instructed not to take tourists there. Please, if you find yourself in Montserrat, view the studio from the Montserrat Volcano Observatory which has a great view of the Ridge property from less than a half mile away (.8 km.) Enjoy the wonderful ambiance of the island and the people there. The gorgeous environment and warm welcomes will provide you with a more vivid and grounded experience of why Montserrat was (and is) such a special place for everyone who was at the studio, much more than visiting a dilapidated and dangerous ruin.

Forty years after their herculean effort to get AIR Montserrat operational, Malcolm and Dave Harries returned to the studio property in the summer of 2019 for the 'Under The Volcano' documentary. Malcolm said, "I'd seen it a couple of times after it had been devastated so I know what I was in for. I don't think Dave had seen it in a long time. He was very moved by what he saw there and he was quite upset by it but as I think as George once said, 'All things pass.'" Dave said that when they tried entering the staff bedrooms, bats were living in the rooms. They found an old power supply for the Neve console in the workshop that had not been shipped out when the console went to A&M 33 years prior. Entering the studio, they noticed that the termites had eaten the entire maple hardwood floor in the control room but had left the wood supports underneath intact. Because the inner walls and roof of the inner building of the studio were concrete, they were intact. Referring to the current state of the studio itself, Dave said, "When we went into that studio, it sounds great. I didn't realize how good it sounded at the time. The termites have eaten the floor but they didn't eat the plywood and all the hard board or any of the acoustic materials. So you [could still] get a great drum sound."

The Studio Facilities In Early 2019
Photo: Brian Sallerson

Old Friends

During my interview with Desmond Riley, he told me a few stories about how his time working with artists in Montserrat led to exciting spontaneous events many years later.

One such story was about how he ended up at Keith Richard's house in Connecticut "by coincidence." He said, "I was in the U.S., me and George [Morgan], and we were walking along in Manhattan somewhere. We hear a car beep [its horn.] We're not looking because no one knows us [in New York.] It was a lady. She works for one of Elton John's offices...She said [excitedly], 'What are you guys doing here? Come, come in the car!' She said that she knows someone that works for Keith [Richards] and she's going to tell them that we're in town. And she did. They got in touch with us...They sent a limousine for me and George...and took us to Connecticut. And you know, as usual, George cooked! [Laughing] We had a big BBQ."

Another tale from Desmond: "I was here in England on holidays again. And I was down just off of Tottenham Court Road and there's a guitar shop. I was just there looking in the shop. Walking around. There's a guitarist, roadie for the Rolling Stones. 'Des! What are you doing here?' At that time, Wembley Stadium was still there, the old one. 'What are you doing here?' I said 'I'm just visiting me parents and me brothers and sisters.' 'Oh my God. We're having a concert at Wembley...Give me your number.' So I gave him my number. He called me two days later and told me to come to Tottenham Court Road. 17 tickets! All VIP passes! I took most of friends of mine to the concert at Wembley. Backstage pass, you know? I tell you...the food, the drink, everything backstage. Then after that, [they said to me,] 'Alright. You're staying with us, you know' [I said,] 'What are you talking about?' [They insisted,] 'No. No No. You're not going' All my friends had gone. I never got back home for two days. We went to the rooftop. It's a hotel...They had an after party there. And then they put me in the Ritz for the next two nights. I couldn't believe it, man...It was real, real fun. It's coincidence as well. There's nothing planned."

Montserrat Hosts One More Artist

John Otway is an English artist, part singer/songwriter and part comedian, with a dash of performance artist thrown in for good measure. He had a minor hit in the 1970s in the U.K. but had little commercial success in the ensuing decades. He jokingly refers to himself as "Rock 'N Roll's Greatest Failure." The interesting thing about John is that he continues to have a rabid, albeit small, fanbase that loves his quirky sense of humor and music. It was this group of dedicated fans that helped John become the last artist to record in Montserrat, almost 30 years after the studio closed.

John had seen a documentary about George Martin and was intrigued about what he had seen about AIR Montserrat. He brought the idea of recording there to his bandmates. John said, "I talked to the band. 'I think we should go to Montserrat.' You had to look it up on Google. Looked on Google images and they're like 'No! [We] can't record there!' But the whole idea was the fact that nobody been back. [We] could be the first people to record here since the Rolling Stones in 1989. That had an appeal because nobody else had done it." John contacted Giles Martin's manager who told John that if he was serious, he had to go to the island and see the condition of the studio for himself. When John came to Montserrat, it was immediately apparent that the studio was in a state of dereliction that would prohibit anyone from safely recording there. Although the studio was not viable for the project, George Martin liked the idea of someone coming back to the island to record music once again. John was not going to give up on the project, so they went back to the drawing board.

Peter Filleul, who had been the keyboardist with the Climax Blues Band when they recorded at AIR Montserrat in 1979, had purchased a home on the island and lived there during the winters. He had been involved with the island community for years and saw the value in helping John with the project. Peter remembered that Olveston House, which was still owned by the Martins, had a basement that was once used as a theater. As such, it had acoustic tiles installed on the walls and was an appropriate size for hosting a band the size of John's. They ran the idea by the Martins who gave their blessing to use the space for John to record.

John, being a very niche artist, did not have the funding for the project so he turned to his fans. A Kickstarter campaign was launched and the fans came together to raise £40,000 for the project. As a thank you, John invited several dozen of his fans to join him in Montserrat during the recording of the album.

Since there was no recording or audio equipment in Olveston House, the endeavor required someone to design the recording setup and install it. John turned to none other than Malcolm Atkin, who agreed to help. Malcolm looked at the space and specified everything that was needed, from air conditioning, to power requirements, to recording gear. Malcolm said that he was paid £150 for the job. He joked when he told me, "But I got a free Caribbean holiday for 3 weeks...hanging out and having a laugh really. [My wife] Debbie wasn't too impressed because I didn't take her. [Laughing]." Again, Malcolm had the opportunity to employ that ever-so-Montserratian "fix and make due mentality" during the recording session. They had not checked the voltage in the recording space in the basement of Olveston House and consequently, a brand-new Marshall amp had "blown up." Being that this was Montserrat, Malcolm was not convinced that they would be able to find the proper replacement part on the island. Much to his surprise, while in a local supermarket, he found that they had a full electronics part department. They had everything you would need to repair almost any kind of gear. When Malcolm inquired about the parts, the woman at the register had no idea about the use or origins of the parts but refused to dispose of them because they might have had a use someday, which is a very Montserratian way of thinking. He bought the resistors for less than $1 and repaired the amp.

The album was recorded over the ensuing weeks with the fans given the opportunity to sing background on one of the songs. Their vocals were recorded at the island's Cultural Center, another extension of the Martin family's enduring influence on the island.

John's album was aptly named "Montserrat." All the recording equipment was left behind for the next artist who, as Yvonne Kelly once said, is brave enough to come down and record in Montserrat.

As an aside, I have an anecdote about this story. In the days leading up to my trip to Montserrat in 2019, I came across the story of John's voyage to Montserrat to record his album. I had never heard of John so I did some cursory research into his career. I took note to follow up on this when I got home after my trip as I thought it was an interesting story. On the second day that I was on the island, I was having breakfast at the Gingerbread Hill restaurant. As I sipped my coffee in the empty café, in walked three people, one who looked remarkably like John Otway, whose pictures I had seen only days before. I walked up and asked the gentleman if he was John, which to my surprise, it was! Absolute serendipity! Two years after recording his record, John had returned to the island to celebrate the engagement of one of his friends. By complete chance, I had crossed paths with the last artist to record in Montserrat...in Montserrat. John, Peter Filleul, and I had a great chat about recording the album "Montserrat" at one of the local bars later that week.

Sad State Of Affairs

So what is the legacy of the studio for the people that worked there and the artists who came to Montserrat to record? Throughout this project, I have been astonished by how much of an influence AIR Montserrat had on people.

Almost universally, it is considered a special time and place for those who were there. So many people's eyes lit up, with broad smiles across their faces when telling me of their stories of the studio. Those who were hesitant to open up about their time there were hesitant, not because any of negative emotions, but because the studio represents such a personal and important time in their lives that they needed to be assured that I would be treating their memories the reverence and respect that they themselves had for AIR Montserrat. With that said, the following are, in their own words, the thoughts of the staff, artists, and locals, relating how they feel about how the current state of the studio makes them feel:

Chef George Morgan: "I miss it everyday, man. Everyday. I wish I could do something again, bring something back...It's a shame...That was it man. That was the dream. The dream! If I were ever wanted to go back, turn the clock back, those were the days."

Stephanie Francis: "When I went up there to AIR Studio [after it closed] and I stood there, I saw it. You know? You hear everything just come back around you. You hear everything but then nothing is there. It was so vibrant. So much life going on. All around the swimming pool. Sometimes the guys, them there relaxing. And be down there playing their games. And that's where [they] used to sit have their lunches upstairs there."

Studio Manager Yvonne Kelly: "I never quite know why people do this to me but there's some pictures on the Internet...If I make a new friend, they obviously deep 'Google' me and then they'll send me these pictures [of the destroyed studio] and I think, 'If my house had burned down, would you send me photographs?' because that's what it's like...you just get an email, it's like, 'Oh my god, Here they are again. Awful pictures."

AIR Engineer Ken Blair: "I try to avoid those pictures to be honest. I don't seek them out certainly. When I first learned that people had got to the studio and had taken pictures, I kind of had a little look...I find them pretty sad because it was a place that used to have so much life, so much vigor, so much creativity and now it's a shell of its original self."

AIR Engineer Matt Butler: "Being a part of the AIR world, it was kind of a sort of strange feeling when the hurricane arrived and the decision was to let it go because it was like 'It's probably for the best' was half of me thinking but of course, you just couldn't imagine, I still can't imagine that it's not there...Of all things to go, AIR Studios Montserrat was not fathomable that it's gone. It's like losing the Houses of Parliament or St. Paul's Cathedral to us Brits."

AIR Engineer Richard Moakes: "[There is] this huge gap to try to explain inside your head to reconcile the fact that you'd been to this place and it's something out of Planet of the Apes...You sort of look at the story of it. You realize that it's something that is just no more and it causes this huge amount of nostalgia and remembrance about the place of what it was back in the heyday."

Dire Straits Technician Ron Eve: "It just looms so large in my life. It was a massively good time. Three months? It sounds ridiculous. You were only there for three months. Yeah. It had such a massive effect on my life."

Midge Ure: "It's horrific...It's like watching an old friend grow old that you haven't seen for 40 years. It's not pleasant. You still recognize the buildings. You recognize what was there but it's lost all of its magic...I prefer to remember it that way as I do my little house...I'd rather keep the memories that I have and remember the good points about it, just like the studio...I don't want to see the ruins of the whole that it used to be. It's just a bit sad really...Even with that thought, the good stuff...being there with George and just being part of something that was a little bit of history. Walking up those stairs with 'E.C. was here' carved on them. [Eric Clapton carved his initials into the wooden studio stairs.] Playing on the pool table that everyone played at. Having dinner on that table that everybody had dinner [at], everybody who is anybody had been there and done this. And that was just glorious. That was just a wonderful thing."

Historian and Poet Howard Fergus: "It's a ruin and it is a pity because it played such a prominent part in the history of the island at a particular time that it really should be a landmark."

Although the current state of AIR Montserrat makes those who I interviewed quite sad, the memories of their time working, playing, and living there glow much brighter than the depressing images of the property as it is today. Perhaps that is why so few of them ever returned to Montserrat. Not only has the studio decayed to the point where it is almost unrecognizable, but Montserrat itself has been forever changed by the natural disasters that have devastated the island, the population, and its economy. In many ways, the island is a shadow of its former self and those who would choose to return would find a quite different place than they remember. I can understand that they did not want to spoil the incredible memories that they made there so many years ago. Montserrat remains as it was in their minds, three decades or more in the past and perhaps it is better that way. What I will say is that the culture of the island that made it such an incredible place in the era of AIR Montserrat endures today. The friendly and welcoming character of Montserrat is still alive and well there despite all the adversity that the islanders have endured. It really shows the incredible character of Montserratians, the character that drew George Martin to the island so many decades ago.

As a fan of the music of the era, as many of you are, I had a very idealized vision of AIR Montserrat at the start of this project. The nostalgia we feel for the decade and the incredible music produced during that era is of deep interest to many of us. Couple that with the pictures that are floating around the Internet: Paul and Stevie in the studio, The Police hanging around the pool, George Martin sitting on the diving board. They only add to the mystique of the studio. Almost 3 years and 100 hours of interviews later, having talked to more than 50 people who built the studio and worked onsite, artists and producers who recorded there, and locals who lived on the island back then, as well having been to Montserrat myself, I have a completely different view of AIR Montserrat today. Yes, famous musicians travelled to a beautiful, idyllic Caribbean island to hang out and record some of the most iconic music of the 80s. It was a fun and creative atmosphere for many of them. But there is so much more depth to the story than what lies beneath the studio's Wikipedia page or the pictures we see on the internet:

-The culture of Montserrat was very important to the studio experience. The friendly, safe, and isolated environment gave it a character not found anywhere else.
-It was a place of very intense work, both for the staff and artists.
-The studio's construction was both a brave and difficult endeavor.
-The party atmosphere was often tempered with soul-crushing boredom.
-Keeping a modern studio up and running thousands of miles from supplies and support was a feat in itself.
-The culture of both AIR and Montserrat contributed to a family-like bond between the staff, the artists, and the islanders.
-Hurricane Hugo, as dramatic and devastating an event as it was for the island, was a convenient place to end the studio's illustrious run.
-As great a studio as it was, it was a financial wash for AIR. Its end was simply a financial decision, driven by changes in the recording industry over the decade of its operation.

So many people are involved in the story of the studio, far beyond just the stars that recorded there and I appreciate all their time spent sharing their experiences of AIR Montserrat, allowing me to capture not only the history of the studio, but their experience of being there. It really was (and still is) a special place to live and work. I hope that I was able to shed some light into the story of AIR Montserrat. It is an important piece of music history, and it was a privilege to record it for posterity. Thanks to all saw the value in preserving the history of the studio and lent a hand (or two) to make this project come to fruition.

[1] Cherry, J. F., Ryzewski, K., & L.J., P. (2013). Archaeologies of Mobility and Movement (M. C. Beaudry & T. G. Parno, Eds.; 2013th ed.). Springer.

THANK YOU!

First and foremost, I want to thank my wife Stacy for supporting me on this crazy lark of a project. Without her, this book would have never seen the light of day.

Next, I wanted to thank everyone who took the time and effort to talk with me about the studio. Your kindness and generosity in granting me an interview cannot be understated. 95% of the entire book comes from your memories and I am humbled that you trusted me with your personal memories of AIR Montserrat.

A huge thank you goes to Dr. Matthew R. Smith. He has been a cheerleader for this project for quite some time. He took many hours to read an early version of the book and offered many thoughtful suggestions, simply as a volunteer that thought that the history of the studio needed to be recorded for posterity. Thank you so much Matt!

AIR Staff

·   Dave Harries- Dave was another big cheerleader for the project from the first time I reached out to him. I could always expect a "How the book coming?" email from Dave every month or two which helped propel me forward when I was feeling frustrated and overwhelmed. I appreciate his help in making this project a reality.
·   Steve and Jan Jackson- They were two of the first AIR staffers I reached out to. I cold called Jan out of the blue and for some reason (and lucky for me), they decided that I was going to be the first journalist they talked to about the studio to in over 40 years. They welcomed me into their home, and they were the first people I interviewed for this project. Five hours later, I emerged from that interview knowing that I could do this. Like Dave, their cheerleading throughout the years has helped keep me going. I like to think I now have some friends in Antigua.
·   Frank Oglethrope- Frank was the first person I reached out to regarding AIR Montserrat. His reply was "Who are you and why do you want to know about the studio?" Frank taught me that the information that I would collecting was not just raw facts but, in fact, personal and private memories and that I needed to respect that fact, that trust would be needed before I would get into the AIR inner circle. Eventually, he invited me to his home and reveled me with terrific stories and hundreds of slides of his time at AIR

Montserrat. His endorsement opened many doors for me within the world of AIR. Many of his pictures grace the pages of this book.

   ·   Malcolm Atkin- I had the privilege of interviewing Malc in his garage/workshop, surrounded by piles of vintage gear including a beautiful MCI console that he was restoring. I really appreciated his candor in talking his most integral role in the creation of the studio.

   ·   Yvonne Robinson (Kelly)- It took a lot of convincing to get Yvonne to agree to an interview as journalists have been on her naughty list for years. But once she realized my sincerity in wanting to record the history of the studio, she invited me into her home and reveled me with stories of her time managing the studio. Her hospitality was most welcome as I was a stranger in a strange land and the grind of running around the U.K. from interview to interview was wearing on me at that time. Tell Bob I said hello!

   ·   Denny Bridges- It took some time to make contact with Denny as he was another AIR staffer who had moved away from AIR many years ago and was no longer in the spotlight. He and his wife welcomed me to their solar powered farm in the English countryside, fed me a delicious dinner, and put me up for the night after a terrific interview. Such great people.

   ·   Carol Weston- Carol is such a humble person. When she started talking with me, she told me, "I'm not sure what I can contribute." This coming from the person who was John Burgess' "right hand woman." What a treasure trove of information! Such a different perspective on AIR Montserrat than those on the technical side of the studio. She was so kind in humoring me with follow-up calls to clarify new leads that I had found. Thanks again Carol.

   ·   Stuart Breed- Stuart's enthusiasm for the project was very welcomed. Such a humorous guy who reveled me with many funny stories of the staff and artists.

   ·   Ken Blair- What a nice fellow. Ken really helped shed some light on the timing of some of the artists' sessions and had some terrific stories of how AIR help launch his long career in the recording industry through his internship at AIR Montserrat.

   ·   Lloyd "X" Francis and Desmond "Micey" Riley- These guys have to be thanked together. The interplay between X and Micey in our interview was such a treat. They are truly two nice, down-to-earth gentlemen. I felt more like I was hanging out with two close friends rather than conducting an interview for a book.

   ·   George "Tappy" Morgan- The last in person interview I had before Covid shut everything down. Tappy and I had a terrific conversation over dinner after he finished up a shift at the hospital he works at in the U.S. As everyone had predicted, he was bigger than life, both in stature and in personality.

   ·   Stephanie and Minetta Francis- These wonderful ladies welcomed me into their homes in both Montserrat and the U.K. Some of my best memories of this project are of Minetta's homemade lemonade and her giving me a tour of her vegetable garden in Montserrat, things that had nothing to do with the studio. Thanks to you both.

- John Silcott- Steve Jackson took the time to arrange and shuttle me to the interview with John. John was so open about his time working at AIR and how grateful he is to AIR for giving him the chance to be successful in life. He welcomed me into one of his radio station stations for the interview and for that, I am thankful.
- Franklyn Allen- There was nothing more Montserrat than interviewing Franklyn at the tiny roadside Treasure Spot Café in Montserrat. With his cousin prepping meals for the evening on the table beside us and friends honking their horns as they drove by, Franklyn regaled me with stories of serving the stars. Such a nice person.
- Geoff Irons
- Steve Culnane
- Chris Mason
- Richard Moakes
- Matt Butler
- Mike Stavrou
- Paul Rushbrooke

Montserratians and Ex-Pats
- David and Maureen Hodd- Ah! Drinking rum on the Hodd's veranda while looking over original copies of the architectural drawings of the studio. A journalistic dream come true. I was so fortunate to meet David before his death in 2019.
- Rose Willock
- Dr. Howard Fergus
- Errol Eid
- Anna Volkle-Dam- Thank you for all of the great photos!
- Danny Sweeney
- Susan Edgecombe
- Peter O. Whitmer
- Mark Bostleman
- Gary Robilotta
- Michael and Julie (Sturge) McNamara
- Michelle Graham

Artists, Producers, and Crew
- Peter Filleul
- Alan Clark
- Chris Kimsey
- Chris Neil
- Chris Thomas
- Deborah Feingold
- Derek Holt
- Hugh Padgham
- John Otway
- Jon Anderson
- Midge Ure
- Mike Batt

- Mo Foster
- Neil Dorfsman
- Ray Bardani
- Ron Eve
- Shelly Yakus
- William Whitman
- Jennifer Maidmen
- Eddie Jobson

Others
- Dr. John Cherry
- Shona Martyn
- Malcom Jackson

I would also like to thank the following people who helped make this journey a little easier:

Deonne Semple, Julian Romeo, The Rotary Club of Montserrat, David Lea and Gingerbread Hill Café, The citizens of Montserrat, Dwain Lovett, Ann Grant, Rachel Robbins at the UK Ministry of Justice, and Maggie Gingerich at the Chesterfield County Library.

RECORDING LIST

As noted by AIR employee Carol Weston, most of the records from AIR Montserrat have been lost. There is no complete list of recordings that can be compiled from AIR documentation. Even if there had been a list of official recordings, there were dozens more that were done off the books for local Montserratian and Caribbean bands as well as local choirs. The studio opened its doors for low or no cost to locals to record, and many of these singles and albums were locally pressed in the Caribbean so no modern comprehensive list of these recordings exists. I have included some of them in the following list of recordings. I expect that I will come across more of these recordings once this book is released. I plan on posting an updated list on my website as more information is obtained.

Since I only have a small subset of the actual dates that bands used the studio, I have listed the release date for each of the albums instead of the recording dates. Also, this list includes recordings that had all or part of the work done on the album at AIR Montserrat. Very few albums were both recorded and mixed at the studio. As was detailed in the book, tracking was done much more frequently in the early years of the studio with more mixing work done in the later years with the introduction of the SSL console. This list includes recordings that had any or all work done at the studio, regardless of how extensive or little AIR Montserrat was utilized for the final product.

1979
- Climax Blues Band- Real To Reel
- America- Silent Letter
- Jimmy Buffet- Volcano
- Caribbean Heet Waves- Disco Party

1980
- Gerry Rafferty- Snakes And Ladders
- UFO- No Place To Run
- Lou Reed- Growing Up Public
- Private Lightning- Private Lightning
- John Townley- Slipping Away (Single)
- Cheap Trick- All Shook Up
- Earth Wind and Fire- Faces
- Roger Daltrey- McVicar Soundtrack
- The Tourists- Luminous Basement
- Nazareth- The Fool Circle

1981
- Alan David- Mainstreet (Single)
- Paul McCartney- Tug Of War
- Little River Band- Time Exposure
- Sheena Easton- Take My Time
- The Police- Ghost In The Machine
- Stray Cats- Gonna Ball

- The Michael Schenker Group- MSG
- Mike Batt- Six Days In Berlin
- Gordon Henderson and U Convention- Self Titled
- Rob de Nijs- De Regen Voorbij

1982
- Elton John- Jump Up!
- Roger Daltrey- Parting Should Be Painless
- Nazareth- 2XS
- Ultravox- Quartet
- Bankie Banx- Sooth Your Soul
- Sheena Easton- Madness, Money, and Music
- Spoons- Nova Heart (Single)

1983
- The Police- Synchronicity
- Pooh- Tropico Del Nord
- Duran Duran- Seven And The Ragged Tiger
- Elton John- Too Low For Zero
- Status Quo- Back To Back

1984
- Orchestral Manoeuvres In The Dark- Junk Culture
- Elton John- Breaking Hearts
- Arrow- Soca Savage
- Sting- demo recordings for Dream of Blue Turtles
- Roby Facchinetti- Self Titled

1985
- Air Supply- Air Supply
- Eric Clapton- Behind The Sun
- Mike + The Mechanics- Self Titled
- Rush- Power Windows
- Midge Ure- The Gift
- Luther Vandross- The Night I Fell In Love
- Dire Straits- Brothers In Arms
- James Taylor- That's Why I'm Here

1986
- Art Garfunkel/Amy Grant/Jimmy Web- The Animal's Christmas
- Ultravox- U-VOX
- Sting- Bring On The Night
- Tommy Keene- Songs From The Film
- Luther Vandross- Give Me The Reason
- King Obstinate- Classics

1987
- Indochine- 7000 Danses

- Sting- ...Nothing Like The Sun
- Rush- Hold Your Fire
- Black Sabbath- The Eternal Idol
- Boy George- Sold
- Takako Okamura- After Tone

1988
- The Fixx- Calm Animals
- Keith Richards- Talk Is Cheap
- Gillian and Glover- Accidentally On Purpose
- Gregory Hines- Self Titled
- Cory Hart- Young Man Running
- Midge Ure- Answers To Nothing

1989
- Complex- Self Titled
- Stephen Bishop- Bowling In Paris
- Anderson Bruford Wakeman Howe- Self Titled
- Simply Red- A New Flame
- Arrow- O' La Soca
- Kassav- Majestik Zouk
- The Rolling Stones- Steel Wheels

No Exact Dates
- Eddy and Eyes Red- Rocky Stuff The Planter
- The Walt Disney Corporation- Recordings for theme parks
- Eddie Jobson- Unreleased album as well as commercial and video soundtracks

PHOTO SECTION

These are various photos that I thought captured the studio and island vibe as well as some of the images of the complex as it was in 2019.

Another Arial Image Of The Studio Complex And Lawn
Photo: Lloyd Francis

Governor Of Monserrat Cuts The "Ribbon" On Opening Day
Handwritten Captions From The Hodd's Photo Album
Photo: David and Maureen Hodd

Studio Stonework
David Hodd Provides His Own Caption
Photo: David and Maureen Hodd

Olveston House
Where Many Musicians, Engineers, and Crew Members Stayed
Photo: Ron Eve

241

Studio Balcony With View Of The Sea
Photo: Frank Oglethorpe

The Front Of The Studio Villa
Photo: Frank Oglethorpe

The Villa Main Room In 1989
Julie Sturge Is In The Foreground. She Was Revisting Her Old Home
Photo: Julie McNamera

One Of The Four Troublesome HVAC Units Used At The Studio
Frozen Up Again
Photo: Frank Oglethorpe

Head Of Housekeeping Minetta Francis
Photo: Frank Oglethorpe

The Small Airport Runway As Seen From Jack Boy Hill
The Hill That Needed To Be Avoided On Approach To The Island
Photo: Ron Eve

Downtown Plymouth
The Soufriere Volcano Looms Over The Capital
Photo: Frank Oglethorpe

Festival In Montserrat
Photo: Frank Oglethorpe

One Of The Incredible Costumes Of Festival
Photo: Frank Oglethorpe

A Typical Local Rum Shack In Montserrat
Photo: Frank Oglethorpe

248

Another Client Car Rescued By AIR Staffers
Photo: Frank Oglethorpe

Luther Vandross Enjoying The Studio Pool
Photo: Frank Oglethorpe

249

X Cuts Some Meat For Bosun As Bosun Looks On
Photo: Frank Oglethorpe

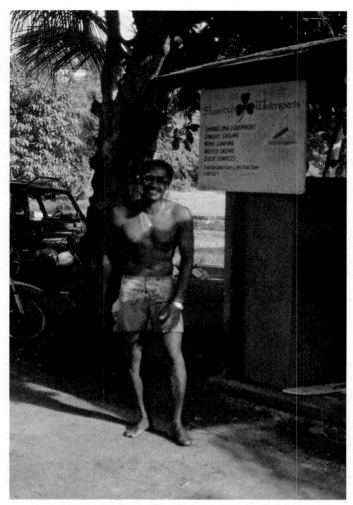

Danny Sweeney Taught Watersports To Many Artists
Photo: Frank Oglethorpe

Danny Sweeney And Sting
Photo: Anna Dam

Danny Sweeney And Sting Windsurfing
Photo: Anna Dam

A Member Of Indochine Uses The Workshop Telephone
Photo: Frank Oglethorpe

Mark Knopfler Gets A Hair Cut At The Studio
Photo: Frank Oglethorpe

Dire Straits Guitar Selection In The Studio Main Room
Photo: Frank Oglethorpe

Dire Straits Share A Laugh
With Malcolm Kelly At The Island's Airport
Photo: Frank Oglethorpe

Beach BBQ With Dire Straits
Photo: Ron Eve

Chef Tappy Morgan Gets Ready For A Beach BBQ
Photo: Ron Eve

Frank Oglethorpe At The Helm
Photo: Frank Oglethorpe

AIR Engineer Matt Butler With Some Good Studio Advice
Photo: Frank Oglethorpe

Studio Staffers Play Pool During Down Time
Photo: Frank Oglethorpe

Andy, Owner Of Village Place, In His Bar In Salem
A Favorite Spot For Many Artists
Photo: Frank Oglethorpe

Bar At Andy's Village Place In 2019
Photo: Brian Sallerson

Andy's Village Place In 2019
A Shell Of Its Former Glory
Photo: Brian Sallerson

Studio Property In 2019
Photo: Brian Sallerson

View Of The Villa Patio Looking Into The Villa Main Room-2019
The Roof Over The Living Room Is Gone And The Front Door Is Hanging Open
Photo: Brian Sallerson

Studio Entrance 2019
Door No Longer Exists
Photo: Brian Sallerson

Gate At The Beginning Of The Studio Drive-2019
Photo: Brian Sallerson

The Studio Property View From The West
Photo: Frank Oglethorpe

Watercolor Painting Of The Studio Villa
Painted By Malcolm Kelly In 1986
Photo: Paul Rushbrooke

Printed in Great Britain
by Amazon

45322461R00149